LEVEL I PRACTICE EXAMS – VOLUME 1

SCHWESER 2013 CFA LEVEL I PRACTICE EXAMS VOLUME 1

©2012 Kaplan, Inc. All rights reserved.

Published in 2012 by Kaplan Schweser.

Printed in the United States of America.

ISBN: 978-1-4277-4224-7 / 1-4277-4224-3

PPN: 3200-2864

Use Your Schweser Online Access Account

All purchasers of the SchweserNotes™ package are sent login information for Online Access in an email. This is your login to view video volumes in the Schweser Library, use the Schweser Study Planner, use Performance Tracker, and (if you purchased the Essential, Premium, or Premium Plus Solutions) join Instructor-led Office Hours. Simply login at www.schweser.com and select "Online Access" to use any of these features. If you need password help, go to www.schweser.com/password or use the "Password Help" link that appears if your login is unsuccessful.

Volume 1 Online Features at a Glance

Links to Curriculum

Within the online answer explanations, we have included page references to the relevant text in both the SchweserNotes and the CFA Institute program texts.

Exam Diagnostics

When you enter your answers in our Performance Tracker utility, you can request a breakdown of your overall score on any one-half (120 question) exam. See how you performed by topic area, study session, or reading. You can also get the Learning Outcome Statement references for questions you answered incorrectly to help you focus your review efforts.

Performance Comparison

When you enter your answers on the page for Performance Tracker, you can find out how your score on each half-exam compares to the scores of others who entered their answers.

HOW TO USE THIS BOOK

Volume 1 is a very important part of the Schweser Study Program. **Don't skip over it.**

You shouldn't take the Level I CFA® Exam without lots of practice answering questions.

Test yourself with these practice exams only after you have completed all the assigned readings. As on the actual CFA exam, assume International Financial Reporting Standards (IFRS) apply unless a question indicates otherwise.

The purpose of these questions is to make sure that you know all the concepts and ideas that are in the assigned readings. If you truly know the material you will do well on the actual exam. While our practice questions cover all the material, **they are not actual exam questions.** Our practice exams are not designed to predict your score on the actual CFA exam, although we try to match the level of difficulty on the exam. Use them to practice and identify those areas in which you need additional work.

Remember though, that CFA Institute tries very hard every year to come up with new and innovative ways to test you. Your only defense against a good exam writer is to actually know the material. Learning the material and how to pace yourself on the exam is what our practice questions are designed to help you do.

The CFA exam is structured so that the morning and afternoon exams are each independent exams covering all topic areas. So, the three 6-hour practice exams here in Volume 1 are really six 3-hour practice exams. This gives you several opportunities to test your progress.

Our recommendations for using this book are:

- After you have finished your first complete review of the assigned reading material, take the morning portion of Practice Exam 1, paying strict attention to the time constraint. Enter your answers online. Performance Tracker will identify your weak spots and point you toward the material you need to review. Go back and study the material related to your weak areas.
- After you have reviewed that material, take the afternoon portion of Practice Exam 1. Again, pay strict attention to the allotted time and review the material related to your weak areas identified by Performance Tracker.
- During the weeks prior to the exam, set aside two days to take Exams 2 and 3. Complete each of these 6-hour exams on one day with only a lunch break between the two halves. This will get you used to doing what you must do on exam day. Again review your weak areas but also look at the explanation for every problem you missed, so it won't happen again.
- Finally, review all of Study Session 1 on the day before the exam. Ethical and Professional Standards and Global Investment Performance Standards will be approximately 15% of the Level I exam. A final review of this material, including all the text and all the examples in the *Standards of Practice Handbook,* will serve you well on exam day.

Don't plan on passing the exam by memorizing questions and answers. Instead, learn the logic behind each of the questions. CFA Institute isn't going to ask you our questions, but they will ask you questions that address the same concepts, logic, and definitions necessary to answer the practice exam questions.

Exam 1
Morning Session

Calculating Your Score

Topic	Maximum Score	Your Score
Ethical and Professional Standards	18	
Quantitative Methods	14	
Economics	12	
Financial Reporting and Analysis	24	
Corporate Finance	10	
Portfolio Management	6	
Equity Investments	12	
Fixed Income	14	
Derivatives	6	
Alternative Investments	4	
Total	120	

The morning and afternoon exams are identically weighted over the topics and readings. You can therefore treat the morning and afternoon exams as independent exams.

If you took more than three hours (180 minutes) to complete this portion of the exam, you should adjust your score downward by one point for each minute you ran over.

Remember: the real exam *will be more difficult* than these practice exams. The main reason for this is the general anxiety and stress that you will be feeling on exam day, coupled with the time pressure you will be under. Many of the questions on this practice exam and the real exam are not individually difficult, so if you take extra time to answer the questions on this practice exam, your score will go up significantly. However, if you want an accurate measure of your potential performance on the exam, adhere to the 3-hour time limit.

After you have finished grading your practice exam, you may find it useful to use the exam questions and recommended solutions for review. Many of these questions were specifically written for your use as study tools. Once again, I feel I should remind you not to rely on memorizing these questions; you are not likely to see them on the actual exam. What you will see on the exam, though, are the concepts, terms, and procedures presented in these questions.

Your actual exam will most likely look different than what you see in this book. Please remember, no study provider knows the content of the actual exam. These practice exams are our best guess as to the structure, content, and difficulty of an actual exam.

Test Answers

1.	A B C		41.	A B C		81.	A B C
2.	A B C		42.	A B C		82.	A B C
3.	A B C		43.	A B C		83.	A B C
4.	A B C		44.	A B C		84.	A B C
5.	A B C		45.	A B C		85.	A B C
6.	A B C		46.	A B C		86.	A B C
7.	A B C		47.	A B C		87.	A B C
8.	A B C		48.	A B C		88.	A B C
9.	A B C		49.	A B C		89.	A B C
10.	A B C		50.	A B C		90.	A B C
11.	A B C		51.	A B C		91.	A B C
12.	A B C		52.	A B C		92.	A B C
13.	A B C		53.	A B C		93.	A B C
14.	A B C		54.	A B C		94.	A B C
15.	A B C		55.	A B C		95.	A B C
16.	A B C		56.	A B C		96.	A B C
17.	A B C		57.	A B C		97.	A B C
18.	A B C		58.	A B C		98.	A B C
19.	A B C		59.	A B C		99.	A B C
20.	A B C		60.	A B C		100.	A B C
21.	A B C		61.	A B C		101.	A B C
22.	A B C		62.	A B C		102.	A B C
23.	A B C		63.	A B C		103.	A B C
24.	A B C		64.	A B C		104.	A B C
25.	A B C		65.	A B C		105.	A B C
26.	A B C		66.	A B C		106.	A B C
27.	A B C		67.	A B C		107.	A B C
28.	A B C		68.	A B C		108.	A B C
29.	A B C		69.	A B C		109.	A B C
30.	A B C		70.	A B C		110.	A B C
31.	A B C		71.	A B C		111.	A B C
32.	A B C		72.	A B C		112.	A B C
33.	A B C		73.	A B C		113.	A B C
34.	A B C		74.	A B C		114.	A B C
35.	A B C		75.	A B C		115.	A B C
36.	A B C		76.	A B C		116.	A B C
37.	A B C		77.	A B C		117.	A B C
38.	A B C		78.	A B C		118.	A B C
39.	A B C		79.	A B C		119.	A B C
40.	A B C		80.	A B C		120.	A B C

Exam 1
Morning Session

Questions 1 through 18 relate to Ethical and Professional Standards.
(27 minutes)

1. Which of the following statements made in a marketing brochure is a violation of the Standards?
    A. "Roger Langley, Chartered Financial Analyst, has been a portfolio manager for ten years and passed all three levels of the CFA examinations on his first attempts."
    B. "Jennifer York has passed the Level II exam and will earn the right to use the CFA designation after completing the Level III exam this June."
    C. "Paul Yeng, CFA, has retired from the firm after 25 years of service. Much of the firm's past success can be attributed to Yeng's efforts as an analyst and portfolio manager."

2. Hedge Funds Unlimited, a global hedge fund, has publicly acknowledged in writing that it has adopted the CFA Institute Code and Standards as its policies. Which of the following is *least likely* a violation of the firm's policies?
    A. An analyst at the firm working overseas uses material nonpublic information as allowed by local law to make investment decisions for discretionary client accounts.
    B. A junior analyst at the firm uses a subscription to his local newspaper and the opinions of his friends and colleagues to make investment recommendations for discretionary client accounts.
    C. A CFA candidate at the firm, who is registered for the Level III exam, includes reference to participation in the CFA program and her status as a Level III candidate in her biographical background.

3. According to the Code and Standards, members and candidates who are involved in distributing an initial public offering (IPO) of equity shares and wish to participate in the IPO:
    A. may participate unless the IPO is oversubscribed.
    B. may not participate because this creates a conflict of interest.
    C. must obtain pre-clearance from a supervisor before participating.

4. Linda Bryant, CFA, is an employee of Roomkin Investment House, which underwrites equity and debt offerings. She has been approached by SimthCo to consult on a private debt placement. According to CFA Institute Standards of Professional Conduct, before Bryant agrees to accept this job, she is required to:
    A. obtain written consent from Roomkin after submitting details of the arrangement.
    B. talk to her immediate supervisor and get her approval to take this consulting job.
    C. inform SimthCo in writing that she will accept the job and provide details of the arrangement to Roomkin in writing.

5. To comply with the Code and Standards, analysts who send research recommendations to clients must:
    A. keep records of all the data and analysis that went into creating the report.
    B. send recommendations only to those clients for whom the investments are suitable.
    C. not send recommendations without including the underlying analysis and basic investment characteristics.

6. Marilyn Walters, CFA, supervises a large group of research analysts. Walters has delegated some of her supervisory responsibilities to her assistant, Amy Brooks, who is a CFA candidate. In carrying out her responsibilities, Brooks has discovered that the firm's compliance system is inadequate and informed Walters, who has not been very supportive of Brooks's efforts to correct the situation. According to CFA Institute Standards of Professional Conduct, Brooks:
    A. must dissociate herself from the firm because the firm is not in compliance with the CFA Institute Standards.
    B. should decline in writing to accept supervisory responsibilities until a reasonable compliance system is adopted.
    C. has satisfied her obligation under the Code and Standards by informing her manager of the situation.

7. Not including the results of terminated accounts when calculating historical performance is recommended by:
    A. both GIPS and the Standard concerning performance presentation.
    B. GIPS, but not by the Standard concerning performance presentation.
    C. neither GIPS nor the Standard concerning performance presentation.

8. Ken Toma, a CFA charterholder and securities analyst for the leisure services industry, has just completed an extensive review of the demand for beach vacations in Hawaii and concluded that the demand will far exceed the supply for the foreseeable future. Toma writes a research report stating, "Based on the fact that the demand for Hawaiian beach vacations will exceed the supply of rooms for the foreseeable future, I recommend the purchase of shares of the Hawaiian Fund, a diversified portfolio of Hawaiian beachfront resorts." If Toma presents this report to his clients, he will have violated the CFA Institute Standards:
   A. because he did not distinguish between fact and opinion.
   B. by failing to have a reasonable and adequate basis for his recommendation.
   C. because he did not consider the suitability of the investment for his clients.

9. Derek Stevens, CFA, manages the pension plan assets of Colors, Inc. When voting proxies for plan equities, Stevens owes a fiduciary duty to:
   A. the plan trustees who hired him.
   B. the plan participants and beneficiaries.
   C. the managers, stockholders, and bondholders of Colors, Inc. equally.

10. Dawn Shields, CFA, decides to change her recommendation on TelSky from "buy" to "sell." In the morning, she mails the revision to all her clients with a known interest in TelSky. That afternoon, one of these clients calls in an order to buy 15,000 shares of TelSky. According to the Standard on fair dealing, Shields:
    A. must accept the order without mentioning the change because the Standard requires her to inform all clients of the change in recommendation simultaneously.
    B. should advise her customer of the change in her recommendation before accepting the order.
    C. must not accept the order until the customer has had time to receive and read the new report.

11. Which of the following is one of the nine major sections of the GIPS standards?
    A. Verification.
    B. Private equity.
    C. Sub-advisers.

12. Edie Pschorr, CFA, notices that a bond is priced at 98.0 in one market and 98.4 in another market. Pschorr places an order to buy a large number of these bonds in the first market and simultaneously places an order to sell the same number of bonds in the second market. The bond's price increases to 98.2 in the first market and decreases to 98.2 in the second market. Are Pschorr's trades a violation of the Code and Standards?
    A. No.
    B. Yes, because they violate the Standard concerning fair dealing.
    C. Yes, because they violate the Standard concerning market manipulation.

13. Greg Hoffman, a Level I CFA candidate, works as an independent securities research consultant. Hoffman has been hired by Hill Manufacturing, Inc. (HMI) to write a research report on their company. After conducting his due diligence, Hoffman writes a report on HMI with a "Buy" recommendation. Hoffman posts the report for purchase on his web site but does not state either on the web site or in the report that HMI paid for the research. According to the Standards that govern independence and objectivity and disclosure of conflicts, Hoffman has violated:
    A. both of these Standards.
    B. neither of these Standards.
    C. only one of these Standards.

14. Rhonda Morrow, CFA, is an analyst for Waller & Madison, a brokerage and investment banking firm. Waller & Madison is a market maker for CorpEast, and Tim Waller, a principal in the firm, sits on CorpEast's board. Morrow has been asked to write a research report on CorpEast. According to the Standard regarding disclosure of conflicts, Morrow:
    A. may write the report without disclosure of Waller's seat on CorpEast's board since he is not writing the report, but she must disclose that Waller & Madison is a market maker in CorpEast shares.
    B. must not write the report and must request that Waller & Madison put CorpEast on their restricted list.
    C. may write the report only if she discloses that Waller & Madison is a market maker in CorpEast shares and that Waller sits on the CorpEast board.

15. John Farr, CFA, has accumulated several pieces of nonpublic information about Cattle Corp. of Omaha from his contacts with the company. Although none of this information is material by itself, when Farr combines it with his own analysis, it leads him to conclude that Cattle Corp. will have an unexpectedly low earnings report this year. Cattle Corp. has not announced this information, and although Farr has contacted the company, it will not confirm his finding. According to CFA Institute Standards of Professional Conduct, Farr:
    A. can use the information to make investment recommendations and decisions.
    B. cannot legally invest, divest, or make recommendations based on this information.
    C. may use the information, but only if his company's compliance officer is able to verify with Cattle Corp. that the material he used was indeed nonmaterial.

16. According to the GIPS standards, which of the following statements is *most accurate*?
    A. Firms are required to obtain independent third-party verification for a claim of GIPS compliance.
    B. GIPS compliant firms are required to maintain written documentation of policies and procedures used to establish and maintain compliance with GIPS.
    C. To initially claim compliance with GIPS, a company must present a minimum of ten years (or since the firm's inception if less than ten years) of GIPS-compliant performance data.

17. Geno Hanson is a portfolio manager at Bigtime Investments. James Ward, an old friend of Hanson's, is an executive recruiter in the same city. Ward refers to Hanson's firm any high-level executives that Ward places locally. In return, Hanson allows Ward to play a round of golf at Hanson's country club for each new client referred. According to the Standard on referral fees, Hanson is required to disclose the arrangement with Ward to:
    A. his employer, all clients, and all prospective clients.
    B. prospective clients referred by Ward, but not to his employer.
    C. his employer and to prospective clients referred by Ward.

18. Yvette Michaelson, a junior analyst for Torborg Investments, covers healthcare and consumer discretionary stocks alongside a senior analyst at the firm. Michaelson inadvertently overhears a conversation between two executives regarding Collective Healthcare's proposed tender offer for Network Healthcare at a 12% premium, which will be announced next week. Michaelson has followed both companies extensively and feels consolidation would be very beneficial for both companies. She tells her senior analyst about the proposed tender offer. According to the Standard concerning material nonpublic information, Michaelson's actions are:
   A. in violation of the Standard.
   B. not in violation of the Standard because she is not trading any securities based on the information.
   C. not in violation of the Standard under the mosaic theory since she has followed both companies extensively, and the tender offer information substantiates her beliefs about the benefits of consolidation.

Questions 19 through 32 relate to Quantitative Methods. (21 minutes)

19. The odds for an event occurring are calculated by dividing:
   A. one by the probability that the event occurs.
   B. the probability that the event does not occur by the probability that an event occurs.
   C. the probability that the event occurs by the probability that the event does not occur.

20. A successful investor has decided to set up a scholarship fund for deserving students at her alma mater. Her plan is for the fund to be capable of awarding $25,000 annually in perpetuity. The first scholarship is to be awarded and paid out exactly four years from today. The funds will be deposited into an account immediately and will grow at a rate of 4%, compounded semiannually, for the foreseeable future. How much money must the investor donate today to fund the scholarship?
   A. $528,150.
   B. $549,487.
   C. $574,253.

21. Which of the following statements about return distributions is *most accurate*?
   A. With positive skewness, the median is greater than the mean.
   B. If skewness is positive, the average magnitude of positive deviations from the mean is smaller than the average magnitude of negative deviations from the mean.
   C. If a return distribution has positive excess kurtosis and the analyst uses statistical models that do not account for the fatter tails, the analyst will underestimate the likelihood of extreme outcomes.

22. An analyst plans to use the following test statistic: $t_{n-1} = \dfrac{\bar{x} - \mu_0}{s / \sqrt{n}}$.

    This test statistic is appropriate for a hypothesis about the:
    A. mean difference of two normal populations.
    B. population mean of a normal distribution with unknown variance.
    C. the equality of two population means of two normally distributed populations based on independent samples.

23. Which of the following statements about covariance and the correlation coefficient is *least accurate*?
    A. Covariance is a measure of how the returns of two assets tend to move together over time.
    B. The correlation coefficient is computed by dividing the covariance of returns on two assets by the individual variances of returns for the two assets.
    C. The covariance of returns between two assets is equal to the correlation between the returns of the two assets, multiplied by the product of their standard deviations of returns.

24. Greg Goldman, research analyst in the fixed-income area of an investment bank, needs to determine the average duration of a sample of twenty 15-year fixed-coupon investment grade bonds. Goldman first categorizes the bonds by risk class and then randomly selects bonds from each class. After combining the bonds selected (bond ratings and other information taken as of March 31 of the current year), he calculates a sample mean duration of 10.5 years. Assuming that the actual population mean duration is 9.7 years, which of the following statements about Goldman's sampling process and sample is *least accurate*?
    A. Goldman is using time-series data.
    B. The sample mean is a random variable.
    C. The sampling error is 0.8 years.

25. The type of technical analysis chart *most likely* to be useful for intermarket analysis is a:
    A. candlestick chart.
    B. point and figure chart.
    C. relative strength chart.

26. If Stock X has a standard deviation of returns of 18.9% and Stock Y has a standard deviation of returns equal to 14.73% and returns on the stocks are perfectly positively correlated, the standard deviation of an equally weighted portfolio of the two is:
    A. 10.25%.
    B. 14.67%.
    C. 16.82%.

27. Over a sample period, an investor gathers the following data about three mutual funds.

Mutual Fund	Risk-Free Rate	Portfolio Return	Portfolio Standard Deviation	Portfolio Beta
P	5%	13%	18%	1.2
Q	5%	15%	20%	1.4
R	5%	18%	24%	1.8

Based solely on the Sharpe measure, an investor would prefer mutual fund:
A. P.
B. Q.
C. R.

28. An investment manager wants to select three analysts from a group of six analysts to receive first-, second-, and third-place awards for outstanding performance. In how many ways can the investment manager make the three awards?
A. 20 ways.
B. 54 ways.
C. 120 ways.

29. Which of the following statements about the central limit theorem is *least accurate*? The:
A. standard deviation of the sample mean is called the standard error of the sample mean.
B. standard error of the sample mean can be estimated by dividing the population standard deviation by $\sqrt{n-1}$.
C. sample means for large sample sizes will have an approximately normal distribution regardless of the distribution of the underlying population.

30. An investment analyst takes a random sample of 100 aggressive equity funds and calculates the average beta as 1.7. The sample betas have a standard deviation of 0.4. Using a 95% confidence interval and a z-statistic, which of the following statements about the confidence interval and its interpretation is *most accurate*? The analyst can be confident at the 95% level that the interval:
A. 1.580 to 1.820 includes the mean of the population beta.
B. 1.622 to 1.778 includes the mean of the population beta.
C. 1.634 to 1.766 includes the mean of the population beta.

31. Which is the correct test statistic for a test of the null hypothesis that a population variance is equal to a chosen value?
    A. *F*-statistic.
    B. *t*-statistic.
    C. Chi-square statistic.

32. From a high of $180, a stock price decreases to a low of $100 and then begins increasing. A technical analyst states that she expects resistance levels to emerge at $140, $150, and $153.33. This analyst is *most likely* forecasting these resistance levels based on:
    A. Fibonacci numbers.
    B. an inverse head and shoulders pattern.
    C. moving average convergence/divergence lines.

Questions 33 through 44 relate to Economics. (18 minutes)

33. To benefit from price discrimination, a monopolist *least likely* needs to have:
    A. a higher-quality product at a premium price and a lower-quality alternative.
    B. a way to prevent reselling between types of consumers.
    C. two identifiable groups of consumers with different price elasticities of demand for the product.

34. Automatic stabilizers are government programs that require no legislation and tend to:
    A. automatically increase spending at the same growth rate as real GDP.
    B. reduce interest rates, thus stimulating aggregate demand.
    C. change the government budget deficit in an opposite direction to economic growth.

35. An economy is in full-employment equilibrium. If the government unexpectedly decreases the tax rate, in the short run the economy is *most likely* to experience:
    A. an increase in employment.
    B. a decrease in the price level.
    C. no change in employment and an increase in the price level.

36. Notasled, Inc., a producer of cafeteria trays, operates in a perfectly competitive market. If the market price of a cafeteria tray is $3.25, Notasled will increase production so long as:
    A. marginal revenue is positive.
    B. marginal cost is less than $3.25.
    C. marginal revenue is greater than $3.25.

37. Three years ago, the U.S. dollar/euro exchange rate was 1.32 USD/EUR. Over the last three years, the price level in the United States has increased by 18%, and the price level in the eurozone has increased by 12%. If the current exchange rate is 1.40 USD/EUR, the real exchange rate over the period has:
    A. increased, and eurozone goods are now more expensive to U.S. consumers.
    B. decreased, and eurozone goods are now more expensive to U.S. consumers.
    C. increased, and U.S. goods are now more expensive to eurozone consumers.

38. Consider a market where quantity supplied = 1,500 – 3 × price, and quantity demanded = 2,000 – 5 × price. With respect to equilibrium price and quantity, there is:
    A. no market equilibrium.
    B. a stable market equilibrium.
    C. an unstable market equilibrium.

39. Which of the following is *most likely* a characteristic of monopolistic competition?
    A. Producer decisions are interdependent.
    B. Each producer offers a differentiated product.
    C. Producers face horizontal demand curves.

40. The Fisher effect describes the relationship among:
    A. savings, investment, the fiscal balance, and the trade balance.
    B. credit expansion, investor expectations, and the business cycle.
    C. nominal interest rates, real interest rates, and expected inflation.

41. Which of the following events is *most likely* to increase short-run aggregate supply (shift the curve to the right)?
    A. Inflation that results in an increase in goods prices.
    B. High unemployment puts downward pressure on money wages.
    C. An increase in government spending intended to increase real output.

42. In recent months, inventory-to-sales ratios have increased unexpectedly and real personal income and the index of industrial production have decreased. Based only on these indicators, in which phase of the business cycle is the economy *most likely* to be?
    A. Peak.
    B. Trough.
    C. Contraction.

43. A government is auctioning 500 newly issued bonds and receives the following bids:

Bidder	Yield	Number of Bonds
Bidder 1	5.25%	200
Bidder 2	5.30%	100
Bidder 3	5.40%	300
Bidder 4	5.45%	400

Bidder 3 receives 200 bonds at a yield of 5.40%. This auction is *best* described as a(n):
   A. second price auction.
   B. ascending price auction.
   C. descending price auction.

44. In the short run, the average product of labor:
   A. is increasing when the total product of labor is increasing.
   B. is at a maximum where it intersects the marginal product of labor curve.
   C. is upward-sloping if the firm is experiencing diminishing marginal returns to labor.

Questions 45 through 68 relate to Financial Reporting and Analysis. (36 minutes)

45. When the Rivers Company filed its corporate tax returns for the first quarter of the current year, it owed a total of $6.7 million in corporate taxes. Rivers paid $4.4 million of the tax bill, but still owes $2.3 million. It also received $478,000 in the second quarter as a down payment towards $942,000 in custom-built products to be delivered in the third quarter. Its financial accounts for the second quarter *most likely* show the $2.3 million and the $478,000 as:

	$2.3 million	$478,000
A.	Income tax payable	Unearned revenue
B.	Income tax payable	Accrued revenue
C.	Deferred tax liability	Accrued revenue

46. Which of the following statements about the appropriate revenue recognition method to use under U.S. GAAP is *most accurate*? Use the:
   A. percentage-of-completion method if the firm cannot reliably estimate the outcome of the project.
   B. completed contract method if ultimate payment is reasonably assured and revenue and costs can be reliably estimated.
   C. installment method if collectability of payments for a sale cannot be reasonably estimated.

47. An analyst gathered the following data about a company:
    - Collections from customers are $5,000.
    - Depreciation is $800.
    - Cash expenses (including taxes) are $2,000.
    - Tax rate = 30%.
    - Net cash increased by $1,000.

    If inventory increases over the period by $800, cash flow from operations equals:
    A. $1,600.
    B. $2,400.
    C. $3,000.

48. Which of the following statements about the indirect method of calculating cash flow from operations is *least accurate*?
    A. Depreciation is added back to net income because it is an expense not requiring cash.
    B. No adjustment is needed to account for changes in accounts receivable because no cash is involved.
    C. No adjustment is needed for the payment of taxes because the tax payment is already in net income.

49. Assuming stable inventory quantities, in a period of:
    A. rising prices, LIFO results in higher ending inventory and FIFO results in higher gross profit.
    B. falling prices, LIFO results in higher gross profit and FIFO results in lower cost of goods sold.
    C. rising prices, LIFO results in higher cost of goods sold and FIFO results in higher working capital.

50. Under which type of pension plan are retirement benefit payments an obligation of the sponsoring firm?
    A. Defined benefit plan only.
    B. Defined contribution plan only.
    C. Both a defined benefit plan and a defined contribution plan.

51. Which of the following is *most likely* presented on a common-size balance sheet or common-size income statement?
    A. Total asset turnover.
    B. Operating profit margin.
    C. Return on common equity.

52. An analyst gathers the following data about a company:
    - The company had 1 million shares of common stock outstanding for the entire year.
    - The company's beginning stock price was $50, its ending price was $70, and its average price was $60.
    - The company had 100,000 warrants outstanding for the entire year. Each warrant allows the holder to buy one share of common stock at $50 per share.

    How many shares of common stock should the company use in computing its diluted earnings per share?
    A. 1,100,000.
    B. 1,083,333.
    C. 1,016,667.

53. Under U.S. GAAP, land owned by the firm is *most likely* to be reported on the balance sheet at:
    A. historical cost.
    B. fair market value minus selling costs.
    C. historical cost less accumulated depreciation.

54. Which of the following items is *least likely* to contain details about various accruals, adjustments, balances, and management assumptions?
    A. Income statement.
    B. Supplementary schedules.
    C. Discussion and analysis by management.

55. A firm presents the following income statement, which complies with the standards under which it must report:

Sales	20,535
Cost of goods sold	14,525
Operating expenses	2,530
Operating income	3,480
Income taxes	1,220
Income from continuing operations	2,260
Extraordinary items, net of tax	(525)
Net income	1,735

Based on the differences between U.S. GAAP and International Financial Reporting Standards, this firm:
A. must report any dividends received as operating cash flows.
B. is permitted to recognize upward revaluations of long-lived assets.
C. cannot have used LIFO as its inventory cost assumption.

56. A permanent difference between pretax and taxable income is *least likely* to arise when a firm:
A. receives tax-exempt interest.
B. uses the installment sales method for financial reporting.
C. pays premiums on life insurance of key employees.

57. According to the IASB Conceptual Framework for Financial Reporting, what are the two fundamental qualitative characteristics of financial statements that make them useful to their users?
A. Timeliness and comparability.
B. Verifiability and understandability.
C. Relevance and faithful representation.

58. A firm uses the first-in first-out (FIFO) cost flow assumption. Compared to gross profit with a periodic inventory system, the firm's gross profit with a perpetual inventory system would be:
A. lower.
B. higher.
C. the same.

59. From the lessee's perspective, compared to an operating lease, a finance lease results in:
A. higher asset turnover.
B. a higher debt-to-equity ratio.
C. lower operating cash flow.

60. A firm needs to adjust its financial statements for a change in the tax rate. Taxable income is $80,000 and pretax income is $120,000. The current tax rate is 50%, and the new tax rate is 40%. The effect on taxes payable of adjusting the tax rate is *closest* to:
A. $4,000.
B. $8,000.
C. $16,000.

61. While motive and opportunity both can lead to accounting fraud, a third important contributing factor is:
A. poor financial controls.
B. a justification of the fraudulent actions.
C. pressure to meet earnings expectations.

62. Which of the following firms is *most likely* to present a liquidity-based balance sheet rather than a classified balance sheet?
A. Banking institution.
B. Manufacturing firm.
C. Chain of retail stores.

63. Two firms in the same industry show the following ratios for the most recent year after all proper adjustments have been made for dilutive securities and differences in financial reporting standards:

	Earnings per Share	Operating Cash Flow per Share
Company Y	$3.50	$2.00
Company Z	$2.00	$3.00

Based only on this information, the better financial performer of these two firms is:
A. Company Y because it has the highest earnings per share.
B. Company Z because it generated the most operating cash flow per share.
C. inconclusive because per-share ratios are not comparable.

64. Granite, Inc. owns a machine with a carrying value of $3.0 million and a salvage value of $2.0 million. The present value of the machine's future cash flows is $1.7 million. The asset is permanently impaired. Granite should:
A. immediately write down the machine to its salvage value.
B. immediately write down the machine to its recoverable amount.
C. write down the machine to its recoverable amount as soon as it is depreciated down to salvage value.

65.   Yamaska Mining issued a 5-year, $50 million face, 6% semiannual bond
       when market interest rates were 7%. The market yield of the bonds was
       8% at the beginning of the next year. What is the initial balance sheet
       liability, and what is the interest expense that the company should report
       for the first half of the second year of the bond's life (the third semiannual
       period)?

Initial liability	Interest expense, first half of year 2
A. $47,920,849	$1,689,853
B. $47,920,849	$1,750,000
C. $50,000,000	$1,500,000

66.   Clement Company has revalued an intangible asset with an indefinite
       life upward by €25 million. In its financial statements, Clement will *most
       likely*:
       A. disclose how it determined the fair value of the intangible asset.
       B. report lower net income in subsequent periods because of increased
          amortization expense on the asset.
       C. report higher assets, net income, and shareholders' equity in the
          most recent period than it would have reported under the cost
          model.

67.   As a result of a recent acquisition, Lombard, Inc. has placed the following
       items on their balance sheet as of the beginning of their fiscal year:

Goodwill	$30 million	
Patent	$10 million	Expires in 10 years.
Trademark	$15 million	Expires in 15 years, renewable at minimal cost.

       If Lombard amortizes intangible assets using the straight line method, the
       amortization expense on these assets for the fiscal year will be:
       A. $1 million.
       B. $2 million.
       C. $3 million.

68.   A firm pays accrued wages with cash. Assuming a current ratio greater
       than one and a quick ratio that is less than one, what will be the impact on
       the current ratio and the quick ratio?
       A. Both ratios will remain the same.
       B. The current ratio will increase and the quick ratio will decrease.
       C. The current ratio will decrease and the quick ratio will increase.

©2012 Kaplan, Inc.

Questions 69 through 78 relate to Corporate Finance. (15 minutes)

69. Responsibilities of a board of directors' nominations committee are *least likely* to include:
     A. recruiting qualified members to the board.
     B. selecting an external auditor for the company.
     C. preparing a succession plan for the company's executive management.

70. The following data applies to LeVeit Company:
     - LeVeit has a target debt-to-equity ratio of 0.5.
     - LeVeit's bonds are currently yielding 10%.
     - LeVeit is a constant growth (5%) firm that just paid a dividend of $3.00.
     - LeVeit's stock sells for $31.50 per share.
     - The company's marginal tax rate is 40%.

     The company's weighted after-tax cost of capital is *closest* to:
     A. 10.5%.
     B. 11.0%.
     C. 12.0%.

71. Timely Taxis, Ltd. has signed a long-term lease for 20 underground parking spots at $150 each per month for its fleet of taxis. The firm currently has 18 taxis in operation and is performing an NPV analysis on the purchase of a 19th taxi. The cost of parking for the 19th taxi is *best* described as a(n):
     A. sunk cost.
     B. opportunity cost.
     C. incremental cost.

72. If a firm uses the weighted average cost of capital (WACC) to discount cash flows of higher than average risk projects, which one of the following will *most likely* occur?
     A. Project NPVs will be understated.
     B. The firm will reject profitable projects.
     C. The overall risk of the firm's investments will rise over time.

73. Michael Robe, CFA, is a junior analyst for a large financial institution and has been preparing an analysis of United Mines, a coal mining company located in the United States. As part of his research, he examines the company's proxy voting and rules and practices. Which of the following policies would be considered the *most* restrictive to shareholders?
    A. Shareholders of United Mines are allowed to cast confidential votes but must be present to do so.
    B. Corporate policy prohibits the use of share blocking prior to United Mines' annual meetings.
    C. United Mines requires shareowner attendance to vote but coordinates the timing of its annual meeting to be held on the same day as other companies in the region.

74. Wreathfield, Inc. is choosing between two mutually exclusive projects. The cash flows for the two projects are below. The firm has a cost of capital of 12%, and the risk of the projects is equivalent to the average risk of the firm.

	0	1	2	3	4	5	6
Project J:	−12,000	4,000	5,000	6,000			
Project K:	−20,000	3,000	3,000	3,000	5,000	8,000	8,000

Wreathfield should accept:
    A. Project J.
    B. Project K.
    C. Neither project J nor project K.

75. To finance a proposed project, Youngham Corporation would need to issue £25 million in common equity. Youngham would receive £23 million in net proceeds from the equity issuance. When analyzing the project, analysts at Youngham should:
    A. not consider the flotation cost because it is a sunk cost.
    B. add the £2 million flotation cost to the project's initial cash outflow.
    C. increase the cost of equity capital to account for the 8% flotation cost.

76. If firms Acme and Butler have the same amount of sales and equal quick ratios, but Acme's receivables turnover is higher, it is *most likely* that:
    A. Butler has better liquidity than Acme.
    B. Butler has a lower cash ratio than Acme.
    C. Acme's average days of receivables is higher than Butler's.

77. Daker Industries reports assets of £140 million and liabilities of £85 million. Daker decides to repurchase 5% of its 11 million outstanding shares through a tender offer at £5 per share when the market price is £4.75. If the tender offer is fully subscribed, the *most likely* effect on the book value of Daker's shares will be to:
    A. increase the book value of Daker shares by 5%.
    B. decrease the book value of Daker shares by 5%.
    C. have no effect on the book value of Daker shares.

78. A firm's optimal capital budget can be found by moving along its investment opportunity schedule until:
    A. it exhausts its capital budget.
    B. average project return is equal to average cost of capital.
    C. the next project's return is less than the marginal cost of capital.

Questions 79 through 84 relate to Portfolio Management. (9 minutes)

79. Which of the following lists major U.S. asset classes from riskiest to least risky based on their returns over the 1926 to 2008 period?
    A. Treasury bills, long-term government bonds, long-term corporate bonds.
    B. Large-cap stocks, long-term corporate bonds, long-term government bonds.
    C. Small-cap stocks, large-cap stocks, long-term corporate bonds.

80. When comparing portfolios that plot on the security market line (SML) to those that plot on the capital market line (CML), a financial analyst would *most accurately* state that portfolios that lie on the SML:
    A. have only systematic risk, while portfolios on the CML have both systematic and unsystematic risk.
    B. are not necessarily well diversified, while portfolios on the CML are well diversified.
    C. are not necessarily priced at their equilibrium values, while portfolios on the CML are priced at their equilibrium values.

81. Which of the following possible portfolios is *least likely* to lie on the efficient frontier?

Portfolio	Expected Return	Standard Deviation
X	9%	12%
Y	11%	10%
Z	13%	15%

    A. Portfolio X.
    B. Portfolio Y.
    C. Portfolio Z.

82. In extending the 3-factor model of Fama and French, the additional factor suggested by Carhart that is often used is:
    A. GDP growth.
    B. price momentum.
    C. market-to-book value.

83. Martin Dean, CFA, is a portfolio manager who is writing an investment policy statement (IPS) for Albert Francis, a new client. The *least likely* reason why Dean should prepare an IPS is to:
    A. set the target asset allocation for Francis's portfolio.
    B. comply with the Code and Standards with regard to suitability.
    C. specify a benchmark against which to measure Dean's performance.

84. An analyst gathered the following data about three stocks:

Stock	Beta	Estimated Return
A	1.5	18.1%
B	1.1	15.7%
C	0.6	12.5%

    If the risk-free rate is 8%, and the market risk premium is 7%, the analyst is *least likely* to recommend buying:
    A. Stock A.
    B. Stock B.
    C. Stock C.

Questions 85 through 96 relate to Equity Investments. (18 minutes)

85. Martin Gomez holds 100 shares of each of the stocks in a price-weighted index and reinvests cash dividends in additional shares. Assuming there are no stock splits, stock dividends, or changes in the makeup of the index, how will Gomez's portfolio return compare with the price return of the index if the low-priced index stocks outperform the high-priced index stocks?
    A. Gomez's portfolio return will be higher.
    B. The price return of the index will be higher.
    C. Gomez's portfolio return will be equal to the price return of the index.

86. Evelyn Stram, CFA, places a good-till-cancelled limit buy order at 86 for a stock. Stram's order specifies:
    A. clearing and validity instructions.
    B. validity and execution instructions.
    C. execution and clearing instructions.

87. The type of equity security that gives its owners the right to vote the shares of, and receive dividends from, a foreign company is *best* described as a:
    A. global depository receipt.
    B. sponsored depository receipt.
    C. fully-owned depository receipt.

88. Ron Egan, CFA, classifies firms in the transportation industry in peer groups that include airlines and bus operators. Egan learns that one of the airlines, Acme, derives half its revenue from its Acme Bus Lines subsidiary. Egan adds Acme to his peer group for bus operators while continuing to include Acme in his peer group for airlines. Is Egan's treatment of Acme appropriate?
    A. Yes.
    B. No, because each company should be included in only one peer group.
    C. No, because the bus operations are not the company's principal business activity.

89. An analyst gathered the following data about a company:
    - A historical earnings retention rate of 60% that is projected to continue into the future.
    - A sustainable return on equity of 10%.
    - A beta of 1.0.
    - The nominal risk-free rate is 5%.
    - The expected market return is 10%.

    If next year's EPS is $2 per share, what value should be estimated for this stock?
    A. $20.00.
    B. $30.50.
    C. $35.45.

90. An analyst makes the following predictions for the coming year:
    - A stock's earnings per share will be $4.
    - The dividend payout will be 55%.
    - Return on equity will be 15%.
    - The required rate of return on the market will be 12%.

    Based on these estimates, the value of the stock is *closest* to:
    A. $32.
    B. $37.
    C. $42.

91.   A high yield bond fund states that through active management, the fund's return has outperformed an index of Treasury securities by 4% on average over the past five years. As a performance benchmark for this fund, the index chosen is:
A. appropriate.
B. inappropriate, because the index return does not reflect active management.
C. inappropriate, because the index does not reflect the actual bonds in which the fund invests.

92.   The change in the intrinsic value of a firm's common stock resulting from an increase in ROE *most likely*:
A. increases the stock's intrinsic value.
B. decreases the stock's intrinsic value.
C. depends on the reason for the increase in ROE.

93.   Which of the following statements about short selling is *least accurate*?
A. A short seller is required to set up a margin account.
B. A short sale involves securities the investor does not own.
C. A short seller loses if the price of the stock sold short decreases.

94.   Compared to an index of 100 U.S. exchange-traded stocks, an index of 100 U.S. government and corporate bonds will *most likely*:
A. reflect equally timely price data.
B. be more difficult to build and maintain.
C. have less turnover among the securities in the index.

95.   Beth Knight, CFA, and David Royal, CFA, are independently analyzing the value of Bishop, Inc. stock. Bishop paid a dividend of $1 last year. Knight expects the dividend to grow by 10% in each of the next three years, after which it will grow at a constant rate of 4% per year. Royal also expects a temporary growth rate of 10% followed by a constant growth rate of 4%, but he expects the supernormal growth to last for only two years. Knight estimates that the required return on Bishop stock is 9%, but Royal believes the required return is 10%. Royal's valuation of Bishop stock is approximately:
A. equal to Knight's valuation.
B. $5 less than Knight's valuation.
C. $5 greater than Knight's valuation.

96.   An industry in the growth phase of the industry life cycle is *most likely* to experience:
A. increasing prices.
B. increasing profitability.
C. intense competition among competitors.

Questions 97 through 110 relate to Fixed Income. (21 minutes)

97.   Consider the following Treasury spot rates expressed as bond equivalent
       yields:

Maturity	Spot Rate
6 months	3.0%
1 year	3.5%
1.5 years	4.0%
2 years	4.5%

       If a Treasury note with two years remaining to maturity has a 5%
       semiannual coupon and is priced at $1,008, the note is:
       A. overpriced.
       B. underpriced.
       C. correctly priced.

98.   Which of the following is an advantage of a callable bond (compared to an
       identical option-free bond) to an investor?
       A. Less reinvestment risk.
       B. Higher yield.
       C. More convexity.

99.   An investor is considering the purchase of Security X, which matures in
       ten years and has a par value of $1,000. During the first five years, X has
       a 6% coupon with quarterly payments. During the remaining five years,
       X has an 8% coupon with quarterly payments. The face value is paid at
       maturity. A second 10-year security, Security Z, has a 6% semiannual
       coupon and is selling at par. Assuming that X has the same bond
       equivalent yield as Z, the price of Security X is *closest* to:
       A. $943.
       B. $1,036.
       C. $1,067.

100.   The yield spreads between corporate bonds and Treasuries are *most
       likely* to decrease if:
       A. liquidity decreases in the market for the bonds.
       B. a credit rating downgrade on the bonds becomes more likely.
       C. investors increase their estimates of the recovery rate on the bonds.

101.   The full price of a bond:
       A. includes accrued interest.
       B. includes commissions and taxes.
       C. is also known as the "clean" price.

102. Which of the following statements regarding sinking funds is *most accurate*?
    A. The specific bonds that will be redeemed on each scheduled date are identified in the indenture.
    B. Sinking fund redemptions can be accomplished by making cash payment to the trustee who will then retire the required proportion of the bonds.
    C. If yields have declined since the bond was issued, companies are likely to choose to retire the required portion of the debt by delivering securities to the trustee.

103. A debt covenant designates one of a holding company's subsidiaries as restricted. Which of the following credit-related considerations does this covenant address?
    A. Credit migration risk.
    B. Structural subordination.
    C. Payments to equity holders.

104. Consider a 25-year, $1,000 par semiannual-pay bond with a 7.5% coupon and a 9.25% YTM. Based on a yield change of 50 basis points, the effective duration of the bond is *closest* to:
    A. 8.73.
    B. 10.03.
    C. 12.50.

105. For a bond currently priced at $1,018 with an effective duration of 7.48, if the market yield moved down 75 basis points, the new price would be approximately:
    A. $961.
    B. $1,075.
    C. $1,094.

106. Which of the following statements about Treasury Inflation Protected Securities (TIPS) is *most accurate*?
    A. Inflation adjustments are made annually.
    B. Yields on TIPS are effectively real rates of interest.
    C. The coupon rate adjusts upward for inflation.

107. Consider a $1,000-face value, 12-year, 8%, semiannual coupon bond with a YTM of 10.45%. The change in value for a decrease in yield of 38 basis points is:
    A. $21.18.
    B. $22.76.
    C. $23.06.

108. The minimum data required to calculate the implied forward rate for three years beginning three years from now is:
    A. the 3-year and 6-year spot rates.
    B. the 4-year, 5-year, and 6-year spot rates.
    C. spot rates at 1-year intervals for the 6-year period.

109. Consider three bonds that are identical in all features except those shown in the following table:

Bond	Embedded Option	Amount Outstanding
A	Call	$20 million
B	Call	$80 million
C	Put	$20 million

The bond *most likely* to have the largest spread to a comparable Treasury security is:
    A. Bond A.
    B. Bond B.
    C. Bond C.

110. A 3-year, 6% coupon, semiannual-pay note has a yield to maturity of 5.5%. If an investor holds this note to maturity and earns a 4.5% return on reinvested coupon income, his realized yield on the note is *closest* to:
    A. 5.46%.
    B. 5.57%.
    C. 5.68%.

Questions 111 through 116 relate to Derivatives. (9 minutes)

111. Janet Powers writes a covered call on a stock she owns, Billings, Inc. The current price of the stock is $45, and Powers writes the call at a strike price of $50. The call option premium is $3.50. Which of the following statements regarding Powers's covered call strategy is *most accurate*?
    A. Powers is trading the stock's upside potential in exchange for current income.
    B. The price of the stock must rise to at least $48.50 before Powers will lose money.
    C. Powers is eliminating downside risk at the same time she is increasing her current income with the covered call strategy.

112. A portfolio manager holds a long position on a forward contract on $20 million face value 81-day T-bills priced at 1.85% on a discount basis. At settlement, 81-day T-bills are priced at 1.95% on a discount basis. If the contract settles in cash, at settlement the portfolio manager will:
    A. pay $4,500.
    B. receive $4,500.
    C. pay $20,000.

113. When comparing the values of two otherwise identical in-the-money options on a stock that pays no dividend, it is *most likely* that a(n):
    A. European call with a lower exercise price will have less value than a European call with a higher exercise price.
    B. American put with a lower exercise price will have more value than an American put with a higher exercise price.
    C. American call with a shorter time to expiration will have less value than an American call with a longer time to expiration.

114. Over-the-counter derivatives are:
    A. standardized and backed by a clearinghouse.
    B. not standardized but are backed by a clearinghouse.
    C. neither standardized nor backed by a clearinghouse.

115. The time value of an option is *most accurately* described as:
    A. increasing as the option approaches its expiration date.
    B. equal to the entire premium for an out-of-the-money option.
    C. the amount by which the intrinsic value exceeds the option premium.

116. An investor long a forward position in a Treasury bill is *most likely* to be concerned about:
    A. default risk.
    B. delivery options the short has.
    C. paying more than expected because the price of the bill rises.

Questions 117 through 120 relate to Alternative Investments. (6 minutes)

117. A hedge fund uses derivative positions to take a long position in the Japanese yen and a short position in the euro. The classification of this hedge fund is *most likely* a(n):
    A. event-driven fund.
    B. macro strategy fund.
    C. quantitative directional fund.

118. Chip Jergen, CFA, is an asset manager who wishes to allocate a percentage of his portfolio to alternative investments. Jergen invests in a security that represents a proportional claim to cash flows from a pool of loans. In which category of alternative investments has Jergen *most likely* invested?
    A. Real estate.
    B. Commodities.
    C. Private equity.

©2012 Kaplan, Inc.

119. Compared to its net asset value (NAV) calculated in accordance with accounting standards, a hedge fund's trading NAV:
    A. will be lower because of adjustments for illiquid positions.
    B. is likely to be higher because of upward bias in model-based security values.
    C. may be higher or lower, reflecting gains or losses on securities designated for short-term trading.

120. The mezzanine financing portion of a leveraged buyout (LBO) is *most likely* to:
    A. represent committed capital.
    B. be convertible to equity or include warrants.
    C. have seniority over other bonds issued to finance the LBO.

EXAM 1
AFTERNOON SESSION

Calculating Your Score

Topic	Maximum Score	Your Score
Ethical and Professional Standards	18	
Quantitative Methods	14	
Economics	12	
Financial Reporting and Analysis	24	
Corporate Finance	10	
Portfolio Management	6	
Equity Investments	12	
Fixed Income	14	
Derivatives	6	
Alternative Investments	4	
Total	120	

The morning and afternoon exams are identically weighted over the topics and readings. You can therefore treat the morning and afternoon exams as independent exams.

If you took more than three hours (180 minutes) to complete this portion of the exam, you should adjust your score downward by one point for each minute you ran over.

Remember: the real exam *will be more difficult* than these practice exams. The main reason for this is the general anxiety and stress that you will be feeling on exam day, coupled with the time pressure you will be under. Many of the questions on this practice exam and the real exam are not individually difficult, so if you take extra time to answer the questions on this practice exam, your score will go up significantly. However, if you want an accurate measure of your potential performance on the exam, adhere to the 3-hour time limit.

After you have finished grading your practice exam, you may find it useful to use the exam questions and recommended solutions for review. Many of these questions were specifically written for your use as study tools. Once again, I feel I should remind you not to rely on memorizing these questions; you are not likely to see them on the actual exam. What you will see on the exam, though, are the concepts, terms, and procedures presented in these questions.

Your actual exam will most likely look different than what you see in this book. Please remember, no study provider knows the content of the actual exam. These practice exams are our best guess as to the structure, content, and difficulty of an actual exam.

Test Answers

1.	(A)	(B)	(C)		41.	(A)	(B)	(C)		81.	(A)	(B)	(C)
2.	(A)	(B)	(C)		42.	(A)	(B)	(C)		82.	(A)	(B)	(C)
3.	(A)	(B)	(C)		43.	(A)	(B)	(C)		83.	(A)	(B)	(C)
4.	(A)	(B)	(C)		44.	(A)	(B)	(C)		84.	(A)	(B)	(C)
5.	(A)	(B)	(C)		45.	(A)	(B)	(C)		85.	(A)	(B)	(C)
6.	(A)	(B)	(C)		46.	(A)	(B)	(C)		86.	(A)	(B)	(C)
7.	(A)	(B)	(C)		47.	(A)	(B)	(C)		87.	(A)	(B)	(C)
8.	(A)	(B)	(C)		48.	(A)	(B)	(C)		88.	(A)	(B)	(C)
9.	(A)	(B)	(C)		49.	(A)	(B)	(C)		89.	(A)	(B)	(C)
10.	(A)	(B)	(C)		50.	(A)	(B)	(C)		90.	(A)	(B)	(C)
11.	(A)	(B)	(C)		51.	(A)	(B)	(C)		91.	(A)	(B)	(C)
12.	(A)	(B)	(C)		52.	(A)	(B)	(C)		92.	(A)	(B)	(C)
13.	(A)	(B)	(C)		53.	(A)	(B)	(C)		93.	(A)	(B)	(C)
14.	(A)	(B)	(C)		54.	(A)	(B)	(C)		94.	(A)	(B)	(C)
15.	(A)	(B)	(C)		55.	(A)	(B)	(C)		95.	(A)	(B)	(C)
16.	(A)	(B)	(C)		56.	(A)	(B)	(C)		96.	(A)	(B)	(C)
17.	(A)	(B)	(C)		57.	(A)	(B)	(C)		97.	(A)	(B)	(C)
18.	(A)	(B)	(C)		58.	(A)	(B)	(C)		98.	(A)	(B)	(C)
19.	(A)	(B)	(C)		59.	(A)	(B)	(C)		99.	(A)	(B)	(C)
20.	(A)	(B)	(C)		60.	(A)	(B)	(C)		100.	(A)	(B)	(C)
21.	(A)	(B)	(C)		61.	(A)	(B)	(C)		101.	(A)	(B)	(C)
22.	(A)	(B)	(C)		62.	(A)	(B)	(C)		102.	(A)	(B)	(C)
23.	(A)	(B)	(C)		63.	(A)	(B)	(C)		103.	(A)	(B)	(C)
24.	(A)	(B)	(C)		64.	(A)	(B)	(C)		104.	(A)	(B)	(C)
25.	(A)	(B)	(C)		65.	(A)	(B)	(C)		105.	(A)	(B)	(C)
26.	(A)	(B)	(C)		66.	(A)	(B)	(C)		106.	(A)	(B)	(C)
27.	(A)	(B)	(C)		67.	(A)	(B)	(C)		107.	(A)	(B)	(C)
28.	(A)	(B)	(C)		68.	(A)	(B)	(C)		108.	(A)	(B)	(C)
29.	(A)	(B)	(C)		69.	(A)	(B)	(C)		109.	(A)	(B)	(C)
30.	(A)	(B)	(C)		70.	(A)	(B)	(C)		110.	(A)	(B)	(C)
31.	(A)	(B)	(C)		71.	(A)	(B)	(C)		111.	(A)	(B)	(C)
32.	(A)	(B)	(C)		72.	(A)	(B)	(C)		112.	(A)	(B)	(C)
33.	(A)	(B)	(C)		73.	(A)	(B)	(C)		113.	(A)	(B)	(C)
34.	(A)	(B)	(C)		74.	(A)	(B)	(C)		114.	(A)	(B)	(C)
35.	(A)	(B)	(C)		75.	(A)	(B)	(C)		115.	(A)	(B)	(C)
36.	(A)	(B)	(C)		76.	(A)	(B)	(C)		116.	(A)	(B)	(C)
37.	(A)	(B)	(C)		77.	(A)	(B)	(C)		117.	(A)	(B)	(C)
38.	(A)	(B)	(C)		78.	(A)	(B)	(C)		118.	(A)	(B)	(C)
39.	(A)	(B)	(C)		79.	(A)	(B)	(C)		119.	(A)	(B)	(C)
40.	(A)	(B)	(C)		80.	(A)	(B)	(C)		120.	(A)	(B)	(C)

Exam 1
Afternoon Session

Questions 1 through 18 relate to Ethical and Professional Standards.
(27 minutes)

1.   Courtney Johnson, CFA, is an independent investment advisor specializing in equity securities. Johnson refers clients seeking fixed income investments to Reliable Securities. Reliable Securities, in turn, provides Johnson with equity research. Although Johnson has not informed her clients of the arrangement with Reliable, Johnson's clients often praise her for obtaining such quality research and for referring them to Reliable for fixed income investments. Has Johnson violated any CFA Institute Standards of Professional Conduct?
    A. Yes, because the soft dollars generated by the arrangement don't benefit all the clients.
    B. No, because Johnson's clients are satisfied with the fixed income advisor that Johnson recommended.
    C. Yes, because Johnson's clients lack sufficient information to evaluate any partiality inherent in her recommendation of Reliable's services.

2.   Russell Finley, CFA, is a managing director at Wilson Brothers, a regional brokerage firm. Finley manages the institutional fixed-income desk and is responsible for 20 employees in both the trading and sales departments. Finley recently called a meeting with the head of trading and the head of sales to review the firm's policies regarding trading by employees in their personal accounts. He instructed the two to review the information with the employees they supervise. A week after the meeting, Finley discovered that a sales assistant made personal trades during a firm "blackout" period on a restricted security. According to the Standards regarding responsibilities of supervisors, the *least appropriate* action for Finley to take is to:
    A. speak directly to the employee and attain assurance that the violation will not be repeated.
    B. begin an investigation to determine the extent of the wrongdoing.
    C. increase the monitoring of the employee's activities at the firm.

3.   Charlotte Stein, a CFA candidate, obtained a copy of a computerized stock selection model designed by a former classmate who is a Wall Street analyst. After spending some time reviewing the program and making some adjustments, Stein showed the new model to her supervisor. Her supervisor said she did a great job and told Stein to incorporate the new model in her next industry review. She called her classmate for permission, and he told her to go ahead and use the model. Stein has:
   A. violated the Standard concerning misrepresentation.
   B. violated the Standard concerning communication with clients.
   C. not violated CFA Institute Standards of Professional Conduct.

4.   Justin Matthews, CFA, is the CFO of a regional bank and serves on the bank's investment committee. The investment committee is considering the appropriate actions to take with regard to the bank's temporary surplus of cash. The committee, composed of analysts and investment personnel, recommends to the bank's CEO that the cash be invested in intermediate-term Treasury notes. Matthews feels that the recommendation is too conservative. However, Matthews is the only member of the independent committee who disagrees with the recommendation. In accordance with CFA Institute Standard of Professional Conduct, Matthews should *most* appropriately:
   A. decline to be associated with the recommendation.
   B. privately express his concerns to his supervisor.
   C. document his difference of opinion with the committee.

5.   Howard Klein, CFA, supervises a group of research analysts, none of whom is a CFA charterholder or CFA candidate. He has attempted on several occasions to get his firm to adopt a compliance system to ensure that applicable laws and regulations are followed. The firm's principals, however, have never adopted his recommendations. According to CFA Institute Standards of Professional Conduct, Klein at this point:
   A. should decline in writing to accept supervisory responsibility until his firm adopts reasonable compliance procedures.
   B. needs to take no action because the employees are not CFA charterholders or CFA candidates.
   C. must resign from the company and document in writing his reasons for doing so.

6. Lisa Crocker, CFA, manages several pension accounts and directs most of her trades through the Zeta Brokerage House. Crocker does this because she believes she gets expedient and low-cost trade execution, and Zeta provides her with excellent research reports used in the management of these accounts. Regional, a small discount brokerage house, has just approached Crocker and said it will execute her trades at half of Zeta's cost. However, Regional does not have a research department. If Crocker declines to switch her business to Regional, has she violated any CFA Institute Standards of Professional Conduct?
   A. Yes, because she has not obtained explicit permission from her clients to use Zeta.
   B. No, if the higher commissions are commensurate with the value of the research services she receives.
   C. Yes, because the Standard concerning loyalty, prudence, and care states that she must minimize trade expenses.

7. Katrina Anderson, CFA, is an investment advisor for Ringfellow Investments, an institutional investment manager with $5 billion in assets under management. Prior to joining Ringfellow, Anderson was in a similar position with a boutique firm that had $500 million in assets under management. Anderson left her previous employer on good terms, did not sign a non-compete agreement, and took no firm materials with her. According to CFA Institute Standards of Professional Conduct, Anderson:
   A. must seek permission from her previous employer before contacting her previous clients at that firm.
   B. may contact clients of her previous firm immediately after ending her employment there.
   C. should not contact clients from her previous employment at all because it would harm her previous employer.

8. Scott Houser, CFA, is a widely known equity analyst whose recommendations often influence share prices. Houser changes his recommendation to "Sell" on Drywall Company and distributes this recommendation only to his clients, many of whom act on the recommendation before it becomes known to the public. Has Houser violated the Code and Standards?
   A. No.
   B. Yes, he has violated the Standard concerning communications with clients.
   C. Yes, he has violated the Standard concerning material nonpublic information.

9. Isabelle Burns, CFA, is an investment advisor for a firm whose client base is composed of high net worth individuals. In her personal portfolio, Burns has an investment in Torex, a company that has developed software to speed up internet browsing. Burns has thoroughly researched Torex and believes the company is financially strong yet currently significantly undervalued. According to the CFA Institute Standards of Professional Conduct, Burns may:

    A. not recommend Torex as long as she has a personal investment in the stock.
    B. recommend Torex to a client, but she must disclose her investment in Torex to the client.
    C. recommend Torex to a client without disclosure as long as it is a suitable investment for the client.

10. Christopher Kim, CFA, is a research analyst for Batts Brothers, an investment banking firm in New York. Kim follows the energy industry and has frequent contact with industry executives. A CEO of a large oil and gas corporation that has previously employed Batts Brothers to underwrite a stock issue has invited Kim to his office to discuss a secondary offering of the company's stock. The CEO wants Batts Brothers to underwrite the stock issue. As an incentive to place the issue quickly with institutional investors, the CEO offers Kim the opportunity to fly on his private jet to his ranch in Texas for an exotic game hunting expedition if Kim's firm can complete the underwriting within one month. According to CFA Institute Standards of Conduct, Kim:

    A. must not accept such lavish benefits, in order to maintain his objectivity.
    B. must obtain written consent from Batts Brothers before accepting the invitation.
    C. may accept the invitation without consent only if he discloses the trip to Batts Brothers before accepting.

11. When GIPS and local laws conflict, in order to be in compliance with GIPS, the investment firm must:

    A. follow local law but disclose the conflict with GIPS.
    B. follow local law, and no additional disclosure is required.
    C. follow GIPS but disclose that this is in conflict with local laws.

12. Kim Vance, a CFA candidate, tells a prospective client, "I may not have a long-term track record, but I am sure you will be satisfied with my performance. Over the three years I have been in the business, my equity-oriented clients have averaged a total return of more than 20% a year." The statement is accurate, but Vance only has a few equity clients, and one of these took a large position in a penny stock (against Vance's advice) and realized a huge gain. This large return caused the average of all of Vance's clients to exceed 20% per year. Without this one investment, the average gain would have been 10% per year. Has Vance violated CFA Institute Standards of Professional Conduct?
    A. Yes, because the statement misrepresents Vance's track record.
    B. No, because it is true and Vance has not assured such returns in the future.
    C. Yes, because the equities composite she mentions does not qualify as a composite.

13. Joseph Drake, CFA, is a portfolio manager for Best Investments. The fixed-income desk at Best has developed a new structured product that produces positive returns in a very wide range of interest rate scenarios. Drake thoroughly reads and evaluates an analytical report about the product and is impressed by its return profile. He faxes the cover page of the analysis, which includes the name of the author, to a client with objectives similar to those that the structured product is designed to meet, and handwrites a note to the client saying, "I think you should act quickly on this!" When the client calls requesting the entire report, Drake informs him that the research is proprietary and cannot be released. With respect to the Standards concerning suitability and communication with clients, Drake is in violation of:
    A. both of these Standards.
    B. neither of these Standards.
    C. only one of these Standards.

14. Brian Farley, CFA, is an independent portfolio manager. Currently, Farley's only client is a $75 million university endowment fund. A representative of the endowment fund calls Farley and places a "Sell" order on a portfolio holding whose management has just issued a negative earnings forecast. Farley also owns the security in his retirement account and immediately decides to sell his position. He places simultaneous "Sell" orders for both the client and his personal account. According to the Standards on fair dealing and priority of transactions, Farley is in violation of:
    A. both of these Standards.
    B. neither of these Standards.
    C. only one of these Standards.

15. Franklin Murphy is a trader and CFA Level III candidate who works for Wellington & Worrel Advisers. When selecting brokers for client trades, Murphy usually selects between Casanova Broker-Dealer (where he receives discounts on personal securities transactions) and Cedrock Brokers (where he receives investment research used in managing client portfolios). Both Casanova and Cedrock charge higher commission rates than other brokers used by Wellington & Worrel, and Cedrock provides more efficient trade execution than other brokers. According to the Standard on loyalty, prudence, and care, Murphy violates the Standard by directing trades to:
    A. Casanova and Cedrock.
    B. Cedrock but not Casanova.
    C. Casanova but not Cedrock.

16. Art Dodd, CFA, is a registered representative with Owens Securities. He is currently in a dispute with one client, Madge Phillips, CFP, about a limit order for her IRA account that she feels was entered incorrectly, resulting in a loss (in her opinion) of $500. Dodd has been allocated 1,000 shares of a new issue that is oversubscribed. He suggests to Phillips that he will give her 250 shares of his allocation if she forgets about the supposed trade error. Further, he offers to buy her dinner at a very nice restaurant that serves an excellent salmon Kulebyaka, which he suggests they pair with a nice 1997 white Cheval-Blanc Signé. According to the Standards of Practice, Dodd has *most likely* violated the Standard concerning:
    A. misconduct.
    B. fair dealing.
    C. additional compensation arrangements.

17. Which of the following is *least likely* one of the nine major topics of the CFA Institute Global Investment Performance Standards (GIPS)?
    A. Real Estate.
    B. Private Equity.
    C. Venture Capital.

18. Graham Carson has served as investment advisor to Ron Grayson, a wealthy philanthropist, for one year. Grayson has called a meeting with Carson to discuss his disappointment with two of the portfolio stocks Carson had chosen last year. Grayson feels that, in both cases, the individual securities possessed greater risk than he had agreed to in the investment policy statement. Carson reviews his notes and files pertaining to the account and sees that, according to his analysis at the time of the recommendations, the portfolio he recommended to Grayson was consistent with the risk and return objectives as well as the constraints of Grayson's portfolio as detailed in Grayson's most recent investment policy statement (IPS). The individual securities, however, were each quite risky and appeared even more so now, since they had performed so poorly. According to the Standard on suitability and the Standard concerning diligence and reasonable basis, Carson is in violation of:
   A. both of these Standards.
   B. neither of these Standards.
   C. only one of these Standards.

Questions 19 through 32 relate to Quantitative Methods. (21 minutes)

19. Five years ago, an investor borrowed $5,000 from a financial institution that charged a 6% annual interest rate, and he immediately took his family to live in Nepal. He made no payments during the time he was away. When he returned, he agreed to repay the original loan plus the accrued interest by making five end-of-year payments starting one year after he returned. If the interest rate on the loan is held constant at 6% per year, what annual payment must the investor make in order to retire the loan?
   A. $1,338.23.
   B. $1,588.45.
   C. $1,638.23.

20. If an investment of $4,000 will grow to $6,520 in four years with monthly compounding, the effective annual interest rate will be *closest* to:
   A. 11.2%.
   B. 12.3%.
   C. 13.0%.

21. An analyst constructs a histogram and frequency polygon of monthly returns for aggressive equity funds over a 20-year period. Which of the following statements about these displays is *most accurate*?
    A. The height of each bar in a frequency polygon represents the absolute frequency for each return interval.
    B. Both a histogram and a frequency polygon provide a graphical display of data found in a frequency distribution.
    C. To construct a histogram, the analyst would plot the midpoint of the return intervals on the x-axis and the absolute frequency for that interval on the y-axis, connecting neighboring points with a straight line.

22. An investor holds a portfolio consisting of one share of each of the following stocks:

Stock	Price at the Beginning of the Year	Price at the End of the Year	Cash Dividend During the Year
X	$20	$10	$0
Y	$40	$50	$2
Z	$100	$105	$4

For the 1-year holding period, the portfolio return is *closest* to:
    A. 6.9%.
    B. 9.1%.
    C. 13.1%.

23. An analyst takes a sample of yearly returns of aggressive growth funds resulting in the following data set: 25, 15, 35, 45, and 55. The mean absolute deviation (MAD) of the data set is *closest* to:
    A. 12.
    B. 16.
    C. 20.

24. A security has annual returns of 5%, 10%, and 15%. The coefficient of variation of the security (using the population standard deviation) is *closest* to:
    A. 0.3.
    B. 0.4.
    C. 0.5.

25. If an analyst concludes that the distribution of a large sample of returns is positively skewed, which of the following relationships involving the mean, median, and mode is *most likely*?
    A. Mean > median > mode.
    B. Mean < median < mode.
    C. Mean > median < mode.

26. An analyst has been hired to evaluate a high-risk project. The analyst estimates the probability that the project will fail in the first year as well as the conditional probability of failure for each of the remaining four years of the project, as follows:

Year	1	2	3	4	5
Failure probability	0.25	0.20	0.20	0.15	0.10

The project will have no payoff if it fails, but it will have a payoff of $20,000 at the end of the fifth year if it succeeds. Because of its high risk, the required rate of return for an investment in this project is 25%. Based on this information, the expected present value of the project is *closest* to:
A. $2,400.
B. $3,010.
C. $5,900.

27. An investor opens an account by purchasing 1,000 shares of stock at $42 per share. One year later, these shares are trading at $55 per share, and the investor purchases 1,000 more shares. At the end of the second year, the shares are trading at $54. The time-weighted rate of return on the account is *closest* to:
A. 7.7%.
B. 13.4%.
C. 16.4%.

28. Which of the following distributions is *most likely* a discrete distribution?
A. A normal distribution.
B. A univariate distribution.
C. A binomial distribution.

29. An investment has a mean return of 15% and a standard deviation of returns equal to 10%. If the distribution of returns is approximately normal, which of the following statements is *least accurate*? The probability of obtaining a return:
A. less than 5% is about 16%.
B. greater than 35% is about 2.5%.
C. between 5% and 25% is about 95%.

30. Which of the following statements about the central limit theorem is *least accurate*?
A. The central limit theorem has limited usefulness for skewed distributions.
B. The mean of the population and the mean of all possible sample means are equal.
C. When the sample size is large, the sampling distribution of the sample means is approximately normal.

31. An analyst takes a random sample of the returns on 225 stocks from a population with a known variance of returns of 100. The standard error of the sample mean return is *closest* to:
    A. 0.44.
    B. 0.67.
    C. 2.26.

32. Which of the following statements about hypothesis testing involving a *z*-statistic is *least accurate*?
    A. The *p*-value is the smallest significance level at which the null hypothesis can be rejected.
    B. A *z*-test is theoretically acceptable in place of a *t*-test for tests concerning a mean when sample size is small.
    C. If the confidence level is set at 95%, the chance of rejecting the null hypothesis when in fact it is true is 5%.

Questions 33 through 44 relate to Economics. (18 minutes)

33. According to the crowding-out effect, the sale of government bonds used to finance excess government spending is *least likely* to:
    A. increase the real interest rate.
    B. reduce private investment spending.
    C. increase the profitability of corporate investment projects.

34. Which of the following statements on the economic implications of trade restrictions is *most accurate*?
    A. Quota rents are the amounts received by the domestic government when it charges for import licenses.
    B. In the importing country, import quotas, tariffs, and voluntary export restraints all decrease producer surplus.
    C. In the case of a quota, if the domestic government collects the full value of the import licenses, the result is the same as that of a tariff.

35. In a demand function, if the price of a complement to Good J decreases, the quantity demanded of Good J:
    A. increases.
    B. decreases.
    C. may increase or decrease.

36. Based on her forecast for the economy, a portfolio manager increases her investments in high-quality bonds and decreases her investments in commodities. The portfolio manager *most likely* expects the economy to experience:
    A. stagflation.
    B. a recessionary gap.
    C. an inflationary gap.

37. The long-run production decision differs from the short-run production decision in that:
    A. fixed costs can be changed in the long run but not the short run.
    B. variable costs can be changed in the long run but not the short run.
    C. variable costs can be changed in the short run but not the long run.

38. Demand for gasoline (in hundreds of liters) at a particular station, as a function of the price of gasoline and the price of bus travel, is $Q_D = 300 - 14 P_{gas} + 2 P_{bus}$. If the price of gasoline per liter (P_{gas}) is 1.50 euros, and the price of a standardized unit of bus travel (P_{bus}) is 12 euros, the cross price elasticity of gasoline demand with respect to the price of bus travel is *closest* to:
    A. 0.01.
    B. 0.08.
    C. 2.00.

39. Which of the following statements about a monopolist is *least accurate*?
    A. The monopolist faces a downward sloping demand curve.
    B. Unlike an oligopolist, a monopolist will always be able to earn economic profit.
    C. A profit-maximizing monopolist will expand output until marginal revenue equals marginal cost.

40. A market has the following characteristics: a large number of independent sellers, each producing a differentiated product; low barriers to entry; producers facing downward sloping demand curves; and demand that is highly elastic. This description *most* closely describes:
    A. an oligopoly.
    B. pure competition.
    C. monopolistic competition.

41. Regarding the cost-push and demand-pull inflation processes, which requires repeated expansionary actions by policymakers to result in inflation?
    A. Both require repeated expansionary actions.
    B. Neither requires repeated expansionary actions.
    C. Only one requires repeated expansionary actions.

42. Accounting profit is often an unsatisfactory performance measure from an economic point of view because it:
    A. does not consider depreciation.
    B. considers marginal costs rather than average costs.
    C. does not consider the opportunity costs of equity capital.

43. Consider two currencies, the WSC and the BDR. The spot WSC/BDR exchange rate is 2.875, the 180-day riskless WSC rate is 1.5%, and the 180-day riskless BDR rate is 3.0%. The 180-day forward exchange rate that will prevent arbitrage profits is *closest* to:
   A. 2.833 WSC/BDR.
   B. 2.854 WSC/BDR.
   C. 2.918 WSC/BDR.

44. The *most likely* effects of the imposition of an effective increase in the minimum wage include:
   A. an increase in the real wage, gains in efficiency, and a decrease in inflation.
   B. increased unemployment, an excess supply of labor at the new wage rate, and a decrease in economic efficiency.
   C. a reduction in non-monetary labor benefits, excess demand for labor, and a shortage of highly skilled workers.

Questions 45 through 68 relate to Financial Reporting and Analysis. (36 minutes)

45. Normal Corp. has a current ratio above 1 and a quick ratio less than 1. Which of the following actions will increase the current ratio and decrease the quick ratio? Normal Corp.:
   A. buys fixed assets on credit.
   B. uses cash to purchase inventory.
   C. pays off accounts payable from cash.

46. A company has a cash conversion cycle of 70 days. If the company's payables turnover decreases from 11 to 10 and days of sales outstanding increase by 5, the company's cash conversion cycle will:
   A. decrease by approximately 8 days.
   B. decrease by approximately 3 days.
   C. increase by approximately 2 days.

47. A manager whose compensation is tied to improving the firm's inventory turnover *most likely* has an incentive to:
   A. overstate assets.
   B. understate earnings.
   C. overstate working capital.

48. Which of the following is *least likely* to be considered an objective of financial market regulation according to the International Organization of Securities Commissions (IOSCO)?
   A. Reduce systemic risk.
   B. Ensure the fairness, efficiency, and transparency of markets.
   C. Develop individual financial regulatory standards for each country to reflect the unique needs of each market.

49. Napa Corp. sells 1-year memberships to its Fine Wine Club for $180. Wine Club members each receive a bottle of white wine and a bottle of red wine, selected by the club director, four times each year at the beginning of each quarter. To properly account for sales of Wine Club memberships, Napa will record:
A. an asset for prepaid sales.
B. a liability for accrued expenses.
C. a liability for unearned revenue.

50. An analyst gathered the following data about a company:
- Net sales $4,000
- Dividends declared   170
- Cost of goods sold   2,000
- Inventory increased by   100
- Accounts payable increased by   300
- Cash expenses for other inputs   500
- Long-term debt principal repayment   250
- Cash tax payments   200
- Purchase of new equipment   300

The company's cash flow from operations, based on these data only, is:
A. $1,200.
B. $1,500.
C. $1,575.

51. Jennifer Frye, CFA, is comparing the financial performance of a firm that presents its results under IFRS to that of a firm that complies with U.S. GAAP. The U.S. firm uses the LIFO method for inventory accounting, and the other firm uses the FIFO method. If Frye performs the appropriate adjustments to make the U.S. firm's financial statements comparable to the firm that reports under IFRS, her adjustments are *least likely* to change the firm's:
A. quick ratio.
B. debt-to-equity ratio.
C. cash conversion cycle.

52. A reconciliation of beginning and ending carrying values for long-lived tangible assets is required for firms reporting under:
A. IFRS.
B. U.S. GAAP.
C. both U.S. GAAP and IFRS.

53. The following data pertains to a company's common-size financial statements.

- Current assets   40%
- Total debt   40%
- Net income   16%
- Total assets $2,000
- Sales $1,500
- Total asset turnover ratio   0.75
- The firm has no preferred stock in its capital structure.

The company's after-tax return on common equity is *closest* to:
A. 15%.
B. 20%.
C. 25%.

54. Which of the following statements about the calculation of earnings per share (EPS) is *least accurate*?
A. Shares issued after a stock split must be adjusted for the split.
B. Options outstanding may have no effect on diluted EPS.
C. Reacquired shares are excluded from the computation from the date of reacquisition.

55. A company has 1,000,000 warrants outstanding at the beginning of the year, each convertible into one share of stock with an exercise price of $50. No new warrants were issued during the year. The average stock price during the period was $60, and the year-end stock price was $45. What adjustment for these warrants should be made, under the treasury stock method, to the number of shares used to calculate diluted earnings per share (EPS)?
A. 0.
B. 166,667.
C. 200,000.

56. Which of the following statements about financial ratios is *most accurate*?
A. A company with a high debt-to-equity ratio will have a return on asssets that is greater than its return on equity.
B. Any firm with a high net profit margin will have a high gross profit margin and vice versa.
C. A company that has an inventory turnover of 6 times, a receivables turnover of 9 times, and a payables turnover of 12 times will have a cash conversion cycle of approximately 71 days.

57. In accounting for a defined benefit pension plan, the amount reported as "prior service cost" refers to the:
    A. total value of benefits already paid to retirees who are still receiving pension payments.
    B. present value of the pension benefits due to employees based on their employment up to the date of the statement.
    C. present value of the increase in future pension benefits from a change in the terms of the pension plan.

58. During an accounting period, a company has the following sequence of transactions with a beginning inventory of zero:

Purchases	Sales
100 units at $210	80 units at $240
90 units at $225	90 units at $250

    The company's cost of goods sold (COGS) using FIFO for inventory accounting, and its ending inventory using LIFO, are *closest* to:

	FIFO COGS	LIFO ending inventory
A.	$36,750	$4,200
B.	$37,050	$4,200
C.	$37,050	$4,500

59. On January 2, a company acquires some state-of-the-art production equipment at a net cost of $14 million. For financial reporting purposes, the firm will depreciate the equipment over a 7-year life using straight-line depreciation and a zero salvage value; for tax reporting purposes, however, the firm will use 3-year accelerated depreciation. Given a tax rate of 35% and a first-year accelerated depreciation factor of 0.333, by how much will the company's deferred tax liability increase in the first year of the equipment's life?
    A. $931,700.
    B. $1,064,800.
    C. $1,730,300.

60. When comparing two firms, an analyst should *most* appropriately adjust the financial statements when they include significant:
    A. acquisition goodwill, if one of the firms reports under IFRS and the other under U.S. GAAP.
    B. property, plant, and equipment, if one of the firms uses accelerated depreciation and the other uses straight-line depreciation.
    C. unrealized losses from securities held for trading, if one of the firms uses fair value reporting for securities investments and the other does not.

61. A software company holds a number of marketable securities as investments. For the most recent period, the company reports that the market value of its securities held for trading decreased by $2 million and the market value of its securities available for sale increased in value by $3 million. Together, these changes in value will:
     A. reduce net income and shareholders' equity by $2 million.
     B. increase shareholders' equity by $1 million and have no effect on net income.
     C. reduce net income by $2 million and increase shareholders' equity by $1 million.

62. Maritza Inc. is involved in an exchange of debt for equity. In which of the following sections of the cash flow statement would Maritza record this transaction?
     A. Investing activities section.
     B. Financing activities section.
     C. Footnotes to the cash flow statement.

63. An analyst calculates the following ratios for Lebicke Company:

	20X6	20X5	20X4
Debt-to-capital ratio	56.3%	56.4%	56.2%
Fixed charge coverage ratio	3.3×	3.4×	3.5×
Interest coverage ratio	4.0×	3.9×	3.8×

     These ratios *most likely* suggest that during the period shown, Lebicke's:
     A. use of operating leases increased.
     B. interest obligations increased faster than earnings.
     C. capital structure became more reliant on equity financing.

64. Analysts reviewing Amber, Inc.'s and Bold, Inc.'s long-term contracting activities observe that Amber's contracts are being accounted for under the percentage-of-completion method while Bold's are being accounted for under the completed contract method. This difference is *least likely* to affect the two companies':
     A. income statements.
     B. statements of cash flows.
     C. assets on the balance sheets.

65. Which of the following statements regarding an audit and a standard auditor's opinion is *most accurate*?
    A. The objective of an audit is to enable the auditor to provide an opinion on the numerical accuracy of the financial statements.
    B. To provide an independent review of a company's financial statements, an independent certified public accounting firm is appointed by the company's management.
    C. The absence of an explanatory paragraph in the audit report relating to the going concern assumption suggests that there are no serious problems that require a close examination of that assumption by the analyst.

66. Two growing firms are identical except that Alfred Company capitalizes costs for some long-lived assets that Canute Company expenses. For these two firms, which of the following financial statement effects is *most likely*? Alfred will show higher:
    A. net income than Canute.
    B. working capital than Canute.
    C. investing cash flow than Canute.

67. A company fails to record accrued wages for a reporting period. What effect will this error have on the company's financial statements?
    A. Assets and liabilities are understated.
    B. Assets and owners' equity are overstated.
    C. Liabilities are understated and owners' equity is overstated.

68. Which of the following statements about the treatment of leases on the lessor's financial statements is *least accurate*?
    A. If the present value of the payments on a finance lease is greater than the carrying value of the asset, the lease is a sales-type lease on the books of the lessor.
    B. In a direct financing lease, the lessor recognizes gross profit at the lease inception, while in a sales-type lease it does not.
    C. To be a finance lease for the lessor, collectibility must be reasonably certain and the lessor must have substantially completed performance.

Questions 69 through 78 relate to Corporate Finance. (15 minutes)

69. Rodgers, Inc. has fixed operating expenses of $2 million and will break even with sales of $5 million. For sales of $7 million, an analyst would estimate the firm's operating income as:
    A. $800,000.
    B. $1,200,000.
    C. $2,000,000.

70. Weights to be used in calculating a company's weighted average cost of capital are *least appropriately* based on:
    A. information from the company about its target capital structure.
    B. the average capital structure weights for companies of a similar size.
    C. the average capital structure weights for companies in the same industry.

71. An accounts receivable aging schedule is *best* used to:
    A. determine how the receivables turnover ratio has changed over time.
    B. identify trends in how well the firm is doing at collecting receivables and converting them to cash.
    C. compare a company's receivables management to those of the average for its industry or for a group of peer companies.

72. Managers of Smith Corporation are reviewing a section of the firm's code of ethics that relates to Board members. Vice president Susan Klepp argues, "Drawing upon the expertise of our Board members by hiring them as consultants is in the shareholders' best interests. However, personal use of company assets by Board members should be limited to those instances that align the incentives of the Board members with those of the firm." With respect to the provisions that should be included in a strong corporate code of ethics, Klepp is:
    A. correct about both provisions.
    B. correct about only one of these provisions.
    C. incorrect about both provisions.

73. A company has 35 million shares outstanding with a current market price of $49.75 per share. The company has maintained a $1.00 per share quarterly dividend for several years, but for the next quarter, management is considering whether to implement a $35 million share repurchase in place of the regular quarterly dividend. Assuming the tax treatments and information effects of either alternative are the same, the net impact of the share repurchase, compared to the payment of a cash dividend, is to:
    A. decrease shareholder wealth.
    B. have no effect on shareholder wealth.
    C. increase shareholder wealth.

74. Ron's Organic Markets has limited access to borrowed funds and must choose among ten independent projects with returns greater than their cost of capital. All the projects under consideration have the same required investment of $2 million, and Ron's has $10 million available for capital investments this year. Which of the following selection criteria is *least likely* to identify the five projects that will produce the greatest expected increase in the value of the firm? Choose the five projects with:
    A. the highest IRRs.
    B. the greatest total NPV.
    C. the largest sum of profitability indexes.

75. Randox Industries has the following investment policy statement: "In order to achieve the safety and liquidity necessary in the investment of excess cash balances, the CFO or his designee may invest excess cash balances in 30-day U.S. Treasury bills, or in banker's acceptances with maturities of less than 31 days or 30-day certificates of deposit, where the credit rating of the issuing bank is A+ or higher." This policy statement is:
   A. inappropriate because it is too restrictive.
   B. appropriate because these are all safe, liquid securities.
   C. inappropriate because both banker's acceptances and certificates of deposit are illiquid.

76. Which of the following is *least* relevant in determining project cash flow for a capital investment?
   A. Sunk costs.
   B. Tax impacts.
   C. Opportunity costs.

77. From a liquidity management perspective, an increase in the number of days of payables is *best* described as:
   A. liquidity neutral.
   B. a drag on liquidity.
   C. a source of liquidity.

78. Which of the following characteristics is *least likely* required to ensure that a company's Board of Directors Audit Committee is adequately representing shareowner interests?
   A. Any conflicts between the external auditor and the firm are resolved in a manner that favors shareholders.
   B. The shareholders vote on whether to approve of the Board's selection of the external auditor.
   C. The committee regularly reviews the performance, independence, skills, and experience of existing board members.

Questions 79 through 84 relate to Portfolio Management. (9 minutes)

79. In choosing asset classes for establishing strategic portfolio allocation across assets, the manager would *most* prefer that:
   A. asset classes are only those with tradable liquid assets.
   B. the asset classes span the broadest universe of investable assets.
   C. correlations of asset returns within an asset class are significantly greater than correlations of asset class returns.

80. Which of the following is *least likely* among the usual investment constraints that should be considered?
   A. Legal and regulatory factors.
   B. Unique needs and preferences.
   C. Adherence to the Standards of Practice.

81.   Given the following correlation matrix, a risk-averse investor would *least* prefer which of the following 2-stock portfolios (all else equal)?

Stock	W	X	Y	Z
W	+1			
X	−0.2	+1		
Y	+0.6	−0.1	+1	
Z	+0.8	−0.3	+0.5	+1

A. W and Y.
B. X and Y.
C. X and Z.

82.   Which type of risk is positively related to expected excess returns according to the CAPM?
A. Unique.
B. Systematic.
C. Diversifiable.

83.   Which of the following statements about the security market line (SML) and capital market line (CML) is *most accurate*?
A. The SML involves the concept of a risk-free asset, but the CML does not.
B. The SML uses beta, but the CML uses standard deviation as the risk measure.
C. Both the SML and CML can be used to explain a stock's expected return.

84.   Becky Scott and Sid Fiona have the same expectations about the risk and return of the market portfolio; however, Scott selects a portfolio with 30% T-bills and 70% invested in the market portfolio, while Fiona holds a leveraged portfolio, having borrowed to invest 130% of his portfolio equity value in the market portfolio. Regarding their preferences between risk and return and their indifference curves, it is *most likely* that:
A. Scott is risk averse but Fiona is not.
B. Fiona's indifference curves are flatter than Scott's.
C. Scott is willing to take on more risk to increase her expected portfolio return than Fiona is.

Questions 85 through 96 relate to Equity Investments. (18 minutes)

85.   An index is composed of three stocks. Their performance in a recent period is as follows:

Stock	Number of Shares Outstanding (Thousands)	Beginning Price	Ending Price	Percent Change
X	100	160	136	–15%
Y	100	80	100	+25%
Z	1,000	60	66	+10%

None of the stocks split during the period. This index will have the smallest percentage increase for the period if it is a(n):
A. value-weighted index.
B. price-weighted index.
C. equal-weighted index using the geometric mean.

86.   A company is *most likely* to earn economic profits if it is operating in an industry characterized by:
A. high industry concentration, high barriers to entry, and low industry capacity.
B. low industry concentration, low barriers to entry, and low industry capacity.
C. low industry concentration, high barriers to entry, and high industry capacity.

87.   Among the types of factors that influence industry growth and profitability, the one that is *most likely* to affect consumer discretionary goods producers more than consumer staples producers is:
A. social factors.
B. demographic factors.
C. macroeconomic factors.

88.   Which form of the efficient markets hypothesis (EMH) implies that an investor can achieve positive abnormal returns on average by using technical analysis?
A. None.
B. Weak form.
C. Weak form or semistrong form.

89. A stock has a steady 5% growth rate in dividends. The required rate of return for stocks of this risk class is 15%. The stock is expected to pay a $1 dividend this coming year. The expected value of the stock at the end of the fourth year is:
     A. $12.16.
     B. $14.21.
     C. $16.32.

90. An investor has long exposure to the risk of the asset underlying an option when taking a:
     A. short position in a put option.
     B. short position in a call option.
     C. long position in a put option.

91. If all other factors remain unchanged, which of the following would *most likely* reduce a company's price/earnings ratio?
     A. The dividend payout ratio increases, and the dividend growth rate increases.
     B. The dividend growth rate increases, and the required rate of return decreases.
     C. The required rate of return increases, and the dividend payout ratio decreases.

92. Porter, Inc. sells 200,000 newly issued shares to two institutions without registering the shares with its country's securities regulators. This transaction is *best* described as being:
     A. illegal.
     B. in the primary market.
     C. in the secondary market.

93. Callable shares *most likely*:
     A. are less risky than noncallable shares.
     B. pay a higher dividend than noncallable shares.
     C. give the investor the right to sell the shares back to the issuer at a specified price.

94. A stop buy order is *most likely*:
     A. used to limit the potential losses on a short sale.
     B. executed if the market price is less than or equal to the specified level.
     C. an order to purchase a security if the price decreases to a specified level.

95. Beachballs, Inc., expects abnormally high earnings for the next three years due to the forecast of unusually hot summers. After the 3-year period, their growth will level off to its normal rate of 6%. Dividends and earnings are expected to grow at 20% for years 1 and 2 and 15% in year 3. The last dividend paid was $1.00. If an investor requires a 10% return on Beachballs, the price she is willing to pay for the stock is *closest* to:
   A. $26.00.
   B. $36.50.
   C. $50.00.

96. If stock markets are semistrong-form efficient, a portfolio manager is *least likely* to create value for investors by:
   A. monitoring clients' needs and circumstances.
   B. allocating invested funds among asset classes.
   C. analyzing financial statements to select undervalued stocks.

Questions 97 through 110 relate to Fixed Income. (21 minutes)

97. An investor who is calculating the arbitrage-free value of a Treasury security should discount each cash flow using the:
   A. risk-free rate.
   B. Treasury spot rate that is specific to its maturity.
   C. Treasury note yield that is specific to its maturity.

98. For an option-free bond, what are the effects of the convexity adjustment on the magnitude (absolute value) of the approximate bond price change in response to an increase in yield and to a decrease in yield?

	Decrease in yield	Increase in yield
A.	Increase in magnitude	Decrease in magnitude
B.	Increase in magnitude	Increase in magnitude
C.	Decrease in magnitude	Increase in magnitude

99. Which of the following statements about different types of bonds is *least accurate*?
   A. Municipal bonds are traded primarily on the New York Stock Exchange.
   B. Tax-backed bonds are backed by the full faith and credit of the issuer.
   C. Government agency issues of federally related institutions are typically backed by the full faith and credit of the U.S. government.

100. A 10%, 10-year bond is sold to yield 8%. One year passes, and the yield remains unchanged at 8%. Holding all other factors constant, the bond's price during this period will have:
   A. increased.
   B. decreased.
   C. remained constant.

101. An analyst is considering a bond for purchase. The bond has a coupon that resets semiannually and is determined by the following formula:

    coupon = 12% – (3.0 × 6-month Treasury bill rate)

    This bond is *most* accurately described as a(n):
    A. step-up note.
    B. inverse floater.
    C. inflation protected security.

102. Exactly one year ago, an investor purchased a $1,000 face value, zero-coupon bond with 11 years remaining to maturity. The YTM (semiannual) was 8.0%. Now, one year later, with market rates unchanged, an investor purchases an annuity that pays $40 every six months for 10 years. The combined value of the two investments based on the 8% semiannual yield is *approximately*:
    A. $966.
    B. $1,000.
    C. $1,456.

103. An analyst gathered the following information about a 15-year bond:
    • 10% semiannual coupon.
    • Effective duration of 7.6 years.

    If the market yield rises 75 basis points, the bond's approximate price change is a:
    A. 5.4% decrease.
    B. 5.4% increase.
    C. 5.7% decrease.

104. Which of the following relationships is *least accurate*?
    A. Premium bond: nominal yield > current yield; current yield > yield to maturity.
    B. Discount bond: coupon rate < yield to maturity; nominal yield < yield to maturity.
    C. Discount bond: current yield < yield to maturity; nominal yield > yield to maturity.

105. An investor most concerned with reinvestment risk would be *least likely* to:
    A. prefer a noncallable bond to a callable bond.
    B. prefer a lower coupon bond to a higher coupon bond.
    C. eliminate reinvestment risk by holding a coupon bond until maturity.

106. For an asset-backed security (ABS), a special purpose vehicle:
   A. sells an asset to the issuing corporation, which then proceeds to issue the ABS.
   B. is a legal entity used to separate assets used as collateral from those of the company seeking financing through an ABS.
   C. acts as an intermediary that purchases an asset from the company issuing an ABS and then resells it to obtain sufficient liquid funds to provide collateral for the ABS.

107. The following interest rate information is observed:

	Spot Rates
1 year	10%
2 years	11%
3 years	12%

   Based on this data, the 2-year forward rate one year from now is *closest* to:
   A. 12%.
   B. 13%.
   C. 14%.

108. Which of the following statements about theories of the yield curve is *most accurate*?
   A. A liquidity preference is not consistent with a flat term structure of interest rates.
   B. The pure expectations theory suggests that an upward-sloping term structure of interest rates is a consequence of investors expecting short-term rates to remain unchanged for a period of time, followed by investors expecting short-term rates to rise for a period of time.
   C. The liquidity preference theory suggests that a downward-sloping term structure of interest rates is due to declining expected short-term rates, and although there is a maturity premium to consider, it is not large enough to offset the expected decline in short-term rates.

109. Bert Reed owns a junior secured bond of a firm that has entered bankruptcy proceedings. Mia Tano owns a senior unsecured bond of the same firm. As a result of the bankruptcy, Reed and Tano each recover 80% of the interest and principal owed on their bonds. This outcome is *least likely* the result of:
   A. an order of the bankruptcy court.
   B. the pari passu ranking of these creditors.
   C. a negotiated settlement among the firm's creditors.

110. Which of the following statements about how various embedded options benefit the issuers or the bondholders is *least accurate*?
A. The accelerated sinking fund provision favors the issuers.
B. The conversion provision favors the bondholders.
C. The option-adjusted spread measures the spread, including the effect of the embedded option.

Questions 111 through 116 relate to Derivatives. (9 minutes)

111. The payoff to the long position in a forward rate agreement (FRA) can be duplicated by which of the following combinations of interest rate options?

	Interest rate call	Interest rate put
A.	Long	Long
B.	Long	Short
C.	Short	Long

112. Which of the following statements about equity forward contracts is *least accurate*?
A. The primary risk managed by equity forwards is the uncertainty about dividend yields.
B. An asset manager can effectively lock in the price of a specific stock at a particular point in time if he can arrange for the sale of a forward contract on the stock through a reputable dealer.
C. A pension fund manager who wants to sell a specific group of stocks in the future can accomplish this either by selling a forward contract on each of the stocks, or by selling a single forward contract on the portfolio of stocks she wants to sell.

113. An investor buys a stock for $40 per share and simultaneously sells a call option on the stock with an exercise price of $42 for a premium of $3 per share. Ignoring dividends and transaction costs, what is the maximum profit the writer of this covered call can earn at expiration?
A. $2.
B. $3.
C. $5.

114. Adam Hickle manages a money market portfolio and anticipates receiving a $10 million deposit in three months. Hickle believes that interest rates will decrease over the next three months and would like to hedge the interest rate risk for his anticipated deposit. Hickle can *best* hedge the risk that interest rates decline over the next three months with a short position in a(n):
A. forward rate agreement.
B. interest rate swap.
C. Eurodollar futures contract.

115. An investor holds a short position in four September gold futures contracts. Each gold futures contract is for delivery of 100 ounces of gold. When the contract was entered into on day zero, the futures price was $350 per ounce. The initial margin is $1,750 per contract, and the maintenance margin is $1,312.50 per contract. The following table gives information on the price of gold for September delivery over a 4-day period:

Day	Closing Futures Price ($)
1	345.50
2	348.75
3	355.50
4	356.25

What will the variation margin be on the first day a margin call is received?
A. $1,800.
B. $2,200.
C. $2,500.

116. What are the minimum values of an American-style and a European-style 3-month call option with a strike price of $80 on a non-dividend-paying stock trading at $86 if the risk-free rate is 3%?

	American	European
A.	$6.00	$6.00
B.	$6.59	$6.00
C.	$6.59	$6.59

Questions 117 through 120 relate to Alternative Investments. (6 minutes)

117. The component of the yield on a long-only commodity futures position that is dependent on whether the contract is in contango or backwardation is the:
A. collateral yield.
B. roll yield.
C. contract yield.

118. With respect to venture capital, the term "mezzanine-stage financing" is used to describe the financing:
A. to prepare for an initial public offering.
B. to initiate commercial manufacturing.
C. that supports product development and market research.

119. Cathy Werner, CFA, is considering adding exposure to hedge funds to her portfolio of traditional investments. Based on historical mean and standard deviation of hedge fund index returns and their correlation with traditional investment returns, Werner estimates the diversification benefits from allocating 5% of portfolio assets to hedge funds. Assuming her calculations are correct, Werner is *most likely* to:
   A. overestimate the potential diversification benefits to the portfolio.
   B. underestimate the potential diversification benefits to the portfolio.
   C. accurately estimate the potential diversification benefits to the portfolio.

120. A private equity firm that wants to receive money from a portfolio company without giving up control of the portfolio company is *most likely* to engage in a:
   A. trade sale.
   B. secondary sale.
   C. recapitalization.

Exam 2
Morning Session

Calculating Your Score

Topic	Maximum Score	Your Score
Ethical and Professional Standards	18	
Quantitative Methods	14	
Economics	12	
Financial Reporting and Analysis	24	
Corporate Finance	10	
Portfolio Management	6	
Equity Investments	12	
Fixed Income	14	
Derivatives	6	
Alternative Investments	4	
Total	120	

The morning and afternoon exams are identically weighted over the topics and readings. You can therefore treat the morning and afternoon exams as independent exams.

If you took more than three hours (180 minutes) to complete this portion of the exam, you should adjust your score downward by one point for each minute you ran over.

Remember: the real exam *will be more difficult* than these practice exams. The main reason for this is the general anxiety and stress that you will be feeling on exam day, coupled with the time pressure you will be under. Many of the questions on this practice exam and the real exam are not individually difficult, so if you take extra time to answer the questions on this practice exam, your score will go up significantly. However, if you want an accurate measure of your potential performance on the exam, adhere to the 3-hour time limit.

After you have finished grading your practice exam, you may find it useful to use the exam questions and recommended solutions for review. Many of these questions were specifically written for your use as study tools. Once again, I feel I should remind you not to rely on memorizing these questions; you are not likely to see them on the actual exam. What you will see on the exam, though, are the concepts, terms, and procedures presented in these questions.

Your actual exam will most likely look different than what you see in this book. Please remember, no study provider knows the content of the actual exam. These practice exams are our best guess as to the structure, content, and difficulty of an actual exam.

Test Answers

#				#				#			
1.	A	B	C	41.	A	B	C	81.	A	B	C
2.	A	B	C	42.	A	B	C	82.	A	B	C
3.	A	B	C	43.	A	B	C	83.	A	B	C
4.	A	B	C	44.	A	B	C	84.	A	B	C
5.	A	B	C	45.	A	B	C	85.	A	B	C
6.	A	B	C	46.	A	B	C	86.	A	B	C
7.	A	B	C	47.	A	B	C	87.	A	B	C
8.	A	B	C	48.	A	B	C	88.	A	B	C
9.	A	B	C	49.	A	B	C	89.	A	B	C
10.	A	B	C	50.	A	B	C	90.	A	B	C
11.	A	B	C	51.	A	B	C	91.	A	B	C
12.	A	B	C	52.	A	B	C	92.	A	B	C
13.	A	B	C	53.	A	B	C	93.	A	B	C
14.	A	B	C	54.	A	B	C	94.	A	B	C
15.	A	B	C	55.	A	B	C	95.	A	B	C
16.	A	B	C	56.	A	B	C	96.	A	B	C
17.	A	B	C	57.	A	B	C	97.	A	B	C
18.	A	B	C	58.	A	B	C	98.	A	B	C
19.	A	B	C	59.	A	B	C	99.	A	B	C
20.	A	B	C	60.	A	B	C	100.	A	B	C
21.	A	B	C	61.	A	B	C	101.	A	B	C
22.	A	B	C	62.	A	B	C	102.	A	B	C
23.	A	B	C	63.	A	B	C	103.	A	B	C
24.	A	B	C	64.	A	B	C	104.	A	B	C
25.	A	B	C	65.	A	B	C	105.	A	B	C
26.	A	B	C	66.	A	B	C	106.	A	B	C
27.	A	B	C	67.	A	B	C	107.	A	B	C
28.	A	B	C	68.	A	B	C	108.	A	B	C
29.	A	B	C	69.	A	B	C	109.	A	B	C
30.	A	B	C	70.	A	B	C	110.	A	B	C
31.	A	B	C	71.	A	B	C	111.	A	B	C
32.	A	B	C	72.	A	B	C	112.	A	B	C
33.	A	B	C	73.	A	B	C	113.	A	B	C
34.	A	B	C	74.	A	B	C	114.	A	B	C
35.	A	B	C	75.	A	B	C	115.	A	B	C
36.	A	B	C	76.	A	B	C	116.	A	B	C
37.	A	B	C	77.	A	B	C	117.	A	B	C
38.	A	B	C	78.	A	B	C	118.	A	B	C
39.	A	B	C	79.	A	B	C	119.	A	B	C
40.	A	B	C	80.	A	B	C	120.	A	B	C

Exam 2
Morning Session

Questions 1 through 18 relate to Ethical and Professional Standards.
(27 minutes)

1. An analyst for a foreign branch of HB Investments, which is based in Lagos, has just issued a recommendation on an IPO. Unknown to the analyst, who is a CFA charterholder, members of her team manipulated the valuation model to increase the newly public company's stock price. She and all of the analysts on the team purchased shares of the oversubscribed IPO for their personal accounts and then purchased the remainder of the firm's allocation of shares for appropriate client accounts, a practice which is permitted by local securities laws. With regard to the Standard on knowledge of the law, the analyst:
    A. did not violate the Standard.
    B. violated the Standard by purchasing the shares of the IPO but not by allowing the report to be published.
    C. violated the Standard by allowing the report to be published and by purchasing the shares of the IPO.

2. Green Investments utilizes the CFA Institute Standards of Professional Conduct as their standards for ethical practice. For purposes of compliance, which of the following is *least likely* a violation of Green Investments' policies?
    A. One of Green Investments' marketing brochures states that several of the firm's portfolio managers passed all three levels of the CFA exam on their first attempts.
    B. At a meeting with potential clients, chief investment officer Bill Ray, CFA, states that he is among an "elite group of the most qualified investment professionals who have earned the right to use the CFA designation."
    C. In interviewing a prospective employee, a portfolio manager at the firm says that the position could be financially rewarding because "CFA charterholders are known to achieve superior performance results."

3.   Charmaine Townsend, CFA, has been managing a growth portfolio for her clients using a screening process that identifies companies that have high earnings growth rates. Townsend has decided that, because of a volatile economy, she is going to adopt a value strategy using a screening process that identifies companies that have low price-earnings multiples. To comply with the Code and Standards, Townsend must:
      A. promptly notify her clients of the change.
      B. get written permission from her clients in advance of the change.
      C. get prompt written acknowledgment of the change from her clients within a reasonable time after the change was made.

4.   Emily Wells, CFA, retail broker for Charthouse Securities, has been asked by a retail client to buy a substantial position in Computo, Inc., a highly speculative company that is working on developing a solar-powered computer. Wells believes that this would be an inappropriate investment for the client. According to the Standard concerning suitability, Wells should take which of the following actions?
      A. Execute the order if her supervisor approves the trade.
      B. Execute the trade in accordance with the client's request, but mark the ticket "Unsolicited."
      C. Seek an affirmative statement from the client that suitability is not a consideration in this trade and refuse to execute the trade without such a statement.

5.   With respect to the Standard on material nonpublic information, information is considered material if it:
      A. has been produced in printed or electronic form.
      B. concerns the issuer of any publicly traded security.
      C. would be likely to affect the price of a security if disclosed.

6.   Laura Grayson, CFA, is a partner in a small investment advisory firm that caters to high net worth individuals. Grayson also manages an investment account for her mother. Her mother's accountant has advised Grayson that, for tax purposes, Grayson should sell her mother's position in Safety Airlines, realizing a large gain, and then immediately repurchase the position. Several of Grayson's clients also hold positions in Safety Airlines. According to the CFA Institute Standards of Professional Conduct, if Grayson follows the advice of the accountant, she:
      A. is not in violation of any Standards.
      B. is in violation of the Standard on fair dealing for not dealing fairly with all clients.
      C. is in violation of the Standard on market manipulation for engaging in a practice that will artificially inflate the trading volume of a security.

7. Judy Dudley, CFA, is an analyst and plans to visit a company that she is analyzing in order to prepare a research report. The Standard related to independence and objectivity:

    A. requires Dudley to pay for her own transportation costs and not to accept any gifts or compensation for writing the report, but allows her to accept accommodations and meals that are not lavish.

    B. requires Dudley not to accept any compensation for writing a research report, but allows her to accept company paid transportation, lodging, and meals.

    C. allows Dudley to accept transportation, lodging, expenses, and compensation for writing a research report, but requires that she disclose such an arrangement in her report.

8. Campbell Hill, CFA, has recently joined a pension fund management company as its Chief Compliance Officer. One of Hill's first priorities in his new position is to formalize the company's investment policies and procedures. Hill distributes a memo stating that effective immediately, material supporting all company research reports will be kept in the company database in electronic form for ten years, while hard copies of the same material will be maintained for one year only. The memo also states that hard copy records of all material supporting investment-related communications with clients must be kept on file for five years (the period mandated by local regulations). With respect to record retention:

    A. neither of Hill's policies violates the Standards.

    B. Hill's policies regarding both research reports and investment-related communications violate the Standards.

    C. Hill's policy regarding investment actions does not violate the Standards, but the policy regarding investment-related communications does because the Standards require records be kept for seven years.

9. In calculating total firm assets for a GIPS-compliant performance statement, Allen Bund, CFA, finds that there is a mix of fee-paying and non-fee-paying accounts, some of which are discretionary and some of which are non-discretionary accounts. Should Bund include non-discretionary accounts and non-fee-paying accounts in the calculation of total firm assets?

	Non-discretionary accounts	Non-fee-paying accounts
A.	Yes	Yes
B.	No	Yes
C.	No	No

10. Dawn Shepard, CFA, is a broker for a regional brokerage firm. Her company's research department has recently changed its recommendation on the common stock of Orlando, Inc., from "Buy" to "Sell." Concurring with the report's analysis, Shepard faxed the change to all her current customers who hold Orlando, Inc., in their accounts. The next day, one of her customers, who had never before expressed an interest in Orlando, calls and places a "Buy" order for 500 shares of Orlando. According to the Standard concerning fair dealing, Shepard, under these circumstances:
    A. has complied with the fair dealing Standard and may accept the order because it is unsolicited.
    B. may accept the order but must advise the customer of the change in recommendation before accepting the order.
    C. may accept the order only if the customer acknowledges in writing that she was notified of the change in the recommendation.

11. Paul James, CFA, is a retail stock broker for a national financial services corporation. James's client base is mainly comprised of small to medium-sized individual accounts. James notices that one client in particular, Chet Young, Ph.D., is particularly adept at picking undervalued stocks. James decides to watch Young's trades and mimic them in his own account. James:
    A. is not in violation of any Standards.
    B. is in violation of the Standard on priority of transactions because he is front running the client's account.
    C. is in violation of the Standard on misconduct because he has misappropriated confidential client information.

12. Nicholas Hart, CFA, is a retail broker for a national financial institution and has a client base composed mainly of high net worth individuals. During the past year, Hart's wife was extremely ill and was hospitalized for several months. Hart was financially responsible for her mounting medical bills and tried to pay them as best as he could. Despite his best efforts to meet his obligations, Hart was forced to declare personal bankruptcy but did not disclose this to any of his clients. According to the CFA Institute Standards of Professional Conduct, Hart:
    A. is not in violation of any Standard.
    B. is in violation of the Standard on communication with clients for not disclosing his bankruptcy to his clients.
    C. is in violation of the Standard on misconduct for personal conduct that reflects adversely on his professional reputation.

13. Marie Marshall, CFA, is a registered representative for Everest Broker-Dealer who maintains a client base of high net worth individuals, trusts, endowments, and foundations. Such clients pay Everest a quarterly fee, as well as commissions on securities transactions. Marshall receives compensation based on the overall success of the firm, along with a recently implemented quarterly bonus based on the trading volume in her clients' accounts. During her annual portfolio reviews with clients, Marshall receives several questions regarding recent increases in portfolio turnover. Marshall truthfully indicates that recent increases in volatility caused the firm to make more tactical investment recommendations in client portfolios but does not mention her potential volume-based bonus. Marshall has violated the Standard concerning:
   A. communication with clients.
   B. additional compensation arrangements.
   C. disclosure of conflicts.

14. Lunar Investment Management is a subsidiary of a larger company, Galaxy Financial. Lunar's CEO, Travis Howry, would like to have Lunar present GIPS-compliant performance data and has taken the steps necessary to ensure that Lunar's performance presentation is compliant. He asks Galaxy's President, Don Wiggins, about Galaxy's interest in presenting GIPS-compliant performance data. Wiggins informs Howry that Galaxy is not interested. Lunar may:
   A. not claim compliance with GIPS because compliance must be made on a company-wide basis.
   B. claim compliance with GIPS as long as Lunar is presented to the public as a distinct business entity.
   C. claim partial compliance with GIPS if Lunar's performance presentations are in compliance but disclose that Galaxy's are not and in which ways.

15. Fred Reilly, CFA, is an investment adviser at a regional office of a national financial institution. A long-term client, Rob Harrison, decides to terminate the relationship and move his company's pension plan and his personal account to another firm. Reilly obliges and completes the paperwork to close the account. As Reilly gathers the files on Harrison's personal account to put into storage, he notices some discrepancies which lead him to suspect that Harrison has engaged in illegal activity with regard to company funds. Which of the following actions is *most appropriate* for Reilly to take under the Standards?
   A. Report his suspicions to outside counsel.
   B. Do nothing since he must maintain the confidentiality of client information even after the client has left the firm.
   C. Inform Harrison's business partners of the suspected illegal activities because he is no longer a client, and they may have legal liability as well.

16. Fred Dean, CFA, has just taken a job as trader for LPC, a large insurance company. One of his first duties in his new position is to execute the purchase of a block of East Street Industries, a firm that is a major client of his previous employer. During his prior employment, Dean was informed directly by East Street's CEO that the company's sales have experienced a sudden drop and are 20% below current analyst estimates. This information has not yet been announced. In reviewing the research report supporting the purchase decision, Dean realizes that the buy decision is based on sales forecasts that he knows are wrong. Which of the following actions would be the *most appropriate* for Dean to take according to CFA Institute Standards of Professional Conduct?

    A. Post the information about the drop in sales on an internet bulletin board to achieve public dissemination and inform his supervisor of the posting.

    B. Contact the CEO and urge him to make the information public and make the trade if he refuses.

    C. Request that the firm place East Street's stock on a restricted list and refuse to make any buy or sell trades of the company's stock.

17. When members and candidates report performance data, according to the Code and Standards, it is:

    A. permissible to leave details out in a brief presentation.

    B. recommended that a minimum of five years performance history be included.

    C. a requirement to present composite performance rather than individual account performance.

18. Bob Sampson is employed by a mid-sized money management firm in Munich. He is the head portfolio manager for a Global Equities fund. The fund has been in existence for eight years. Beginning this year, the firm has decided to present performance information in compliance with the Global Investment Performance Standards (GIPS). To claim GIPS compliance, the firm must present at least:

    A. eight years of GIPS-compliant performance information.

    B. five years of GIPS-compliant performance information with no additional disclosure required for prior years.

    C. five years of GIPS-compliant performance information and may include non-compliant performance information since inception in the "Disclosures" section.

Questions 19 through 32 relate to Quantitative Methods. (21 minutes)

19.   An investor wants to receive $10,000 annually for ten years with the first payment five years from today. If the investor can earn a 14% annual return, the amount that she will have to invest today is *closest* to:
A. $27,091.
B. $30,884.
C. $52,161.

20.   Which of the following statements about the frequency distribution shown below is *least accurate*?

Return Interval	Frequency
0% to 5%	10
> 5% to 10%	20
> 10% to 15%	30
> 15% to 20%	20

A. The return intervals are mutually exclusive.
B. The cumulative absolute frequency of the fourth interval is 20.
C. The relative frequency of the second return interval is 25%.

21.   A contrarian technical analyst is *most likely* to be bullish based on a:
A. low put-call ratio.
B. high volatility index.
C. low mutual fund cash position.

22.   An investor in a mutual fund earns a 25% return the first year, loses 25% in the second year, gains 30% in the third year, and then loses 30% in the fourth year. The average annual compound growth rate of this investment is *closest* to:
A. −3.9%.
B. 0.0%.
C. 5.6%.

23.   An analyst obtains the following annual returns for a group of stocks: 10%, 8%, 7%, 9%, 10%, 12%, 11%, 10%, 30%, and 13%. This distribution:
A. has a median greater than its mode.
B. is skewed to the right, and the mean is less than the median.
C. is skewed to the right, and the mean is greater than the mode.

24. An analyst gathers the following data about the mean monthly returns of three securities:

Security	Mean Monthly Return	Standard Deviation
X	0.9	0.7
Y	1.2	4.7
Z	1.5	5.2

Which security has the highest level of relative risk as measured by the coefficient of variation?
A. X.
B. Y.
C. Z.

25. The median of a distribution is *least likely* equal to the:
A. second quartile.
B. third quintile.
C. fifth decile.

26. Which of the following statements about probability concepts is *most accurate*?
A. Subjective probability is a probability that is based on personal judgment.
B. A conditional probability is the probability that two or more events happen concurrently.
C. An empirical probability is one based on logical analysis rather than on observation or personal judgment.

27. Which of the following is *least likely* an underlying assumption of technical analysis?
A. Supply and demand are governed solely by rational behavior.
B. Actual shifts in supply and demand can be observed in market price behavior.
C. Prices for individual securities and the market tend to move in trends that persist for long periods of time.

28. Alex White, CFA, is examining a portfolio that contains 100 stocks that are either value or growth stocks. Of these 100 stocks, 40% are value stocks. The previous portfolio manager had selected 70% of the value stocks and 80% of the growth stocks. What is the probability of selecting a stock at random that is either a value stock or was selected by the previous portfolio manager?
A. 28%.
B. 76%.
C. 88%.

29. Which of the following statements about the normal distribution is *least accurate*? The normal distribution:
     A. has a mean of zero and a standard deviation of one.
     B. is completely described by its mean and standard deviation.
     C. is bell-shaped, with tails extending without limit to the left and to the right.

30. A manager forecasts a bond portfolio return of 10% and estimates a standard deviation of annual returns of 4%. Assuming a normal returns distribution and that the manager is correct, there is a:
     A. 90% probability that the portfolio return will be between 3.2% and 17.2%.
     B. 95% probability that the portfolio return will be between 2.16% and 17.84%.
     C. 32% probability that the portfolio return will be between 6% and 14%.

31. An investment has an expected return of 10% with a standard deviation of 5%. If the returns are normally distributed, the chance of losing money is *closest* to:
     A. 2.5%.
     B. 5.0%.
     C. 16.0%.

32. Which of the following statements about sampling and estimation is *least accurate*?
     A. Sampling error is the difference between the observed value of a statistic and the value it is intended to estimate.
     B. A simple random sample is a sample obtained in such a way that each element of the population has an equal probability of being selected.
     C. The central limit theorem states that the sample mean for a large sample size will have a distribution that is the same as the distribution of the underlying population.

Questions 33 through 44 relate to Economics. (18 minutes)

33. The crowding-out effect suggests that:
     A. government borrowing will lead to an increase in private savings.
     B. as government spending increases, so will incomes and taxes, and the higher taxes will reduce both aggregate demand and output.
     C. greater government deficits will drive up interest rates, thereby reducing private investment.

34. Depreciation of a country's currency will be more effective in reducing its trade deficit if:
     A. its imports do not have good substitutes.
     B. its exports are primarily luxury goods.
     C. its exports represent a small portion of foreign consumer expenditures.

35.　At the equilibrium levels of output and price in a competitive industry without taxes:
　　　A.　consumer and producer surplus are equal.
　　　B.　both consumer and producer surplus are maximized.
　　　C.　the sum of producer and consumer surplus is maximized.

36.　Which of the following does the U.S. central bank *most often* use to change the money supply?
　　　A.　The discount rate.
　　　B.　Open market operations.
　　　C.　The required reserve ratio.

37.　The price of milk in a country increases from €1.00 per liter to €1.10 per liter, and the quantity supplied does not change. This suggests the elasticity of the short-run supply of milk in this country is equal to:
　　　A.　infinity, and supply is perfectly elastic.
　　　B.　zero, and supply is perfectly inelastic.
　　　C.　infinity, and supply is perfectly inelastic.

38.　In the short run, will an increase in the money supply increase the price level and real output?
　　　A.　Both will increase in the short run.
　　　B.　Neither will increase in the short run.
　　　C.　Only one will increase in the short run.

39.　The law of diminishing marginal returns explains:
　　　A.　the shape of the long-run average cost curve.
　　　B.　the upward sloping portion of the short-run marginal cost curve.
　　　C.　the upward sloping portion of the long-run marginal cost curve.

40.　A firm in a perfectly competitive market will tend to expand its output as long as:
　　　A.　its marginal revenue is positive.
　　　B.　the market price is greater than the marginal cost.
　　　C.　its marginal revenue is greater than the market price.

41.　Unlike members of free trade areas, customs union members:
　　　A.　adopt a single currency.
　　　B.　remove barriers to trade with all members.
　　　C.　adopt uniform trade restrictions with non-members.

42.　In utility analysis, a consumer's optimal bundle of goods lies on an indifference curve that is:
　　　A.　most preferred by the consumer.
　　　B.　tangent to the consumer's budget line.
　　　C.　contained within the consumer's opportunity set.

43. Reasons why the unemployment rate is a lagging indicator of the business cycle *least likely* include:
     A. discouraged workers who begin seeking work.
     B. action lag in the implementation of unemployment insurance.
     C. high costs to employers of frequently hiring or firing employees.

44. A natural monopoly is *most likely* to exist when:
     A. economies of scale are great.
     B. average total cost increases as output increases.
     C. a single firm owns essentially all of a productive resource.

Questions 45 through 68 relate to Financial Reporting and Analysis. (36 minutes)

45. Which of the following statements about types of nonrecurring items under U.S. GAAP is *least accurate*?
     A. Unusual or infrequent items are included in income from continuing operations.
     B. Extraordinary items are unusual and infrequent items that are reported net of taxes and included in nonrecurring income from continuing operations.
     C. Discontinued operations are reported net of taxes below income from continuing operations.

46. A company has the following sequence of events regarding its stock:
     • The company had 1,000,000 shares outstanding at the beginning of the year.
     • On June 30, the company declared and issued a 10% stock dividend.
     • On September 30, the company sold 400,000 shares of common stock at par.

     The number of shares that should be used to compute basic earnings per share at year end is:
     A. 1,000,000.
     B. 1,100,000.
     C. 1,200,000.

47. An analyst has found that a firm's cash conversion cycle has decreased significantly over the past year and suspects accounting manipulation of cash flows. The *least likely* way for the company to have decreased its cash conversion cycle is by:
     A. financing payables.
     B. stretching out payables.
     C. securitization of receivables.

48. Time-series analysis of a firm's common-size balance sheets reveals the following data:

	20X3	20X4	20X5
Current assets	20%	22%	25%
Inventory	8%	9%	11%
Short-term debt	10%	11%	12%
Long-term debt	24%	21%	18%

Based only on the data provided, an analyst can conclude that the firm's:
A. debt ratio is decreasing.
B. quick ratio is decreasing.
C. inventory/sales ratio is increasing.

49. Which of the following statements about the analysis of cash flows is *least accurate*?
A. Interest payments on debt are not a financing cash flow under U.S. GAAP.
B. Both the direct and indirect methods involve adding back noncash items such as depreciation and amortization.
C. When using the indirect method, an analyst should add any losses on the sales of fixed assets to net income.

50. A company that reports under U.S. GAAP and changes its inventory cost assumption from weighted average cost to last-in first-out is required to apply this change in accounting principle:
A. retrospectively, and disclose the new cost flow method being used.
B. prospectively, and explain the reasons for the change in the financial statement disclosures.
C. retrospectively, and explain the reasons for the change in the financial statement disclosures.

51. An analyst gathered the following data about a company:

	20X6	20X7
EBIT margin (EBIT / revenue)	0.15	0.10
Asset turnover (revenue / assets)	1.5	1.8
Leverage multiplier (assets / equity)	1.5	1.6
Tax burden (net income / EBT)	0.7	0.7
Interest burden (EBT / EBIT)	0.85	0.85

The company's return on equity:
A. decreased because the company's profit margin decreased.
B. increased because the company's asset turnover and leverage increased.
C. remained constant because the company's decreased profit margin was just offset by increases in asset turnover and leverage.

52. For which of the following investments in securities is a firm *most likely* to report unrealized gains or losses on its income statement?
A. Preferred stock, which the firm classifies as available-for-sale.
B. Five-year bonds, which the firm purchased in a private placement.
C. Listed call options, which the firm intends to exercise at expiration.

53. Bentlom Company's common-size financial statements show the following information:
- Earnings after taxes   15%
- Current liabilities   20%
- Equity   45%
- Sales $800
- Cash   10%
- Total assets $2,000
- Accounts receivable   15%
- Inventory   20%

Bentlom's long-term debt-to-equity ratio and current ratio are *closest* to:

	Long-term debt-to-equity ratio	Current ratio
A.	78%	2.25
B.	88%	2.50
C.	98%	2.75

54. Consider a manufacturing company and a financial services company. Interest expense is *most likely* classified as a non-operating component of income for:
   A. both of these companies.
   B. neither of these companies.
   C. only one of these companies.

55. The two primary assumptions in preparing financial statements under IFRS are:
   A. accrual and going concern.
   B. reasonable accuracy and accrual.
   C. going concern and reasonable accuracy.

56. Compared to an operating lease, a capital lease will have what effects on operating income (earnings before interest and taxes) and net income in the first year?
   A. Both will be lower.
   B. Both will be higher.
   C. One will be lower and one will be higher.

57. An analyst gathered the following data about a company:
   - 1,000 common shares are outstanding (no change during the year).
   - Net income is $5,000.
   - The company paid $500 in preferred dividends.
   - The company paid $600 in common dividends.
   - The average market price of their common stock is $60 for the year.
   - The company had 100 warrants (for one share each) outstanding for the entire year, exercisable at $50.

   The company's diluted earnings per share is *closest* to:
   A. $4.42.
   B. $4.55.
   C. $4.83.

58. Which of the following sources of information should an analyst consider the *least* reliable?
   A. Form 10-Q.
   B. Proxy statement.
   C. Corporate press release.

59. A company takes a $10 million impairment charge on a depreciable asset in 20X3. The *most likely* effect will be to:
   A. increase reported net income in 20X4.
   B. decrease net income and taxes payable in 20X3.
   C. increase return on equity and operating cash flow in 20X4.

60. Xanos Corporation faced a 50% marginal tax rate last year and showed the following financial and tax reporting information:
    - Deferred tax asset of $1,000.
    - Deferred tax liability of $5,000.

    Based only on this information and the news that the tax rate will decline to 40%, Xanos Corporation's:
    A. deferred tax asset will be reduced by $400 and deferred tax liability will be reduced by $2,000.
    B. deferred tax liability will be reduced by $1,000 and income tax expense will be reduced by $800.
    C. deferred tax asset will be reduced by $200 and income tax expense will be reduced by $1,000.

61. East Company incurs $110,000 of costs to establish technological feasibility of a new software application it hopes to sell and $90,000 of costs to develop the application. West Company incurs $110,000 of research costs related to a new product and $90,000 of development costs for the product. If East reports under U.S. GAAP and West reports under IFRS, these projects will:
    A. increase East's total assets more the West's total assets.
    B. increase West's total assets more than East's total assets.
    C. have the same effects on East's and West's total assets.

62. A company that capitalizes costs instead of expensing them will have:
    A. higher income variability and higher cash flows from operations.
    B. lower cash flows from investing and lower income variability.
    C. lower cash flows from operations and higher profitability in early years.

63. Under accrual accounting, the payment of $15,000 at the end of fiscal year 20X8 for a special advertising campaign that will run for the first three months of 20X9 would affect the 20X8 financial statements by decreasing cash by $15,000 and generating a $15,000 increase in:
    A. advertising expense.
    B. a prepaid asset account.
    C. a prepaid liability account.

64. Al Pike, CFA, is analyzing Red Company by projecting pro forma financial statements. Pike expects Red to generate sales of $3 billion and a return on equity of 15% in the next year. Pike forecasts that Red's total assets will be $5 billion and that the company will maintain its financial leverage ratio of 2.5. Based on these forecasts, Pike should project Red's net income to be:
    A. $100 million.
    B. $300 million.
    C. $500 million.

65. A company issues $10 million in 8% annual-pay, 5-year bonds, when the market rate is 8.25%. The initial balance sheet liability and liability one year from the date of issue are *closest* to:

Initial liability	Liability one year later
A. $9,900,837	$9,917,656
B. $10,000,000	$9,975,000
C. $10,099,163	$10,082,344

66. Which of the following items would affect owners' equity and also appear on the income statement?
   A. Dividends paid to shareholders.
   B. Unrealized gains and losses on trading securities.
   C. Unrealized gains and losses on available-for-sale securities.

67. Copper, Inc., had $4 million in bonds outstanding that were convertible into common stock at a conversion rate of 100 shares per $1,000 bond. In 20X1, all of the outstanding bonds were converted into common stock. Copper's average share price for 20X1 was $15. Copper's statement of cash flows for the year ended December 31, 20X1, should *most likely* include:
   A. a footnote describing the conversion of the bonds into common stock.
   B. cash flows from financing of +$4 million from issuance of common stock and –$4 million from retirement of bonds.
   C. cash flows from financing of +$6 million from issuance of common stock and –$4 million from retirement of bonds and cash flows from investing of –$2 million for a loss on retirement of bonds.

68. During a period of falling costs of manufacturing, which of the following inventory cost formulas would result in the greatest reported net income?
   A. LIFO.
   B. FIFO.
   C. Average cost.

Questions 69 through 78 relate to Corporate Finance. (15 minutes)

69. An analyst identifies the following cash flows for an average-risk project:
   - Year 0   –$5,000
   - Years 1–2 $1,900
   - Year 3 $2,500
   - Year 4 $2,000

   If the company's cost of capital is 12%, the project's discounted payback period is *closest* to:
   A. 2.5 years.
   B. 3.0 years.
   C. 3.9 years.

70. Mary Miller, CFA, manages the short-term cash position for Young Company. Miller can invest in one of three securities that will mature in 180 days: a Treasury bill priced at 97.5% of par, commercial paper with a bond-equivalent yield of 5.10%, and a 6-month certificate of deposit that will return 2.5% over the 180-day holding period. Miller should purchase the:
    A. Treasury bill.
    B. commercial paper.
    C. certificate of deposit.

71. Which of the following is the *least appropriate* method for estimating a firm's before-tax cost of debt capital?
    A. Use the market yield on bonds with a rating and maturity similar to the firm's existing debt.
    B. Assume the firm's cost of debt capital is equal to the yield to maturity on its publicly traded debt.
    C. Use the coupon rate on the firm's most recently issued debt.

72. Which of the following types of companies are *more likely* to use the payback method to evaluate capital projects?
    A. European companies and private companies.
    B. Asian companies and larger companies.
    C. European companies and larger companies.

73. Sarah Evens has been studying the effects of takeover defenses on shareholder value. Evens is evaluating various uses of golden parachutes, poison pills, and greenmail, all of which can affect share value. Good corporate governance requires a careful review of a firm's takeover defenses. When conducting this review, Evens should *most likely* consider which of the following a negative factor?
    A. In a hostile bidder situation, the board would be willing to pay cash to such a bidder to preserve the company's independence.
    B. Shareholders have voted down an amendment to the bylaws that would have provided a poison pill.
    C. A change of control issue would not trigger the interest of a local government.

74. The following information applies to World Turn Company:
    - 10% rate of interest on newly issued bonds.
    - 7% growth rate in earnings and dividends.
    - The last dividend paid was $0.93.
    - Shares sell for $16.
    - Stock's beta is 1.5.
    - Market risk premium is 6%.
    - Risk-free rate of interest is 5%.
    - The firm is in a 40% marginal tax bracket.

    If the appropriate risk premium relative to the bond yield is 4%, World Turn's equity cost of capital using the dividend discount model is *closest* to:
    A. 12.8%.
    B. 13.2%.
    C. 14.0%.

75. The committee charged with recommending a compensation package for members of a firm's board of directors has recommended that in addition to compensation of $10,000 for each board meeting attended, board members (1) will be able to use one of the firm's corporate jets up to twice each year and (2) will receive a finder's fee of 0.1% if they identify an acquisition target that the firm acquires while the member is still on the board. Are these policies consistent with good corporate governance practices?
    A. Both policies are consistent with good corporate governance.
    B. Neither policy is consistent with good corporate governance.
    C. Only one of these policies is consistent with good corporate governance.

76. Which of the following is *least likely* a problem associated with the internal rate of return (IRR) method of choosing investment projects?
    A. Using IRR to rank mutually exclusive projects assumes reinvestment of cash flows at the IRR.
    B. For independent projects, the IRR and NPV can lead to different investment decisions.
    C. If the project has an unconventional cash flow pattern, the result can be multiple IRRs.

77. Break points in a firm's marginal cost of capital schedule are *best* interpreted as representing the:
    A. maximum amounts of debt, preferred stock, and common stock the firm can issue.
    B. amounts of new securities a firm would need to issue to take advantage of flotation cost discounts.
    C. amounts of capital expenditure at which the company's weighted average cost of capital increases.

78.   A financial advisor makes the following statements about dividends: (1) With respect to dividends, an investor should be indifferent between purchasing a stock before or after the payment date because on the payment date the value of the shares will fall by approximately the amount of the dividend; (2) The holder-of-record date occurs two business days before the ex-dividend date. Are the advisor's statements accurate?
        A. Both of these statements are accurate.
        B. Neither of these statements is accurate.
        C. Only one of these statements is accurate.

Questions 79 through 84 relate to Portfolio Management. (9 minutes)

79.   In a case where a client's capacity to bear risk is significantly less than the client's expressed willingness to bear risk, the *most appropriate* action for a financial advisor is to:
        A. counsel the client and attempt to change his attitude towards risk.
        B. base the assessment of risk tolerance in the IPS on client's ability to bear risk.
        C. attempt to educate the client about investment risk and correct any misconceptions.

80.   Which of the following statements about risk is *most accurate*?
        A. The capital market line plots expected return against market risk.
        B. The efficient frontier plots expected return against unsystematic risk.
        C. The security market line plots expected return against systematic risk.

81.   A portfolio manager is constructing a new equity portfolio consisting of a large number of randomly chosen domestic stocks. As the number of stocks in the portfolio increases, what happens to the expected levels of systematic and unsystematic risk?

	Systematic risk	Unsystematic risk
A.	Increases	Remains the same
B.	Decreases	Increases
C.	Remains the same	Decreases

82.   The risk-free rate is 5% and the expected market return is 15%. A portfolio manager is estimating a return of 20% on a stock with a beta of 1.5. Based on the SML and the analyst's estimate, this stock is:
        A. properly valued.
        B. overvalued.
        C. undervalued.

83. Refusing to invest in companies that sell tobacco products, alcohol, or products that are harmful to the environment would constitute a set of investment restrictions that *best* illustrates which of the following investment constraints?
    A. Regulatory factors.
    B. Unique needs and preferences.
    C. Legal restrictions.

84. Rolly Parker, CFA, has managed the retirement account funds for Misto Inc. for the last two years. Contributions and withdrawals from the account are decided by Misto's CFO. The account history is as follows, with account values calculated before same-date deposits and withdrawals:

Jan 1, 20X1	Beginning portfolio value	$10 million
Jul 1, 20X1	Account value	$11.2 million
Jul 1, 20X1	Deposit of cash	$1.2 million
Jan 1, 20X2	Account value	$12.5 million
Jan 1, 20X2	Withdrawal of cash	$0.6 million
Dec 31, 20X2	Account value	$15 million

    The appropriate annual return to use in evaluating the manager's performance is *closest* to:
    A. 9%.
    B. 19%.
    C. 22%.

Questions 85 through 96 relate to Equity Investments. (18 minutes)

85. Which of the following statements about types of orders is *least accurate*?
    A. Market orders are orders to buy or sell at the best price available.
    B. Limit orders are orders to buy or sell at or away from the market price.
    C. A stop buy order is typically used to protect a short position in a security and is placed below the current market price.

86. A stock has the following data associated with it:
    - A required rate of return of 14%.
    - A return on equity of 15%.
    - An earnings retention rate of 40%.

    The stock's justified price-to-earnings ratio is *closest* to:
    A. 5.0.
    B. 6.7.
    C. 7.5.

87. The required rate of return used in the dividend discount model is *least likely* to be affected by a change in the:
   A. expected rate of inflation.
   B. real risk-free rate of return.
   C. growth rate of earnings and dividends.

88. High return on invested capital and high pricing power are *most likely* to be associated with an industry that has:
   A. high capacity.
   B. low barriers to entry.
   C. high concentration.

89. With regard to the implications of stock market efficiency for technical analysis and fundamental analysis, if market prices are:
   A. weak-form efficient, technical analysis that depends only on past trading data should be of limited or no value.
   B. semistrong-form efficient, fundamental analysis using the top-down approach should yield consistently superior returns.
   C. semistrong-form efficient, fundamental analysis using only publicly available market information should generate abnormal returns after considering risk and transaction costs.

90. The following data pertains to a firm's common stock:
   - The stock will pay no dividends for two years.
   - The dividend three years from now is expected to be $1.
   - Dividends are expected to grow at a 7% rate from that point onward.

   If an investor requires a 17% return on this investment, how much will the investor be willing to pay for this stock now?
   A. $6.24.
   B. $7.31.
   C. $8.26.

91. A stock's price currently is $100. An analyst forecasts the following for the stock:
   - The normalized trailing price earnings (P/E) ratio will be 12×.
   - The stock is expected to pay a $5 dividend this coming year on projected earnings of $10 per share.

   If the analyst were to buy and hold the stock for the year, the projected rate of return based on these forecasts is *closest* to:
   A. 15%.
   B. 20%.
   C. 25%.

92. Which of the following statements about short sales is *least accurate*?
    A. Proceeds from short sales cannot be withdrawn from the account.
    B. The short seller must pay the lender of the stock any dividends paid by the company.
    C. The short seller is required to replace the borrowed securities within six months of a short sale.

93. Which of the following firms' earnings are likely to exhibit the greatest degree of sensitivity to the business cycle?
    A. Furniture producer with high fixed costs as a proportion of total costs.
    B. Entertainment producer with high variable costs as a proportion of total costs.
    C. Food and beverage producer with high fixed costs as a proportion of total costs.

94. The type of share voting *most likely* to result in significant minority shareholders having an approximately proportional representation on the board of directors is:
    A. statutory voting.
    B. weighted voting.
    C. cumulative voting.

95. Which of the following indexes is *most likely* to be rebalanced on a regular basis?
    A. Price-weighted index.
    B. Equal-weighted index.
    C. Market-capitalization weighted index.

96. Over the most recent period, Ladden Materials has seen slow growth, increased competition, and declining profitability in its industry. The phase of the industry life cycle for Ladden's industry is *most likely*:
    A. mature.
    B. decline.
    C. shakeout.

Questions 97 through 110 relate to Fixed Income. (21 minutes)

97. Other things equal, for option-free bonds:
    A. a bond's value is more sensitive to yield increases than to yield decreases.
    B. the value of a long-term bond is more sensitive to interest rate changes than the value of a short-term bond.
    C. the value of a low-coupon bond is less sensitive to interest rate changes than the value of a high-coupon bond.

98. Which of the following is *least likely* a reason that floating rate bonds may trade at prices different from their par values?
   A. A time lag exists between the rate change in the market and the time when the coupon rate is reset.
   B. The fixed quoted margin on the floating rate security may differ from the margin required by the market.
   C. Resetting interest rates makes floating rate bonds more susceptible to the price risk that results from changing interest rates.

99. An investor in the 28% tax bracket is considering buying one of the following securities:
   - A fully taxable Treasury security offering a 6.0% yield.
   - A municipal bond priced at par offering a 4.0% yield.

   The taxable-equivalent yield on the municipal bond is *closest* to:
   A. 2.9%.
   B. 4.3%.
   C. 5.6%.

100. Which of the following statements about debt securities is *most accurate*?
   A. Insured bonds are bonds collateralized by an escrow of securities guaranteed by the U.S. government.
   B. Tax-backed municipal bonds are supported through revenues generated from projects that are funded in whole or in part with the proceeds of the original bond issue.
   C. A collateralized mortgage obligation is a derivative of a passthrough security with a payment structure that redistributes risk among investors in various tranches.

101. An investor has a 1-year, semiannual, 10% coupon bond which is priced at $1,025. If the 6-month spot rate on a bond-equivalent basis is 8%, the 1-year theoretical spot rate as a BEY is:
   A. 6.4%.
   B. 7.3%.
   C. 8.0%.

102. The credit rating agency practice of "notching" is *best* described as:
   A. assigning different ratings to different debt issues from the same issuer.
   B. downgrading or upgrading the rating of a debt issue or issuer by one increment.
   C. adding a plus or minus sign to a rating to indicate a positive or negative outlook.

103. A bond priced at par ($1,000) has a modified duration of 8 and a convexity of 50. If interest rates fall 50 basis points, the new price will be *closest* to:
    A. $1,041.25.
    B. $958.75.
    C. $875.00.

104. Which of the following statements regarding mortgage-backed securities (MBS) and collateralized mortgage obligations (CMOs) is *most accurate*?
    A. MBS are created from CMOs.
    B. Creating CMOs does not reduce the overall prepayment risk of a mortgage passthrough security.
    C. The prepayment option of an MBS benefits the security holder.

105. Which of the following statements about embedded options is *least accurate*?
    A. An investor benefits when a floating rate bond has an interest rate floor.
    B. The prepayment right granted with a mortgage favors the issuer/borrower.
    C. If the market value of a putable bond falls below the par value, the issuer will likely exercise the option.

106. A $1,000 par, semiannual-pay bond is trading for 89.14, has a coupon rate of 8.75%, and accrued interest of $43.72. The clean price of the bond is:
    A. $847.69.
    B. $891.40.
    C. $935.12.

107. An investor is considering floating-rate debt and other investments to protect against unexpected increases in inflation. Her friend suggests Treasury Inflation Protected Securities (TIPS) because the coupon rate is adjusted for inflation semiannually. The friend also states on-the-run Treasury issues have narrower bid-ask spreads than other Treasury issues. Are the friend's statements correct?
    A. Both of these statements are correct.
    B. Neither of these statements is correct.
    C. Only one of these statements is correct.

108. For a domestic investor purchasing foreign bonds:
    A. appreciation of both the asset and the foreign currency benefits the domestic investor.
    B. depreciation of both the asset and the foreign currency benefits the domestic investor.
    C. appreciation of the asset and depreciation of the foreign currency benefit the domestic investor.

109. Reinvestment risk is *least likely*:
   A. minimized with zero-coupon bond issues.
   B. more problematic for those investors with longer time horizons.
   C. more problematic when the current coupons being reinvested are relatively small.

110. Which of the following statements regarding yield spreads is *least accurate*? The:
   A. option cost in percentage terms can be computed by subtracting the OAS from the zero-volatility spread.
   B. nominal yield spread measures the difference between the YTM on a risky bond and the YTM on a Treasury bond of similar maturity.
   C. zero-volatility spread is the constant spread that is added to each Treasury spot rate to equate the present value of a bond's cash flows to the price of an otherwise identical option-free bond.

Questions 111 through 116 relate to Derivatives. (9 minutes)

111. Which of the following statements about call options is *least accurate*?
   A. The buyer of a call option has an obligation to perform.
   B. A call option is in the money when the strike price is below the stock price.
   C. The lower the strike price relative to the stock's underlying price, the more the call option is worth.

112. Exchange-traded options are *most likely* to be available on:
   A. currencies.
   B. individual stocks.
   C. government bonds.

113. A 3-year annual-pay currency swap takes place between a New Zealand company with New Zealand dollars (NZD) and a U.S. company with U.S. dollars (USD). The New Zealand company swaps NZD for USD on which it makes end-of-period payments based on the rate in effect at the beginning of each period. The U.S. company makes fixed-rate payments in NZD.
   • The fixed swap rate at the initiation of the swap was 7%; at the end of the swap it was 8%.
   • The variable rate at the end of year 1 was 6%, at the end of year 2 was 8%, and at the end of year 3 was 7%.
   • At the beginning of the swap, one million USD were exchanged at a NZD/USD rate of 2.
   • At the end of the swap period, the exchange rate was NZD/USD 1.5.

   At the end of year 2, the:
   A. New Zealand company gives the U.S. company USD 60,000.
   B. U.S. company gives the New Zealand company USD 80,000.
   C. New Zealand company gives the U.S. company USD 80,000.

©2012 Kaplan, Inc.

114. A dealer arranges an equity swap with a mutual fund. The notional principal on the swap is $50 million and quarterly payments have been scheduled. The mutual fund agrees to pay the dealer the return on the S&P 400 Midcap Index, which is currently at 1,038.4. Three months later it is 1,052.5. The dealer pays a fixed rate of 5.5% to the mutual fund, with payments made on the basis of 91 days in the period and 365 days in the year. What is the net payment and who makes it?
    A. Dealer pays $6,687.
    B. Dealer pays $1,364,546.
    C. Mutual fund pays $6,687.

115. Which of the following statements about futures and forwards is *most accurate*? Futures:
    A. are subject to default risk, but forwards are not.
    B. are individualized contracts, but forwards are standardized.
    C. require that traders post margin in order to trade, but forwards typically require no cash transaction until the delivery date.

116. Which of the following statements about futures markets is *most accurate*?
    A. Hedgers accept market risk in exchange for expected profits.
    B. The futures exchange establishes the minimum price fluctuation for each contract.
    C. The role of the clearinghouse is to take an active position in the market to maintain a fair and orderly market by providing liquidity when the normal flow of orders is not adequate.

Questions 117 through 120 relate to Alternative Investments. (6 minutes)

117. An investor can gain exposure to alternative investments by purchasing:
    A. convertible bonds of a high-yield issuer.
    B. a mortgage-backed security.
    C. an exchange-traded fund that tracks an emerging market index.

118. Which of the following is *least likely* a benefit of fund of funds (FOF) investing?
    A. FOFs may permit access to otherwise unavailable hedge funds.
    B. FOFs allow investors to diversify the risks of holding a single hedge fund.
    C. The fee is generally quite reasonable since the investor only pays the manager of the FOF.

119. A private equity firm that provides equity capital to a publicly traded company to finance the company's restructuring, but does not take the company private, is *best* described as engaging in:
    A. angel investing.
    B. mezzanine financing.
    C. private investment in public equity.

120. Which provision of a hedge fund's incentive fees is designed to prevent investors from paying multiple incentive fees for the same performance?
    A. Hurdle rate.
    B. High water mark.
    C. 2-and-20 structure.

Exam 2
Afternoon Session

Calculating Your Score

Topic	Maximum Score	Your Score
Ethical and Professional Standards	18	
Quantitative Methods	14	
Economics	12	
Financial Reporting and Analysis	24	
Corporate Finance	10	
Portfolio Management	6	
Equity Investments	12	
Fixed Income	14	
Derivatives	6	
Alternative Investments	4	
Total	120	

The morning and afternoon exams are identically weighted over the topics and readings. You can therefore treat the morning and afternoon exams as independent exams.

If you took more than three hours (180 minutes) to complete this portion of the exam, you should adjust your score downward by one point for each minute you ran over.

Remember: the real exam *will be more difficult* than these practice exams. The main reason for this is the general anxiety and stress that you will be feeling on exam day, coupled with the time pressure you will be under. Many of the questions on this practice exam and the real exam are not individually difficult, so if you take extra time to answer the questions on this practice exam, your score will go up significantly. However, if you want an accurate measure of your potential performance on the exam, adhere to the 3-hour time limit.

After you have finished grading your practice exam, you may find it useful to use the exam questions and recommended solutions for review. Many of these questions were specifically written for your use as study tools. Once again, I feel I should remind you not to rely on memorizing these questions; you are not likely to see them on the actual exam. What you will see on the exam, though, are the concepts, terms, and procedures presented in these questions.

Your actual exam will most likely look different than what you see in this book. Please remember, no study provider knows the content of the actual exam. These practice exams are our best guess as to the structure, content, and difficulty of an actual exam.

Test Answers

1.	A	B	C		41.	A	B	C		81.	A	B	C
2.	A	B	C		42.	A	B	C		82.	A	B	C
3.	A	B	C		43.	A	B	C		83.	A	B	C
4.	A	B	C		44.	A	B	C		84.	A	B	C
5.	A	B	C		45.	A	B	C		85.	A	B	C
6.	A	B	C		46.	A	B	C		86.	A	B	C
7.	A	B	C		47.	A	B	C		87.	A	B	C
8.	A	B	C		48.	A	B	C		88.	A	B	C
9.	A	B	C		49.	A	B	C		89.	A	B	C
10.	A	B	C		50.	A	B	C		90.	A	B	C
11.	A	B	C		51.	A	B	C		91.	A	B	C
12.	A	B	C		52.	A	B	C		92.	A	B	C
13.	A	B	C		53.	A	B	C		93.	A	B	C
14.	A	B	C		54.	A	B	C		94.	A	B	C
15.	A	B	C		55.	A	B	C		95.	A	B	C
16.	A	B	C		56.	A	B	C		96.	A	B	C
17.	A	B	C		57.	A	B	C		97.	A	B	C
18.	A	B	C		58.	A	B	C		98.	A	B	C
19.	A	B	C		59.	A	B	C		99.	A	B	C
20.	A	B	C		60.	A	B	C		100.	A	B	C
21.	A	B	C		61.	A	B	C		101.	A	B	C
22.	A	B	C		62.	A	B	C		102.	A	B	C
23.	A	B	C		63.	A	B	C		103.	A	B	C
24.	A	B	C		64.	A	B	C		104.	A	B	C
25.	A	B	C		65.	A	B	C		105.	A	B	C
26.	A	B	C		66.	A	B	C		106.	A	B	C
27.	A	B	C		67.	A	B	C		107.	A	B	C
28.	A	B	C		68.	A	B	C		108.	A	B	C
29.	A	B	C		69.	A	B	C		109.	A	B	C
30.	A	B	C		70.	A	B	C		110.	A	B	C
31.	A	B	C		71.	A	B	C		111.	A	B	C
32.	A	B	C		72.	A	B	C		112.	A	B	C
33.	A	B	C		73.	A	B	C		113.	A	B	C
34.	A	B	C		74.	A	B	C		114.	A	B	C
35.	A	B	C		75.	A	B	C		115.	A	B	C
36.	A	B	C		76.	A	B	C		116.	A	B	C
37.	A	B	C		77.	A	B	C		117.	A	B	C
38.	A	B	C		78.	A	B	C		118.	A	B	C
39.	A	B	C		79.	A	B	C		119.	A	B	C
40.	A	B	C		80.	A	B	C		120.	A	B	C

Exam 2
Afternoon Session

Questions 1 through 18 relate to Ethical and Professional Standards. (27 minutes)

1. Recommended procedures to comply with the Standard concerning priority of transactions are *least likely* to include:
   A. blackout periods.
   B. limited front-running by employees.
   C. disclosure to clients of the firm's policies in regard to personal investing.

2. Juan Perez, CFA, is a research analyst for a large Wall Street brokerage firm where he follows the pharmaceuticals industry. While a large pharmaceuticals convention is in town, Perez happens to be in a restaurant where several analysts he has never met before are discussing their investment recommendations. Perez overhears the analysts agree that PharmCo, Inc. is a strong "Buy," but cannot hear the details of why they are recommending purchasing stock in the company. The next day, Perez changes his "Sell" recommendation on PharmCo to "Buy," based solely on the conversation he overheard between the analysts the night before. Perez *most likely* violated the Standard concerning:
   A. diligence and reasonable basis.
   B. preservation of confidentiality.
   C. material nonpublic information.

3. Allen Winkler, CFA, an equity analyst, recently had lunch with his former professor, Kim Thompson. Thompson told him about a new theoretical stock valuation model she designed. Upon returning to his office, Winkler recreated Thompson's model and revised it slightly. He then tested the revised model using historical stock prices from Standard & Poor's (S&P) equity databases. The results were so impressive that his supervisors decided to create a small new fund called the Technical Fund directed toward their technically oriented clients. In the fund's prospectus, Winkler included a discussion of the model and the results of his tests. According to the Standard on misrepresentation, is Winkler required to credit Thompson for having developed the original model and S&P as the source of the data?
   A. Both of these sources must be cited.
   B. Neither of these sources must be cited.
   C. Only one of these sources must be cited.

4. Donald Smith, CFA, has been assigned by his employer to analyze Braden Corporation. Prior to joining his current firm, Smith worked as an investment banker and received options on 1,000 shares of Braden stock as part of his compensation for assisting the company with a large secondary offering. The options are currently at-the-money and will expire in two years. In addition, Smith has been speaking with Braden about a consulting arrangement in which Smith would be paid to work with Braden's investor relations department to improve the flow of information to the firm's current and prospective shareholders. If Smith writes a report on Braden Corporation, Smith:
    A. must disclose the options to clients, prospects, and his employer, but needs not disclose the consulting agreement because it has not yet been finalized.
    B. only needs to disclose the options to clients and prospects and disclose the consulting agreement to his employer.
    C. must disclose both the options and the consulting agreement to clients, prospects, and his employer.

5. Fran Lester, CFA, lives in a country that permits equity brokers to receive shares in oversubscribed IPOs only with their employer's permission. She works as a broker for a firm doing business in another country, which does not require brokers to get such permission for any IPOs. If Lester's firm is distributing shares of an oversubscribed IPO in her firm's country, can Lester receive shares in the IPO?
    A. No, not under any circumstances.
    B. Yes, but she must obtain permission from her employer.
    C. Yes, because applicable law in her firm's country permits it.

6. Diane Harris, a CFA Institute member, is a portfolio manager for Worldwide Investments. Robert Cline, one of her clients, offered her the use of his condominium in Aspen for one week in February if the performance of his portfolio is at least two percentage points above that of the S&P 500 during the next 12 months. Immediately after learning about the offer, Harris informed her manager of all terms of this agreement in writing and received verbal consent to the arrangement. At the end of the year, Harris met the performance criteria set by Cline and accepted the vacation. Did Harris violate the Standard concerning additional compensation arrangements?
    A. Yes, because written consent from her employer is required.
    B. No, because Harris notified and received consent from her employer to enter the arrangement.
    C. No, because bonuses from clients for doing her job well do not create any conflict of interest.

7. Stan White, CFA, heads the marketing department of a large brokerage firm, American Securities. He reports directly to the president of the firm, who has mandated that beginning this year, the firm must present all past performance results in accordance with the Global Investment Performance Standards. Which of the following statements is an acceptable indication of American Securities' compliance with the Global Investment Performance Standards?
   A. American Securities has prepared and presented this report in compliance with the Global Investment Performance Standards (GIPS®).
   B. American Securities has prepared and presented this report utilizing the calculation methodologies of the Global Investment Performance Standards (GIPS®).
   C. American Securities has presented this report in compliance with the Global Investment Performance Standards (GIPS®). Please reference "Disclosures" for exceptions.

8. Betty Cantor, a CFA Institute member, was about to issue a neutral report on HLC Corporation, a high-tech firm, when she talked to Donald Watson, her former manager and mentor, who is now with another investment firm. Watson is very bullish on HLC and tells Cantor that "everyone knows HLC is going to experience a major stock price increase over the next year." Cantor knows Watson has been an exceptionally insightful analyst in the high-tech sector. According to the CFA Institute Standards of Practice Handbook, is it acceptable for Cantor to change her recommendation to a "Buy" based on the comments of Watson?
   A. Yes, because based on experience, Watson's views are generally correct.
   B. No, because Watson's comments could be considered inside information.
   C. No, because she does not have a reasonable basis for recommending this stock.

9. Six months ago, Tom Hayes, CFA, left his position as a portfolio manager and accepted a position as senior portfolio manager at a smaller boutique firm. One of Hayes's first recommendations at his new job is Selldex. He had researched and recommended the stock six months ago while employed at his old firm, and he still believes it has great investment potential. He recreates his Selldex research using information from public sources and makes the recommendation. According to the CFA Institute Standards of Practice, Hayes's actions:
   A. are not in violation of any Standard.
   B. are in violation because his previous employer paid for the original research.
   C. are in violation because the research he did at his old employer is the employer's property.

10. The CFA Institute Code of Ethics *most likely* requires members and candidates to:
    A. not engage in activity which compromises the integrity of CFA Institute.
    B. stay informed on applicable laws and regulations that pertain to their respective areas of business.
    C. act with competence, integrity, and in ethical manner when dealing with the public, clients, employers, employees, and other market participants.

11. Craig Boone, a Level I CFA candidate, is a trader on the fixed income desk at a large financial institution. He has observed that one of the salesmen on the desk has been reallocating some trades at the end of the day, giving better execution to a large client at the expense of several smaller clients, a practice Boone suspects is illegal. The salesman tells Boone this is a common practice and that the firm's senior management is aware of it. If Boone makes a personal record of the activity, takes it home for his personal files, and subsequently reveals it to regulatory authorities, he would:
    A. be in violation of the Standards for breaching his duty of loyalty to his employer.
    B. be in violation of the Standards for disclosing confidential information.
    C. not be in violation of any Standards.

12. WEB, an investment-banking firm, is the principal underwriter for MTEX's upcoming debenture issue. Lynn Black, CFA, is an analyst with WEB, and she learned from an employee in MTEX's programming department that a serious problem was recently discovered in the software program of its major new product line. In fact, the problem is so bad that many customers have canceled their orders with MTEX. Black checked the debenture's prospectus and found no mention of this development. The red herring prospectus has already been distributed. According to the CFA Institute Standards of Professional Conduct, Black's *best* course of action is to:
    A. inform her immediate supervisor at WEB of her discovery.
    B. take no action because this is material nonpublic information.
    C. notify potential investors of the omission on a fair and equitable basis.

13. Which of the following statements about a CFA charterholder or candidate is in compliance with the Code and Standards?
     A. As a CFA charterholder, I provide superior performance in managing client portfolios.
     B. I hold the CFA charter, a designation recognized around the world in the investment management and research industry.
     C. I have registered as a CFA candidate because the mastering the CFA curriculum will improve my investment performance.

14. Mary Walters, CFA, is a trust officer at a regional branch of Money Center bank. She has entered into a referral agreement whereby she will refer clients to Bob Sear, a tax attorney who she believes is the best in the business. Sear has told Walters that he will do the tax work on her children's trust, created by their grandparents, in return for such referrals. According to the CFA Institute Code and Standards, Walters should disclose the arrangement to:
     A. her employer only.
     B. prospective clients she refers only.
     C. both her employer and prospective clients she refers.

15. Ronaldo Jenkins, CFA, is chief investment officer of Windwatch Advisors, a discretionary investment advisory firm. With over 15 years experience in various asset classes, Jenkins is head of Windwatch's proxy voting committee. He serves on the boards of several non-profit organizations and public companies and advises local municipal governments. During a recent search for an investment bank for a fixed income offering on behalf of a municipality, Jenkins learns in confidence that an investment bank, which is a large subsidiary of a publicly traded commercial bank owned by Windwatch clients, is experiencing financial difficulties and will be shut down. According to the CFA Institute Standards of Professional Conduct, Jenkins is *least likely* permitted to:
     A. share the information received about the investment bank with his compliance officer.
     B. approach the investment bank about making public disclosure of the financial difficulties and pending closure.
     C. share the information received about the investment bank with Windwatch's head of equity investments for informational purposes as a shareholder of the parent commercial bank.

16. Mary Woods, CFA, is a client services and marketing manager for LAM Asset Management, which has managed domestic equity and fixed income assets for more than 20 years. In an effort to diversify its business, LAM hires two international equity portfolio managers and requires Woods and other employees to take a 2-week course on international equity portfolios, client servicing, and marketing. Subsequently, Woods prepares a marketing presentation regarding LAM's international equity capabilities, citing experienced portfolio managers and a proven track record, and she assures returns above the long-term risk-free rate of return based on 20 years' investment experience in managing client portfolios. Regarding her marketing activities for LAM's international equity product, Woods has:

   A. violated CFA Institute Standards of Professional Conduct by compromising her fiduciary duty to LAM's domestic equity clients.
   B. violated CFA Institute Standards of Professional Conduct by misrepresenting the services that LAM could provide and the firm's qualifications in international equity.
   C. not violated CFA Institute Standards of Professional Conduct since Woods's marketing of the product fulfilled LAM's fiduciary duty to create diversified portfolios for clients, balancing portfolio returns with an appropriate level of risk.

17. While visiting Cassori Company, Mark Ramsey, CFA, overhears management make comments that are not public information but are not really meaningful by themselves. Combining this information with his own analysis and other outside sources, Ramsey decides to change his recommendation on Cassori from "Buy" to "Sell." According to the CFA Institute Standards of Professional Conduct, Ramsey:

   A. must not issue his report until Cassori's management makes their comments public.
   B. may issue his "Sell" report because the facts are nonmaterial, but should maintain a file of the facts and documents leading to this conclusion.
   C. must report these events to his immediate supervisor and legal counsel, since they have become material in combination with his analysis.

18. Compliance with the Global Investment Performance Standards *least likely* requires firms to:

   A. include all fee-paying and non-fee-paying accounts in at least one composite.
   B. document in writing the policies and procedures used to comply with GIPS.
   C. specifically define what constitutes the firm that is claiming compliance.

Questions 19 through 32 relate to Quantitative Methods. (21 minutes)

19.   Jim Franklin recently purchased a home for $300,000 on which he made a down payment of $100,000. He obtained a 30-year mortgage to finance the balance on which he pays a fixed annual rate of 6%. If he makes regular, fixed monthly payments, what loan balance will remain just after the 48th payment?
   A. $186,109.
   B. $189,229.
   C. $192,444.

20.   An investor purchased a $10,000, 5-year corporate note one year ago for $10,440. The note pays an annual coupon of $600. Over the past year, the note's annual yield-to-maturity has dropped by 1%. What total return did the investor earn over the year?
   A. 8.5%.
   B. 9.0%.
   C. 9.5%.

21.   An investor holds a portfolio consisting of one share of each of the following stocks:

Stock	Price at the Beginning of the Year	Price at the End of the Year	Cash Dividend During the Year
A	$10	$20	$0
B	$50	$60	$1
C	$100	$110	$4

   For the 1-year holding period, the portfolio total return is *closest* to:
   A. 15.79%.
   B. 18.42%.
   C. 21.88%.

22.   Which of the following measurement scales provides the *least* information?
   A. Ratio.
   B. Ordinal.
   C. Nominal.

23.   An analyst observes the following four annual returns: $R_1 = +10\%$, $R_2 = -15\%$, $R_3 = 0\%$, and $R_4 = +5\%$. The average compound annual rate over the four years is *closest* to:
   A. -5.0%.
   B. -0.5%.
   C. 0.0%.

24. Given the observations 45, 20, 30, and 25, the mean absolute deviation is *closest* to:
   A. 0.0.
   B. 7.5.
   C. 13.3.

25. An investor wants to buy a condominium in Florida. The value of her portfolio is currently $1,000,000, and she needs $100,000 in one year for the down payment. She doesn't mind decreasing her capital as long she has $950,000 remaining in her portfolio after the down payment is made. She is considering two new portfolios for her holdings. The details on the two portfolios are:

	Expected Annual Return	Standard Deviation of Returns
Portfolio 1	17%	15%
Portfolio 2	12%	10%
Portfolio 3	8%	6%

   According to Roy's Safety-First criterion, the portfolio she would prefer is:
   A. Portfolio 1.
   B. Portfolio 2.
   C. Portfolio 3.

26. A technical analyst is *most likely* to expect an uptrend in prices to continue if:
   A. converging trendlines form a triangle pattern on a price chart.
   B. the 14-day relative strength index increases from 70 to 80.
   C. the uptrend line acts as a resistance level when the price approaches it.

27. Adam Farman has been asked to estimate the volatility of a technology stock index. He has identified a statistic which has an expected value equal to the population volatility and has determined that increasing his sample size will decrease the sampling error for this statistic. Based only on these properties, his statistic can *best* be described as:
   A. unbiased and efficient.
   B. unbiased and consistent.
   C. efficient and consistent.

28. According to Chebyshev's inequality, the minimum proportion of observations falling within three standard deviations of the mean for a negatively skewed distribution is *closest* to:
    A. 68%.
    B. 75%.
    C. 89%.

29. The following table summarizes the results of a poll taken of CEOs and analysts about the economic impact of a pending piece of legislation:

Group	Predict Positive Impact	Predict Negative Impact
CEOs	40	30
Analysts	70	60

    What is the probability that a randomly selected individual from this group will be either an analyst or someone who thinks this legislation will have a positive impact on the economy?
    A. 0.75.
    B. 0.80.
    C. 0.85.

30. A researcher has investigated the returns over the last five years to a long-short strategy based on mean reversion in equity returns volatility. His hypothesis test led to rejection of the hypothesis that abnormal (risk-adjusted) returns to the strategy over the period were less than or equal to zero at the 1% level of significance. He would *most* appropriately decide that:
    A. his firm should employ the strategy for client accounts because the abnormal returns are positive and statistically significant.
    B. while the abnormal returns are highly significant statistically, they may not be economically meaningful.
    C. as long as the estimated statistical returns are greater than the transactions costs of the strategy, his firm should employ the strategy for client accounts.

31. An analyst decides to select 10 stocks for her portfolio by placing the ticker symbols for all the stocks traded on the New York Stock Exchange in a large bowl. She randomly selects 20 stocks and will put every other one chosen into her 10-stock portfolio. The analyst used:
    A. dual random sampling.
    B. simple random sampling.
    C. stratified random sampling.

32. Which of the following tests would generally be considered a nonparametric test?
    A. Whether a sample is random or not.
    B. Large sample test of the value of a population mean.
    C. Value of the variance of a normal population.

Questions 33 through 44 relate to Economics. (18 minutes)

33. Assume the exchange rate between the Trotter (TRT) and the Roeckl (RKL) is 5.50 TRT/RKL and the exchange rate between the Roeckl and the Passage (PSG) is 8.00 RKL/PSG. The cross rate between the PSG and the TRT is *closest* to:
    A. 0.0227 PSG/TRT.
    B. 0.6875 PSG/TRT.
    C. 44.00 PSG/TRT.

34. Which of the following statements about methods of calculating gross domestic product is *most accurate*?
    A. Except for a statistical discrepancy, the income and expenditure approaches to calculating GDP should result in the same value for economic output.
    B. Because it includes activity at all stages of production, the sum-of-value-added method results in a better estimate of GDP than the value-of-final-output method.
    C. Value-of-final-output is used to calculate GDP under the expenditure approach, while sum-of-value-added is used to calculate GDP under the income approach.

35. The J-curve, in the context of trade between two countries, refers to the fact that when the domestic country has a trade deficit:
    A. appreciation of the domestic currency initially leads to a decrease in the trade deficit but will increase the trade deficit in the long term.
    B. an increase in domestic inflation will initially increase the trade deficit but will decrease the trade deficit in the long term.
    C. appreciation of the foreign currency will initially increase the trade deficit but will decrease the trade deficit in the long term.

36. Which of the following organizations is the *most* focused on promoting economic growth and reducing poverty by offering both monetary and technical assistance?
    A. World Bank.
    B. World Trade Organization.
    C. International Monetary Fund.

©2012 Kaplan, Inc.

37. The quantity theory of money states that in a full employment economy, any increase in the supply of money in excess of the rate of growth of real GDP will lead to a proportional increase in:
    A. the price level.
    B. velocity.
    C. real GDP.

38. Akor is a country that has chosen to use a conventional fixed peg arrangement as the country's exchange rate regime. Under this arrangement, Akor's exchange rate against the currency to which it pegs:
    A. is market-determined.
    B. will be equal to the peg rate.
    C. may fluctuate around the peg rate.

39. The supply function for a good is: quantity supplied = –170 + 10 × price. If the market price is 25, the value of producer surplus is:
    A. 320.
    B. 640.
    C. 2,000.

40. Which of the following statements about a monopolist is *most accurate*? A monopolist will:
    A. maximize the average profit per unit sold.
    B. charge the highest price for which it can sell its product.
    C. produce where marginal revenue equals marginal cost.

41. Assume that the supply of ethanol is relatively more elastic than the demand for ethanol. Compared to an initial competitive equilibrium in the market for ethanol, the imposition of a per-gallon tax on producers of ethanol will *most likely* decrease:
    A. producer surplus by the total amount of tax collected.
    B. producer surplus by less than it reduces consumer surplus.
    C. the sum of consumer and producer surplus by the amount of tax collected.

42. Under what conditions is inflation *most likely* to shift wealth from lenders to borrowers?
    A. Only when inflation is unexpected.
    B. Only when inflation is unexpected and negative.
    C. When inflation is either unexpected or expected.

43. The short-run supply curve for a firm under perfect competition is the firm's:
    A. marginal cost curve above average total cost.
    B. marginal cost curve above average variable cost.
    C. average variable cost curve above marginal revenue.

44. Long-run aggregate supply is *least likely* to be affected by changes in the:
    A. prices of raw materials inputs.
    B. quantity of labor in the economy.
    C. level of technology.

Questions 45 through 68 relate to Financial Reporting and Analysis. (36 minutes)

45. In accrual accounting, the matching principle states that:
    A. an entity should recognize revenues only when received and expenses only when they are paid.
    B. transactions and events producing cash flows are allocated only to time periods in which the cash flows occur.
    C. expenses incurred to generate revenue are recognized in the same time period as the revenue.

46. Which of the following statements about revenue recognition methods is *most accurate*?
    A. The completed contract method under U.S. GAAP recognizes long-term contract revenue only as each phase of production is complete.
    B. The percentage of completion method recognizes profit corresponding to the costs incurred as a proportion of estimated total costs.
    C. The installment method recognizes sales when cash is received, but no profit is recognized until cash collected exceeds costs.

47. A company changes from an incorrect method of accounting to an acceptable one. Which of the following statements about this change is *most accurate*?
    A. It requires restatement of any prior period results that are presented in the current financial statements.
    B. It is a change in accounting principle and is reported below the line net of taxes.
    C. It is an unusual or infrequent item and is reported in net income from continuing operations.

48. An analyst who believes a firm's management is manipulating the cash flow statement should *most* appropriately reclassify financing cash outflows as operating cash outflows if the firm has:
    A. financed its payables.
    B. securitized receivables.
    C. repurchased stock to offset dilution.

49. An analyst gathers the following information:
    - Net income $100
    - Decrease in accounts receivable   30
    - Depreciation   25
    - Increase in inventory   17
    - Increase in accounts payable   10
    - Decrease in wages payable   5
    - Increase in deferred taxes   17
    - Sale of fixed assets   150
    - Purchase of fixed assets   340
    - Profit from the sale of fixed assets   5
    - Dividends paid out   35
    - Sale of new common stock   120

    Based on the above information, the company's cash flow from operations under U.S. GAAP is:
    A. $155.
    B. $165.
    C. $182.

50. Which of the following statements about cash flow is *least accurate*? Under U.S. GAAP, cash flow from:
    A. operations includes cash operating expenses and changes in working capital accounts.
    B. financing includes the proceeds of debt issued and from the sale of the company's common stock.
    C. investing includes interest income from investment in debt securities.

51.   An analyst gathered the following data about a company:
    *   The company had 500,000 shares of common stock outstanding for the entire year.
    *   The company's beginning stock price was $40, its ending price was $60, and its average price over the year was $50.
    *   The company has 120,000 warrants outstanding for the entire year.
    *   Each warrant allows the holder to buy one share of common stock at $45 per share.

How many shares of common stock should the company use in computing its diluted earnings per share?
    A. 488,000.
    B. 500,000.
    C. 512,000.

52.   Books Forever, Inc., uses short-term bank debt to buy inventory. Assuming an initial current ratio that is greater than 1, and an initial quick (or acid test) ratio that is less than 1, what is the effect of these transactions on the current ratio and the quick ratio?
    A. Both ratios will decrease.
    B. Neither ratio will decrease.
    C. Only one ratio will decrease.

53.   Which of the following statements regarding the financial statement reporting of leases is *most accurate*?
    A. Under an operating lease, the lessee treats the entire lease payment as a cash outflow from operations.
    B. The lessee's current ratio is the same whether a lease is treated as an operating or finance lease.
    C. At the inception of a direct financing lease, the lessor recognizes gross profit.

54.   Which of the following statements about expenses and intangible assets is *least accurate*?
    A. Advertising fees are generally expensed as incurred.
    B. In most countries, research and development costs are capitalized.
    C. Intangible assets are initially entered on the balance sheet at their purchase prices when they are acquired from an outside entity.

55.   Which of the following accounting practices is *most likely* to decrease reported earnings in the current period?
    A. Using the straight-line method of depreciation instead of an accelerated method.
    B. Capitalizing advertising expenses rather than expensing them in the current period.
    C. Using LIFO inventory cost methods during a period of rising prices.

56. Which of the following statements about dilutive securities is *most accurate*?
   A. A simple capital structure is one that contains only common stock and antidilutive securities.
   B. A dilutive security is one that will cause earnings per share to decrease if it is converted into common stock.
   C. Warrants are antidilutive if their exercise price is less than the stock price at the end of the period.

57. As of January 1, a company had 22,500 $10 par value common shares outstanding. On July 1, the company repurchased 5,000 shares. The company also has 11,000, 10%, $100 par value preferred shares. If the company's net income is $210,000, its diluted earnings per share is *closest* to:
   A. $5.00.
   B. $7.50.
   C. $10.00.

58. In periods of rising prices and stable or increasing inventory quantities, compared with companies that use LIFO inventory accounting, companies that use the FIFO method will have:
   A. higher COGS and lower taxes.
   B. higher net income and higher taxes.
   C. lower inventory balances and lower working capital.

59. Rowlin Corporation, which reports under IFRS, wrote down its inventory of electronic parts last period from its original cost of €28,000 to net realizable value of €25,000. This period, inventory at net realizable value has increased to €30,000. Rowlin should revalue this inventory to:
   A. €28,000 and report a gain of €3,000 on the income statement.
   B. €30,000 and report a gain of €3,000 on the income statement.
   C. €30,000 and report a gain of €5,000 on the income statement.

60. Under IFRS, remeasurements related to defined benefit pension plans are initially recognized in:
   A. net income in the current period.
   B. other comprehensive income and are not amortized to income.
   C. other comprehensive income and amortized over time to income.

61. In the early years of an asset's life, a firm that chooses an accelerated depreciation method instead of using straight-line depreciation will tend to have:
   A. lower net income and lower equity.
   B. higher return on equity and higher return on assets.
   C. lower depreciation expense and lower turnover ratios.

62. Which of the following definitions used in accounting for income taxes is *least accurate*?
    A. Income tax expense is current period taxes payable adjusted for any changes in deferred tax assets and liabilities.
    B. A valuation allowance is a reserve against deferred tax assets based on the likelihood that those assets will not be realized.
    C. A deferred tax liability is created when tax expense is less than taxes payable and the difference is expected to reverse in future years.

63. From the extended (5-part) DuPont equation, which of the following components describes the equation EBT / EBIT?
    A. Tax burden.
    B. Interest burden.
    C. Financial leverage.

64. Under U.S. GAAP, which of the following statements about the financial statement effects of issuing bonds is *least accurate*?
    A. Issuance of debt has no effect on cash flow from operations.
    B. Periodic interest payments decrease cash flow from operations by the amount of interest paid.
    C. Payment of debt at maturity decreases cash flow from operations by the face value of the debt.

65. When an increase in the tax rate is enacted, deferred tax:
    A. assets and liabilities both increase in value.
    B. assets decrease in value and deferred tax liabilities increase in value.
    C. liability and asset accounts are maintained at historical tax rates until they reverse.

66. A manufacturing firm shuts down production at one of its plants and offers the facility for rent. Based on the market for similar properties, the firm determines that the fair value of the plant is €500,000 more than its original cost. If this firm uses the cost model for plant and equipment and the fair value model for investment property, should it recognize a gain on its income statement?
    A. Yes, because the plant will be reclassified as investment property.
    B. No, because the increase in value does not reverse a previously recognized loss.
    C. No, because the firm must continue to use the cost model for valuation of this asset.

67. Under U.S. GAAP, an asset is considered impaired if its book value is:
    A. less than its market value.
    B. greater than the present value of its expected future cash flows.
    C. greater than the sum of its undiscounted expected cash flows.

68. Which of the following pairs of general categories are *least likely* to be considered in the formulas used by credit rating agencies to determine the capacity of a borrower to repay a debt?
    A. Operational efficiency; leverage.
    B. Margin stability; availability of collateral.
    C. Leverage; scale and diversification.

Questions 69 through 78 relate to Corporate Finance. (15 minutes)

69. Which of the following statements about the component costs of capital is *least accurate*?
    A. The cost of common equity is the required rate of return on common stock.
    B. The cost of preferred stock is the preferred dividend divided by the preferred's par value.
    C. The after-tax cost of debt is based on the expected yield to maturity on newly issued debt.

70. Project X has an internal rate of return (IRR) of 14%. Project Y has an IRR of 17%. Both projects have conventional cash flow patterns (all inflows after the initial cash outflow). If the required rate of return is:
    A. 14%, the net present value (NPV) of Project Y will exceed the NPV of Project X.
    B. greater than 17%, Project Y will have a shorter payback period than Project X.
    C. 10%, both projects will have a positive NPV, and the NPV of Project Y will exceed the NPV of Project X.

71. AlcoBanc owns a piece of property that is under consideration for a new bank branch. Which of the following is *least likely* a relevant incremental cash flow in analyzing a capital budgeting project? The:
    A. interest costs of a loan for the property purchase.
    B. business gained at other branches due to new customers at the proposed site.
    C. $150,000 AlcoBanc could get if they sold the property instead of building a new branch.

72. Jay Construction Company is considering whether to accept a new bridge-building project. Jay will use the pure-play method to estimate the cost of capital for the project, using Cass Bridge Builders as a comparable company. To calculate the project beta, Jay should:
    A. estimate Cass's cost of equity capital and apply it to the project.
    B. use the CAPM equation, substituting Cass's equity beta for its own.
    C. adjust Cass's equity beta for any difference in leverage between Cass and Jay.

73. Which of the following would *most likely* indicate deterioration of a firm's working capital management?
    A. An increase in days of payables outstanding.
    B. An increase in days of receivables outstanding.
    C. A decreased amount of cash and cash equivalents.

74. Hanson Aluminum, Inc. is considering whether to build a mill based around a new rolling technology the company has been developing. Management views this project as being riskier than the average project the company undertakes. Based on their analysis of the projected cash flows, management determines that the project's internal rate of return is equal to the company's marginal cost of capital. If the project goes forward, the company will finance it with newly issued debt with an after-tax cost less than the project's IRR. Should management accept or reject this project?
    A. Accept, because the project returns the company's cost of capital.
    B. Accept, because the marginal cost of the new debt is less than the project's internal rate of return.
    C. Reject, because the project reduces the value of the company when its risk is taken into account.

75. Which of the following is *least likely* an important requirement of good corporate governance?
    A. Members of the board should serve staggered, multiple-year terms.
    B. A board should be composed of at least a majority of independent board members.
    C. Board members should have appropriate experience and expertise relevant to the company's business.

76. Pannonia Enterprises, Inc. (PEI) has a target capital structure of 40% debt with 60% equity. PEI's pretax cost of debt will remain at 9% until the firm raises more than $200,000 in new debt capital, at which point its pretax cost of debt will increase to 9.5%. PEI's cost of equity will increase when more than $400,000 in equity capital is raised. PEI's break point for debt capital is *closest* to:
    A. $200,000.
    B. $500,000.
    C. $666,667.

©2012 Kaplan, Inc.

77. For a profitable company, issuing debt in order to retire common stock will *most likely*:
    A. increase both net income and return on equity.
    B. decrease both operating income and net income.
    C. increase both the level and variability of return on equity.

78. Robel Company, which pays no dividends, carries out a 3-for-5 reverse split of its common shares. How will this transaction affect Robel's forecasts of its net cash position?
    A. No effect because this transaction does not affect future cash flows.
    B. More net cash in both the short-term forecast and the long-term forecast.
    C. No effect on the short-term forecast but less net cash in the long-term forecast.

Questions 79 through 84 relate to Portfolio Management. (9 minutes)

79. A stock has a beta of 0.9 and an estimated return of 10%. The risk-free rate is 7%, and the expected return on the market is 11%. According to the CAPM, this stock:
    A. is overvalued.
    B. is undervalued.
    C. is properly valued.

80. An analyst gathers the following data about the returns for two stocks.

	Stock A	Stock B
E(R)	0.04	0.09
σ^2	0.0025	0.0064

    $Cov_{A,B} = 0.001$

    The correlation between the returns of Stock A and Stock B ($\rho_{A,B}$) is *closest* to:

    A. 0.25.
    B. 0.50.
    C. 0.63.

81. In which step of the portfolio management process does an investment manager rebalance the portfolio to its target asset allocation percentages?
    A. Analysis step.
    B. Feedback step.
    C. Execution step.

82. Which of the following possible portfolios cannot lie on the efficient frontier?

Portfolio	Expected Return	Standard Deviation
1	8%	6%
2	10%	6%
3	14%	12%
4	14%	16%

   A. Portfolio 3 only.
   B. Portfolios 1 and 4.
   C. Portfolios 2 and 3.

83. Which of the following pairs refer to the same type of risk?
   A. Total risk and the variance of returns.
   B. Systematic risk and firm-specific risk.
   C. Undiversifiable risk and unsystematic risk.

84. Greenbaum, Inc. stock pays no dividend and currently trades at $54. Based on the CAPM and assuming an expected return on the market of 12% and a risk-free rate of 8%, the expected price for Greenbaum one year from now is $62. The beta of Greenbaum shares is *closest* to:
   A. 1.5.
   B. 1.6.
   C. 1.7.

Questions 85 through 96 relate to Equity Investments. (18 minutes)

85. A financial market is said to be operationally efficient if:
   A. transactions costs are low.
   B. prices adjust quickly to new information.
   C. it results in resources being allocated to their most productive uses.

86. The weak form of the efficient market hypothesis (EMH) implies that:
   A. no one can achieve abnormal returns using market information.
   B. insiders, such as specialists and corporate board members, cannot achieve abnormal returns on average.
   C. investors cannot achieve abnormal returns, on average, using technical analysis, after adjusting for transaction costs and taxes.

87. Which of the following statements about alternative investment indexes is *most accurate*?
    A. An investor can replicate a commodity index by making direct investments in the underlying physical commodities.
    B. Real Estate Investment Trust indexes track the prices of shares of publicly traded companies that invest in mortgages or real property.
    C. Hedge fund indexes accurately represent the investment performance of the hedge fund industry.

88. The present value of an equity security's future cash flows is *most likely* to be significantly different from the company's:
    A. book value per share.
    B. market value per share.
    C. intrinsic value per share.

89. An analyst is valuing a company's perpetual preferred stock that pays a $6 annual dividend. The company's bonds currently yield 7.5% and preferred shares are selling to yield 75 basis points below the company's bond yield. The value of the preferred stock is *closest* to:
    A. $72.
    B. $80.
    C. $89.

90. An investor buys a stock at $32 a share and deposits 50% initial margin. Assume that the maintenance margin is 25%, the stock pays no dividends, and transaction costs and interest on the margin loan are zero. The price at which the investor would receive a margin call is *closest* to:
    A. $16.
    B. $21.
    C. $24.

91. The risk-free rate is 5%, and the expected return on the market index is 15%. A stock has a:
    • Beta of 1.0.
    • Dividend payout ratio of 40%.
    • Return on equity (ROE) of 15%.

    If the stock is expected to pay a $2.50 dividend, its intrinsic value using dividend discount model is *closest* to:
    A. $27.77.
    B. $41.67.
    C. $53.33.

92. Which of the following industries is *best* described as non-cyclical and defensive?
    A. Energy.
    B. Technology.
    C. Consumer staples.

93. Which of the following scenarios is inconsistent with efficient financial markets?
    A. An analyst's buy recommendations have returned 2% more than the broad market index, on average.
    B. Johnson, Inc. reports an increase of 8% in its earnings from a year earlier, and its stock price declines 5% on the news.
    C. Earl Baker, an investor, earns consistently superior risk-adjusted returns by buying stocks when most investment advisors are pessimistic and selling stocks when most investment advisors are optimistic.

94. The holder of the type of security that has a priority in liquidation less than that of bonds or promissory notes issued by the company but ahead of that of common stock is *most likely* to have:
    A. no voting rights.
    B. statutory voting rights.
    C. cumulative voting rights.

95. Transactions costs incurred from portfolio rebalancing are *most likely* to be highest for funds that track:
    A. price-weighted indexes.
    B. value-weighted indexes.
    C. equal-weighted indexes.

96. A stock that currently does not pay a dividend is expected to pay its first dividend of $1.00 five years from today. Thereafter, the dividend is expected to grow at an annual rate of 25% for the next three years and then grow at a constant rate of 5% per year thereafter. The required rate of return is 10.3%. The value of the stock today is *closest* to:
    A. $20.65.
    B. $22.72.
    C. $23.87.

Questions 97 through 110 relate to Fixed Income. (21 minutes)

97. Which of the following statements about bond call features is *least accurate*? Embedded call options in callable bonds:
    A. expose investors to additional reinvestment rate risk.
    B. create risk because they add uncertainty to the bond's cash flow pattern.
    C. can be valued using the difference between the zero-volatility spread and the nominal spread.

98. All else equal, which of the following is *least likely* to increase the interest rate risk of a bond?
    A. A longer maturity.
    B. Inclusion of a call feature.
    C. A decrease in the YTM.

99. One year ago, an investor purchased a 10-year, $1,000 par value, 8% semiannual coupon bond with an 8% yield to maturity. Now, one year later, interest rates remain unchanged at 8%. If the investor sells the bond today (immediately after receiving the second coupon payment, and with no transaction costs), he will have:
    A. a capital gain of $80.
    B. a capital loss of $80.
    C. no capital gain or loss.

100. Which of the following assets is *most likely* to represent high-quality collateral in credit analysis?
    A. Goodwill.
    B. Trademarks.
    C. Deferred tax assets.

101. A company has two $1,000 face value bonds outstanding both selling for $701.22. The first issue has an annual coupon of 8% and 20 years to maturity. The second bond has the same yield to maturity as the first bond but has only five years remaining until maturity. The second issue pays interest annually as well. What is the annual interest payment on the second issue?
    A. $18.56.
    B. $27.18.
    C. $37.12.

102. If a bond has a convexity of 60 and a modified duration of 10, the convexity adjustment (to a duration-based approximation) associated with a 25 basis point interest rate decline is *closest* to:
    A. −2.875%.
    B. −2.125%.
    C. +0.0375%.

103. A semiannual-pay bond is callable in five years at $1,080. The bond has an 8% coupon and 15 years to maturity. If an investor pays $895 for the bond today, the yield to call is *closest* to:
    A. 9.3%.
    B. 10.2%.
    C. 12.1%.

104. Recent economic data suggest an increasing likelihood that the economy will soon enter a recessionary phase. What is the *most likely* effect on the yields of lower-quality corporate bonds and on credit spreads of lower-quality versus higher-quality corporate bonds?
    A. Both will increase.
    B. Both will decrease.
    C. One will increase and one will decrease.

105. Which of the following statements regarding provisions for paying off bonds is *least accurate*?
    A. Nonrefundable bonds can be callable.
    B. "Serial bonds" refers to an issue with several staggered maturity dates.
    C. A sinking fund provision gives the company the option to retire portions of the bond issue prior to maturity.

106. Which of the following statements regarding the risks inherent in bonds is *most accurate*?
    A. Interest rate risk is the risk that the coupon rate will be adjusted downward if market rates decline.
    B. The reinvestment rate assumption in calculating bond yields is generally not significant to the bond's yield.
    C. Default risk deals with the likelihood that the issuer will fail to meet its obligations as specified in the indenture.

107. If an investor wants only investment grade bonds in her portfolio, she would be *least likely* to purchase a(n):
   A. 2-year municipal bond rated A–.
   B. 3-year municipal bond rated BB.
   C. 15-year, semiannual coupon corporate bond rated BBB.

108. An investor is choosing between a 10% corporate bond and a 6% municipal bond with similar risk and similar maturity. What is the marginal tax rate that will make the investor indifferent between the two bonds?
   A. 20%.
   B. 40%.
   C. 60%.

109. Changes in a fixed-coupon bond's cash flows associated with changes in yield would be reflected in the bond's:
   A. effective duration.
   B. modified duration.
   C. Macaulay duration.

110. Four non-convertible bonds have the indicated yield spreads to Treasury securities:

	Maturity	Nominal Spread	Zero-Volatility Spread	Option-Adjusted Spread
Bond W	2 years	156 bp	155 bp	130 bp
Bond X	3 years	173 bp	174 bp	199 bp
Bond Y	5 years	188 bp	189 bp	164 bp
Bond Z	10 years	202 bp	201 bp	226 bp

Based on these spreads, it is *most likely* that:
   A. Bond X is callable, and Bond Y is putable.
   B. Bond W is callable, and Bond Z is putable.
   C. Bond Z is callable, and the spot yield curve is inverted.

Questions 111 through 116 relate to Derivatives. (9 minutes)

111. Three months ago, Jen Baker purchased one American put option contract on Mechor Corporation for $4 per option share. Baker also owns 100 shares of Mechor. The following data applies to Baker's position:
    - Option strike price $60
    - Stock price on date of option purchase $60
    - Stock price today $52
    - Time to option expiry from today   1 month

    Given only the above data, if Baker exercises her option today, the profit/loss (from the date of the option purchase) on Baker's combined stock/put position is:
    A. –$800.
    B. –$400.
    C. $800.

112. Two Level I CFA candidates are discussing futures and make the following statements:

    Candidate 1: Futures are traded using standardized contracts. They require margin and incur interest charges on the margin loan.

    Candidate 2: If the margin balance falls below the maintenance margin amount due to a change in the contract price for the underlying assets, the investor must add funds to bring the margin back up to the initial margin requirement.

    Are the candidates' statements correct or incorrect?
    A. Both statements are correct.
    B. Neither statement is correct.
    C. Only one of the statements is correct.

113. Which of the following statements for puts at expiration is *least accurate*? The:
    A. put buyer's maximum loss is the put option's premium.
    B. maximum loss to the writer of a put is the strike price less the premium.
    C. put holder will exercise the option whenever the stock's price is greater than the exercise price.

©2012 Kaplan, Inc.

114. Which of the following is *least likely* a way to close a futures position?
    A. Canceling the position on the floor of the exchange.
    B. Taking on an opposite position to bring the net position to zero.
    C. Privately negotiating the terms of the transaction with a trader with an opposite position and delivering the asset and closing the contract off the floor of the exchange.

115. At the expiration of a LIBOR-based forward rate agreement (FRA), the party that holds the short position in the FRA will:
    A. lend money to the party that holds the long position at the rate specified in the FRA.
    B. borrow money from the party that holds the long position at the rate specified in the FRA.
    C. receive a payment if LIBOR is below the rate specified in the FRA.

116. Other things equal, a decrease in the value of a put option on a stock is *most likely* consistent with which of the following changes in the risk-free rate and stock return volatility?

	Risk-free rate	Volatility
A.	Increase	Decrease
B.	Decrease	Increase
C.	Decrease	Decrease

Questions 117 through 120 relate to Alternative Investments. (6 minutes)

117. Which of the following strategies is *most likely* to be pursued by a private equity fund?
    A. Use debt financing to acquire control of a publicly traded firm.
    B. Buy convertible bonds and sell short the equity of the bond issuer.
    C. Influence a firm's policies by gaining a seat on its board of directors.

118. Which of the following is *least likely* a type of hedge fund strategy?
    A. Event-driven.
    B. Market-neutral.
    C. Exchange-traded.

119. Compared with purchasing commodities, long positions in commodity derivatives offer the benefit of:
    A. no storage costs.
    B. convenience yield.
    C. better correlation with spot prices.

120. A manager establishes a long commodity futures position and deposits Treasury bills to meet the initial margin requirement. If this futures market is in backwardation, the position is *most likely* to have a negative:
    A. roll yield.
    B. price return.
    C. collateral yield.

EXAM 3
MORNING SESSION

Calculating Your Score

Topic	Maximum Score	Your Score
Ethical and Professional Standards	18	
Quantitative Methods	14	
Economics	12	
Financial Reporting and Analysis	24	
Corporate Finance	10	
Portfolio Management	6	
Equity Investments	12	
Fixed Income	14	
Derivatives	6	
Alternative Investments	4	
Total	120	

The morning and afternoon exams are identically weighted over the topics and readings. You can therefore treat the morning and afternoon exams as independent exams.

If you took more than three hours (180 minutes) to complete this portion of the exam, you should adjust your score downward by one point for each minute you ran over.

Remember: the real exam *will be more difficult* than these practice exams. The main reason for this is the general anxiety and stress that you will be feeling on exam day, coupled with the time pressure you will be under. Many of the questions on this practice exam and the real exam are not individually difficult, so if you take extra time to answer the questions on this practice exam, your score will go up significantly. However, if you want an accurate measure of your potential performance on the exam, adhere to the 3-hour time limit.

After you have finished grading your practice exam, you may find it useful to use the exam questions and recommended solutions for review. Many of these questions were specifically written for your use as study tools. Once again, I feel I should remind you not to rely on memorizing these questions; you are not likely to see them on the actual exam. What you will see on the exam, though, are the concepts, terms, and procedures presented in these questions.

Your actual exam will most likely look different than what you see in this book. Please remember, no study provider knows the content of the actual exam. These practice exams are our best guess as to the structure, content, and difficulty of an actual exam.

Test Answers

1. (A) (B) (C)	41. (A) (B) (C)	81. (A) (B) (C)
2. (A) (B) (C)	42. (A) (B) (C)	82. (A) (B) (C)
3. (A) (B) (C)	43. (A) (B) (C)	83. (A) (B) (C)
4. (A) (B) (C)	44. (A) (B) (C)	84. (A) (B) (C)
5. (A) (B) (C)	45. (A) (B) (C)	85. (A) (B) (C)
6. (A) (B) (C)	46. (A) (B) (C)	86. (A) (B) (C)
7. (A) (B) (C)	47. (A) (B) (C)	87. (A) (B) (C)
8. (A) (B) (C)	48. (A) (B) (C)	88. (A) (B) (C)
9. (A) (B) (C)	49. (A) (B) (C)	89. (A) (B) (C)
10. (A) (B) (C)	50. (A) (B) (C)	90. (A) (B) (C)
11. (A) (B) (C)	51. (A) (B) (C)	91. (A) (B) (C)
12. (A) (B) (C)	52. (A) (B) (C)	92. (A) (B) (C)
13. (A) (B) (C)	53. (A) (B) (C)	93. (A) (B) (C)
14. (A) (B) (C)	54. (A) (B) (C)	94. (A) (B) (C)
15. (A) (B) (C)	55. (A) (B) (C)	95. (A) (B) (C)
16. (A) (B) (C)	56. (A) (B) (C)	96. (A) (B) (C)
17. (A) (B) (C)	57. (A) (B) (C)	97. (A) (B) (C)
18. (A) (B) (C)	58. (A) (B) (C)	98. (A) (B) (C)
19. (A) (B) (C)	59. (A) (B) (C)	99. (A) (B) (C)
20. (A) (B) (C)	60. (A) (B) (C)	100. (A) (B) (C)
21. (A) (B) (C)	61. (A) (B) (C)	101. (A) (B) (C)
22. (A) (B) (C)	62. (A) (B) (C)	102. (A) (B) (C)
23. (A) (B) (C)	63. (A) (B) (C)	103. (A) (B) (C)
24. (A) (B) (C)	64. (A) (B) (C)	104. (A) (B) (C)
25. (A) (B) (C)	65. (A) (B) (C)	105. (A) (B) (C)
26. (A) (B) (C)	66. (A) (B) (C)	106. (A) (B) (C)
27. (A) (B) (C)	67. (A) (B) (C)	107. (A) (B) (C)
28. (A) (B) (C)	68. (A) (B) (C)	108. (A) (B) (C)
29. (A) (B) (C)	69. (A) (B) (C)	109. (A) (B) (C)
30. (A) (B) (C)	70. (A) (B) (C)	110. (A) (B) (C)
31. (A) (B) (C)	71. (A) (B) (C)	111. (A) (B) (C)
32. (A) (B) (C)	72. (A) (B) (C)	112. (A) (B) (C)
33. (A) (B) (C)	73. (A) (B) (C)	113. (A) (B) (C)
34. (A) (B) (C)	74. (A) (B) (C)	114. (A) (B) (C)
35. (A) (B) (C)	75. (A) (B) (C)	115. (A) (B) (C)
36. (A) (B) (C)	76. (A) (B) (C)	116. (A) (B) (C)
37. (A) (B) (C)	77. (A) (B) (C)	117. (A) (B) (C)
38. (A) (B) (C)	78. (A) (B) (C)	118. (A) (B) (C)
39. (A) (B) (C)	79. (A) (B) (C)	119. (A) (B) (C)
40. (A) (B) (C)	80. (A) (B) (C)	120. (A) (B) (C)

EXAM 3
MORNING SESSION

**Questions 1 through 18 relate to Ethical and Professional Standards.
(27 minutes)**

1.   Adam Schute, CFA, is on a conference call with the CFO of an investment banking client with his phone speaker on and his door open. As a result, salesmen and traders overhear the CFO describing problems with production target dates that have not been publicly disclosed. The salesmen relay this information to clients and the traders reduce their positions in the stock. With respect to the Standard on material nonpublic information, Schute has:
    A.   not violated the Standard because he has not acted on the information, but the traders and salesmen have violated the Standard.
    B.   violated the Standard because he should have taken steps to prevent the dissemination of the information.
    C.   violated the Standard by not making the information public when he realized others had overheard the call.

2.   Peter Wellington references his status as a "CFA candidate" in current client presentation materials. Wellington completed the Level II CFA examination two years ago, regularly reads research materials prepared by CFA Institute, and attends continuing education seminars for employees who are CFA charterholders. Wellington plans to register for the Level III CFA exam next year. Wellington's reference to his status as a CFA candidate in presentation materials:
    A.   does not violate any CFA Institute Standards of Professional Conduct.
    B.   violates the Standard on conduct as a CFA Institute Member or CFA Candidate.
    C.   violates the Standard on reference to the CFA Institute, the CFA Designation, and the CFA Program.

3. Which of the following statements relating to the Global Investment Performance Standards (GIPS®) is *least accurate*?
    A. Only investment management firms may claim compliance with GIPS.
    B. GIPS represent standards to which members of CFA Institute and CFA candidates must adhere.
    C. To claim GIPS compliance, a firm must present at least five years (or since its inception if less than five years) of annual investment performance that complies with GIPS.

4. When Ed Michaels, CFA, accepted the compliance officer position at a broker-dealer two years ago, he wrote compliance procedures and made all covered employees aware of the procedures. A report by an external auditor found that on several occasions over the past two years, two different employees traded in recommended securities ahead of trades made in managed client accounts. Michaels fires both employees and recirculates the written compliance procedures that explain clearly which activities are prohibited. Michaels has violated the Standard concerning:
    A. loyalty by firing the employees instead of restricting their activities.
    B. misconduct because he was associated with the unethical activity.
    C. responsibilities of supervisors by failing to implement reasonable procedures to detect violations.

5. Ralph Malone, CFA, is an investment adviser at a multinational finance corporation. He has many wealthy individuals among his clients, including a trust account that benefits three of his immediate family members. The research department of Malone's firm issues a "buy" recommendation on a stock that would be a suitable investment for several client accounts, including the family trust account. Which of the following would be considered a violation of the Standard concerning priority of transactions?
    A. The firm gives clients time to act on the new recommendation, but does not make its recommendation public before buying 100,000 shares for its own account.
    B. Malone trades on the family account shortly after his firm's clients have been informed of the buy recommendation.
    C. Malone waits to trade for the family account until four days after his firm's clients have been informed of the buy recommendation.

6. Patricia Nelson, CFA, was informed by one of her clients that if Nelson could get the performance of the client firm's pension portfolio above that of the Standard & Poor's average by year end, the client would give her a free trip to Singapore to visit the firm's offices. If Nelson agrees to this arrangement, which of the following actions complies with CFA Institute Standards of Professional Conduct? Nelson:
    A. must inform her employer of this agreement but does not need consent.
    B. may inform her employer by e-mail of this agreement and must receive written consent.
    C. must inform her employer of this agreement but may accept it with verbal consent.

7. John Anderson's company is participating in an acquisition. To speed up the process, his manager gives him a report from another company's analyst, also working on the project, and tells Anderson to put it on company letterhead and distribute the report by the end of the day. If Anderson, who is a CFA Institute member, complies, he will violate the Standard on:
    A. misrepresentation.
    B. material nonpublic information.
    C. communication with clients and prospective clients.

8. Roger Smith, CFA, has been invited to join a group of analysts in touring the riverboats of River Casino Corp. For the tour, River Casino has arranged chartered flights from casino to casino since commercial flight schedules are not practical for the group's time schedule. River Casino has also arranged to pay for the analysts' lodging for the three nights of the tour. According to CFA Institute Standards of Professional Conduct, Smith:
    A. may accept the arrangements as they are.
    B. may accept the flight but is required to pay for his lodging.
    C. is required to pay for his flight and lodging.

9. Samuel Parkin, a principal of Argor Advisers, is in charge of preparing the firm's performance history in accordance with GIPS. Parkin is careful to include every portfolio managed into a composite for reporting. At the end of each year, he assigns each portfolio to a single composite. He calculates the total return on each portfolio and averages them to calculate the composite performance for the year. With respect to his assignment of portfolios to composites and his calculation of composite total returns, has Parkin violated the requirements of GIPS?
    A. Both of these actions violate GIPS.
    B. Neither of these actions violates GIPS.
    C. Only one of these actions violates GIPS.

10. Susan Smart, CFA, is about to change her "buy" recommendation on RollinsCo to "sell." RollinsCo had been growing rapidly over the past year, but Smart believes the growth potential is now gone. Smart sells the shares held in her discretionary client accounts and in her own personal account before issuing her report. According to the Standards that concern fair dealing and priority of transactions, Smart violated:
    A. both of these Standards.
    B. neither of these Standards.
    C. only one of these Standards.

11. Matt Jacobs, CFA, is an investment adviser to several university endowment funds. Jacobs previously recommended to a client that he buy shares in Timeco. The shares have underperformed the market this year, and the client has spoken with Jacobs about closing out the position. Jacobs firmly believes Timeco is still a worthy investment and that the client should not sell. Since the stock is thinly traded, Jacobs buys 1,000 Timeco shares in his personal account in order boost the company's share price, with the intent of reversing the trade a few days later. After making the purchase, the share price rises, allowing Jacobs to convince his client to hold on to his Timeco shares. Has Jacobs violated the Standard on market manipulation?
    A. No, because he made the trades for the benefit of his client.
    B. Yes, because he intended to interfere with the market price of Timeco.
    C. Yes, because he failed to consider the stock's current price in relation to its true value.

12. William Rex, CFA, distributes materials referencing his performance results since he is the only portfolio manager at the firm he has founded. In the presentation, Rex includes five years of investment performance, four of which were with a previous employer. The presentation does not make a distinction between the first four years and the most recent year of performance. Also included in the presentation are simulated results of a stock selection model Rex has recently developed and tested. The fact that the results are simulated is disclosed in the presentation. Has Rex violated any CFA Institute Standards of Professional Conduct?
    A. No.
    B. Yes, failing to disclose that four years of his performance results were with another employer is a violation, but including the simulated results is acceptable.
    C. Yes, both failing to disclose that four years of his performance results were with another employer and including the simulated results are violations.

13. Tony Roberts, CFA, is a portfolio manager at Delta Securities. He suspects a colleague, who is not a member or candidate, of ongoing activities that, while not illegal under local law, violate CFA Institute Standards of Professional Conduct. Roberts and the colleague both report to the same managing director at Delta and are both currently being considered for a promotion to senior portfolio manager. According to the CFA Institute Standards of Professional Conduct, Roberts:
    A. is required to dissociate from the activities that violate the Code and Standards if they continue.
    B. is not required to act because the Code and Standards do not apply to non-members.
    C. must report the suspected violations of the Code and Standards first to his supervisor and then to CFA Institute.

14. Judy Blush is a CFA candidate and is recommending the purchase of a mutual fund that invests solely in long-term U.S. Treasury bonds (T-bonds) to one of her clients. She states that, "Since the U.S. government guarantees payment of both the bond's principal and interest, risk of loss with this investment is virtually zero." Blush's actions violated:
    A. the Standard on misrepresentation.
    B. the Standard on communication with clients and prospective clients.
    C. none of the CFA Institute Standards of Professional Conduct.

15. Which of the following actions is *least likely* a violation of the Standard concerning conduct as Members and Candidates in the CFA Program?
    A. A member anonymously posts a disparaging comment about CFA Institute policies on an internet message board.
    B. A member fails to disclose a formal complaint from a client on her annual Professional Conduct Statement.
    C. A candidate discusses which topics were emphasized on the June Level I CFA exam with a candidate for the December exam.

16. Lilly Marlow is an elderly widow with a moderate risk tolerance who depends on her investment portfolio to meet her living expenses. Marcus Pate, CFA, has been her investment adviser for years and has always managed Marlow's account to her satisfaction. Pate has a lunch meeting with Marlow quarterly and has always used their discussions as a basis for selecting investments for her account, over which he has full discretion to set the investment strategies. Pate often invests in risky derivative strategies to increase the return on Marlow's account. As Marlow's son is reviewing her recent year-end statement, he is shocked to discover that Pate has invested a significant amount of the account's assets in currency derivatives. According to the CFA Institute Standards, Pate is:
    A. in violation of the Standard concerning suitability.
    B. in violation of the Standard on communication with clients and prospective clients.
    C. not in violation of any Standard because Marlow has been satisfied with the portfolio performance to date.

17. Jarrett Rogers, CFA, recommends investment advisers to high net worth individuals. Investment advisers pay Rogers a portion of their investment management fees as compensation for client referrals. When a client inquires with Rogers about his criteria for recommending managers, Rogers indicates that managers are selected based only on historical investment performance versus a universe of comparable peer investment managers, but he does not mention the compensation paid by the investment advisers. Rogers has *most likely* violated the Standard concerning:

A. referral fees.
B. misrepresentation.
C. fair dealing.

18. Byron Bell, CFA, is an investment manager for Sally Fillmore, president of the local branch of First Bank. Fillmore, in a conversation with Bell's trading assistant, mentions that she is considering moving her account to another investment manager and confides that she has been diagnosed with the early signs of Alzheimer's disease. The trading assistant relays the conversation to Bell. According to the CFA Institute Code and Standards, the trading assistant is:

A. not in violation of any Standard.
B. in violation of the Standard concerning preservation of confidentiality by disclosing confidential client information.
C. in violation of the Standard concerning loyalty, prudence, and care by putting her employer's interests before the client's.

Questions 19 through 32 relate to Quantitative Methods. (21 minutes)

19. A client is celebrating his 50th birthday today and wants to start saving for his anticipated retirement at age 65. He wants to be able to withdraw $20,000 from his savings account on his 66th birthday and each year for 19 more years after that.

     After extensive research, the client determines that he can invest his money in an account that offers 5% interest per year with quarterly compounding. He wants to make equal annual payments on each birthday into the account—the first payment on his 51st birthday and the last on his 65th birthday.

     In addition, the client's employer will contribute $2,000 to the account each year (beginning on the client's 51st birthday) as part of the company's profit-sharing plan (a total of 15 contributions).

     The amount the client must deposit personally into the account each year on his birthday to enable him to make the desired withdrawals at retirement is *closest* to:
     A. $9,375.
     B. $9,459.
     C. $11,400.

20. A company reports its past six years' earnings growth at 10%, 14%, 12%, 10%, –10%, and 12%. The company's average compound annual growth rate of earnings is *closest* to:
     A. 7.7%.
     B. 8.0%.
     C. 8.5%.

21. The following table summarizes the results of a poll (hypothetically) taken of CFA charterholders and CFA candidates regarding the importance of a continuing education requirement after the CFA designation is obtained:

Group	In Favor of a Continuing Education Requirement	Against a Continuing Education Requirement
CFA charterholders	235	765
CFA candidates	180	820

     Given the information that a member of the group is in favor of a continuing education requirement, what is the probability that she is a CFA candidate?
     A. 18%.
     B. 37%.
     C. 43%.

22.   Stephen Kroller, CFA, analyzes international equity funds. Kroller constructs a sample of international equity mutual funds that have at least a 10-year performance history. Based on the returns of the funds in his sample, Kroller concludes that international equity funds outperformed their comparable U.S. stock indexes over the 10-year period. Kroller's sample and test results are *most likely* subject to:
A. look-ahead bias.
B. time period bias.
C. survivorship bias.

23.   Which of the following statements about common probability distributions is *least accurate*?
A. A probability distribution specifies the probabilities of the possible outcomes of a random variable.
B. In a binomial probability distribution, each observation has only two possible outcomes that are mutually exclusive.
C. A normal distribution is a discrete symmetric probability distribution that is completely described by two parameters: its mean and variance.

24.   For a binomial random variable with a 40% probability of success on each trial, the expected number of successes in 12 trials is *closest* to:
A. 4.8.
B. 5.6.
C. 7.2.

25.   Which of the following statements about the univariate, multivariate, and standard normal distributions is *least accurate*?
A. A univariate distribution describes a single random variable.
B. A multivariate distribution specifies the probabilities for a group of related random variables.
C. The standard normal random variable, denoted Z, has mean equal to one and variance equal to one.

26.   An investor is considering investing in one of the three following portfolios:

Statistical Measures	Portfolio X	Portfolio Y	Portfolio Z
Expected annual return	12%	17%	22%
Standard deviation of return	14%	20%	25%

If the investor's minimum acceptable return is 5%, the optimal portfolio using Roy's safety-first criterion is:
A. Portfolio X.
B. Portfolio Y.
C. Portfolio Z.

27. An analyst is testing the hypothesis that the variance of monthly returns for Index L equals the variance of monthly returns for Index M based on samples of 50 monthly observations. The sample variance of Index L returns is 0.085, whereas the sample variance of Index M returns is 0.084. Assuming the samples are independent and the returns are normally distributed, which of the following represents the *most appropriate* test statistic?

   A. $\dfrac{\text{sample variance of Index L}}{\text{sample variance of Index M}}$.

   B. $\dfrac{\text{variance of Index L} - \text{variance of Index M}}{\text{standard error of squared differences}}$.

   C. $\dfrac{(\text{degrees of freedom}) \times (\text{Index L sample variance})}{\text{Index M sample variance}}$.

28. If the probability of event J multiplied by the probability of event K is not equal to the joint probability of events J and K, then events J and K are *most likely:*
   A. dependent events.
   B. independent events.
   C. mutually exclusive events.

29. Alan Barnes, CFA, is interested in the expected quarterly return on FTSE 100 stock index. He has data for the last five years and calculates the average return on the index over the last 20 quarters. This average return:
   A. is different from the statistic he is trying to estimate by the amount of the sampling error.
   B. overstates the return because he should divide by the square root of 20 when using a mean value.
   C. overstates the expected return because he should have used the geometric mean and not the simple average.

30. Which of the following statements regarding the significance level of a hypothesis test is *most accurate*?
   A. Given a significance level of 5%, a test will reject a true null hypothesis 5% of the time.
   B. If the significance level of a test is 5%, it will yield the correct decision about the null hypothesis 95% of the time.
   C. If the significance level of a test is 95%, it will yield the correct decision about the null hypothesis 95% of the time.

31. A researcher needs to choose a probability distribution for the price of an asset that is quite volatile in order to simulate returns outcomes. She has a program that will generate random variables from any of a variety of distributions. The *most appropriate* distribution for her to select to generate the asset price distribution is a:
    A. normal distribution.
    B. lognormal distribution.
    C. Student's *t*-distribution.

32. An investor is interested in the following piece of property:
    - The property will cost $200,000 at time zero.
    - It will provide cash flows of $50,000 in year 1, $60,000 in year 2, $70,000 in year 3, and $80,000 in year 4.
    - A $20,000 investment will be required in year 5 as the property will have some environmental contamination and will have to be restored to its original condition.

    What is the NPV of the project if the investor's required rate of return is 10%?
    A. −$10,144.
    B. $14,693.
    C. $15,232.

Questions 33 through 44 relate to Economics. (18 minutes)

33. If investors' expected future incomes increase and the demand for financial capital increases, other things equal:
    A. the equilibrium interest rate will rise.
    B. the equilibrium interest rate will fall.
    C. these two factors will have opposing effects on the equilibrium interest rate.

34. Assume that the required reserve ratio is 20%, and banks currently have no excess reserves. If the Federal Reserve then buys $100 million of Treasury bills from the banks, the money supply could potentially increase by:
    A. $20 million.
    B. $100 million.
    C. $500 million.

35. If a minimum wage is set above the equilibrium wage in the labor market, what is the *most likely* effect?
    A. The minimum wage will have no effect on the quantity of labor employed.
    B. Firms will use less than the economically efficient amount of capital.
    C. There will be excess supply of labor, and unemployment will increase.

36. The country of Hokah uses 30 units of labor to produce a unit of cheese and 35 units of labor to produce a unit of leather. The country of Ymer uses 25 units of labor to produce a unit of cheese and 20 units of labor to produce a unit of leather. Which of the following statements is *most accurate*?
    A. Ymer's opportunity cost of one unit of leather is 0.80 units of cheese.
    B. Hokah's opportunity cost of one unit of cheese is 1.167 units of leather.
    C. Ymer has an absolute and a comparative advantage in both cheese and leather.

37. As output quantities expand in an industry with a downward-sloping long-run industry supply curve, what is the *most likely* long-run effect on the equilibrium selling price per unit of the industry's output?
    A. Increase, because of upward pressure on input prices.
    B. Decrease, because of lower input costs per unit of output.
    C. No effect, because selling price is only affected in the short run.

38. If the government regulates a natural monopoly and enforces an average cost pricing, what are the effects on output quantity and price compared to an unregulated natural monopoly?
    A. Both are lower under average cost pricing.
    B. Both are higher under average cost pricing.
    C. One is higher and one is lower under average cost pricing.

39. Assume that one year ago, the exchange rate between the Japanese yen and the euro was 100 JPY/EUR, and the exchange rate between the Japanese yen and the U.S. dollar was 80 JPY/USD. Current exchange rates are 104.2 JPY/EUR and 76.6 JPY/USD. Which of the following statements is *most accurate*?
    A. The USD has depreciated relative to the EUR.
    B. The JPY has depreciated 4.2% relative to the EUR.
    C. The current U.S. dollar to euro exchange rate is approximately 1.25 USD/EUR.

40. Oligopolists have an incentive to cheat on collusive agreements in order to:
    A. avoid competitive practices.
    B. increase their individual share of the joint profit.
    C. restrict output and put upward pressure on price.

41. An increase in the supply of cars is *most likely* to be caused by a(n):
    A. increase in wages.
    B. decrease in price of steel.
    C. decrease in the price of cars.

42. With respect to the IS-LM model, in an LM curve the real interest rate is:
    A. positively related to real income, holding the real money supply constant.
    B. held constant, resulting in excess savings being positively related to real income.
    C. negatively related to real income, holding the marginal propensity to save constant.

43. An individual sees her income rise from $80,000 to $88,000, and along with it, her consumption of Good X has decreased from eight dozen packages per year to six dozen packages per year. Good X should be classified as a(n):
    A. normal good.
    B. Veblen good.
    C. inferior good.

44. The Keynesian view suggests that the government can reduce aggregate demand by using:
    A. restrictive fiscal policy to shift the government budget toward a surplus (or smaller deficit).
    B. restrictive fiscal policy to shift the government budget toward a deficit (or a smaller surplus).
    C. expansionary fiscal policy to shift the government budget toward a surplus (or a smaller deficit).

Questions 45 through 68 relate to Financial Reporting and Analysis. (36 minutes)

45. Which of the following is *least likely* to be considered a barrier to developing one universally recognized set of reporting standards?
    A. Differences of opinion among various regulatory bodies.
    B. Reluctance of firms to adhere to a single set of reporting standards.
    C. Political pressure from stakeholders affected by reporting standards.

46. Which of the following items affects owners' equity but is not included as a component of net income?
    A. Depreciation.
    B. Dividends received on shares of another company classified as available for sale.
    C. Foreign currency translation gains and losses.

47. A company's financial statement data for the most recent year include the following:

    - Net income $100
    - Depreciation expense   25
    - Purchase of machine   50
    - Sale of company trucks   30
    - Sale of common stock   45
    - Decrease in accounts receivable   10
    - Increase in inventory   20
    - Issuance of bonds   25
    - Increase in accounts payable   15
    - Increase in wages payable   10

    Based only on these items, cash flow from financing activities is *closest* to:
    A. $70.
    B. $85.
    C. $140.

48. A firm that rents DVDs to customers capitalizes the cost of newly released DVDs that it purchases and depreciates them over three years to a value of zero. Based on the underlying economics of the DVD rental business, the *most appropriate* method of depreciation for the firm to use on its financial statements is:
    A. straight-line.
    B. declining balance.
    C. units-of-production.

49. The item "noncontrolling interest" included as a component of equity represents the portion of a subsidiary the parent company:
    A. does not own.
    B. owns, if less than 20% of the subsidiary's common stock.
    C. owns, if less than 50% of the subsidiary's common stock.

50. An analyst gathered the following information about a company:

    - Cash flow from operations $800
    - Purchase of plant and equipment   40
    - Sale of land   30
    - Interest expense   80
    - Depreciation and amortization   100
    - The company has a tax rate of 35% and prepares its financial statements under U.S. GAAP.

    The company's free cash flow to the firm (FCFF) is *closest* to:
    A. $840.
    B. $870.
    C. $940.

51. For which of the following balance sheet items is a change in market value *most likely* to affect net income?
    A. Debt securities issued by the firm.
    B. Debt securities that the firm intends to hold until maturity.
    C. Securities held with the intent to profit over the short term.

52. IFRS and U.S. GAAP are *most* similar in their requirements for:
    A. extraordinary items.
    B. discontinued operations.
    C. valuation of fixed assets.

53. A company using LIFO reports the following:
    - Cost of goods sold was $27,000.
    - Beginning inventory was $6,500, and ending inventory was $6,200.
    - The beginning LIFO reserve was $1,200.
    - The ending LIFO reserve was $1,400.

    The *best* estimate of the company's cost of goods sold on a FIFO basis would be:
    A. $21,300.
    B. $26,800.
    C. $27,500.

54. Which of the following items is *best* described as a listing of all the journal entries in order of their dates?
    A. Trial ledger.
    B. General ledger.
    C. General journal.

55. An analyst gathered the following data about a company:
    - 1,000,000 shares of common are outstanding at the beginning of the year.
    - 10,000 6% convertible bonds (conversion ratio is 20 to 1) were issued at par June 30 of this year.
    - The company has 100,000 warrants outstanding all year with an exercise price of $25 per share.
    - The average stock price for the period is $20, and the ending stock price is $30.

    If the convertible bonds are considered dilutive, the number of shares of common stock that the analyst should use to calculate diluted earnings per share is:
    A. 1,000,000.
    B. 1,100,000.
    C. 1,266,667.

56.   During periods of rising prices:
       A. LIFO COGS > Weighted Average COGS > FIFO COGS.
       B. LIFO COGS > Weighted Average COGS < FIFO COGS.
       C. LIFO COGS < Weighted Average COGS < FIFO COGS.

57.   Which of the following statements about calculating earnings per share
       (EPS) in simple versus complex capital structures is *least* accurate?
       A. If convertible bonds are dilutive, the numerator in the diluted EPS
          calculation is increased by the interest expense on the bonds.
       B. If convertible preferred stock is dilutive, the convertible preferred
          dividends must be added back to the numerator to calculate diluted
          EPS.
       C. The denominator in the basic EPS equation contains the number of
          shares of common stock issued, weighted by the days that the shares
          have been outstanding.

58.   In the period when a firm makes an expenditure, capitalizing the
       expenditure instead of recognizing it as an expense will result in
       higher:
       A. debt-to-equity and debt-to-assets ratios.
       B. net income and have no effect on total cash flows.
       C. cash flow from investing and lower cash flow from operations.

59.   Which of the following ratios is a component of the original (three-part)
       DuPont equation?
       A. Asset turnover.
       B. Gross profit margin.
       C. Debt-to-equity ratio.

60.   Harding Corp. has a permanently impaired asset. The difference between
       its carrying value and the present value of its expected cash flows should
       be written down immediately and:
       A. reported as an operating loss.
       B. charged directly against retained earnings.
       C. reported as a non-operating loss in other comprehensive income.

61.   If market interest rates have changed materially since a firm issued
       a bond, and the firm uses the effective interest rate method, how is a
       change in the market value of the firm's debt *most likely* to be reported
       in the firm's financial statements?
       A. The gain or loss in market value must be calculated and disclosed
          in the footnotes to the financial statements.
       B. Net income and equity are unaffected, but the change may be
          discussed in management's commentary.
       C. Net income is unaffected, but the change in market value is
          recorded in other comprehensive income.

62. Which of the following statements regarding deferred taxes is *least* accurate?
    A. A permanent difference is a difference between taxable income and pretax income that will not reverse.
    B. A deferred tax asset is created when a temporary difference results in taxable income that exceeds pretax income.
    C. Deferred tax assets and liabilities are not adjusted for changes in tax rates.

63. A firm that reports its lease of a conveyer system as an operating lease must disclose:
    A. only the annual lease payment.
    B. minimum lease payments for each of the next five years and the sum of lease payments more than five years in the future.
    C. minimum lease payments for each of the next ten years and the sum of lease payments more than ten years in the future.

64. Meyer Company increases the promised payments for all employees in its defined benefit pension plan. Under which financial reporting standards would Meyer recognize past service costs in its income statement for the period?
    A. IFRS only.
    B. U.S. GAAP only.
    C. Both IFRS and U.S. GAAP.

65. Jordan Loney, CFA, issues a "sell" recommendation on Sullivan Company because she suspects accounting fraud. Loney writes, "Sullivan has an unstable and complex organizational structure with unclear lines of authority. Rapid turnover of key employees in its information systems and accounting units have made Sullivan's internal monitoring controls ineffective." Which condition of the "fraud triangle" has Loney detected at Sullivan?
    A. Opportunity.
    B. Incentives and pressures.
    C. Attitudes and rationalizations.

66. Of the following methods of examining the uncertainty of financial outcomes around point estimates, which answers hypothetical questions about the effect of changes in a single variable and which uses assumed probability distributions for key variables?

	Hypothetical questions	Probability distributions
A.	Sensitivity analysis	Simulation
B.	Scenario analysis	Simulation
C.	Scenario analysis	Sensitivity analysis

67. Information about a company's financial position at a point in time is *most likely* found in the:
    A. balance sheet.
    B. income statement.
    C. cash flow statement.

68. A dealer of large earth movers that leases the machinery to its customers is *most likely* to treat the leases as:
    A. operating leases, and account for inventory using last-in first-out.
    B. sales-type leases, and account for inventory using specific identification.
    C. direct financing leases, and account for inventory using weighted average cost.

Questions 69 through 78 relate to Corporate Finance. (15 minutes)

69. Business risk is *best* described as resulting from the combined effects of a firm's:
    A. financial risk and sales risk.
    B. sales risk and operating risk.
    C. operating risk and financial risk.

70. An analyst gathered the following information about a capital budgeting project:
    - The proposed project cost $10,000.
    - The project is expected to increase pretax net income and cash flow by $3,000 in each of the next eight years.
    - The company has 50% of its capital in equity at a cost of 12%.
    - The pretax cost of debt capital is 6%.
    - The company's tax rate is 33%.

    The project's net present value is *closest* to:
    A. $1,551.
    B. $6,604.
    C. $7,240.

71. To protect shareholders' long-term interests, the *most appropriate* characteristic for a board of directors is that:
    A. the board meets regularly with management present.
    B. the majority of board members are not firm executives.
    C. board members represent firm suppliers, customers, or pension advisers.

72. The amount of a company's optimal capital budget is *most accurately* determined by the point on the company's investment opportunity schedule:
    A. where the amount of new capital raised is at its minimum.
    B. where it intersects the company's marginal cost of capital curve.
    C. where the expected return on the next potential project is at its maximum.

73. A company is *most likely* faced with a drag on liquidity if its:
    A. weighted average collection period increases from 42 days to 46 days.
    B. largest vendor changes its invoice terms from "3/10 net 30" to "3/10 net 60."
    C. inventory turnover was below the industry average last year and is above the industry average this year.

74. A firm with earnings per share of $2 decides to repurchase a portion of its shares at their market price of $25. The firm's after-tax cost of debt is 6% and the firm earns a 2% after-tax yield on its excess cash. When the firm repurchases shares, its earnings per share will:
    A. increase if the firm funds the repurchase with debt or uses excess cash to repurchase the shares.
    B. decrease if the firm funds the repurchase with debt or uses excess cash to repurchase the shares.
    C. decrease if the firm funds the repurchase with debt, but increase if the firm uses excess cash to repurchase the shares.

75. Faye Harlan, CFA, is estimating the cost of common equity for Cyrene Corporation. She prepares the following data for Cyrene:
    - Price per share = $50.
    - Expected dividend per share = $3.
    - Expected retention ratio = 30%.
    - Expected return on equity = 20%.
    - Beta = 0.89.
    - Yield to maturity on outstanding debt = 10%.
    - The expected market rate of return is 12% and the risk-free rate is 3%.

    Based on these data, Harlan determines that Cyrene's cost of common equity is 14%. Harlan *most likely* arrived at this estimate by using the:
    A. dividend discount model approach.
    B. capital asset pricing model approach.
    C. bond yield plus risk premium approach.

76. Quixote Co. and Sisyphus Co., two similar-sized competitors, have had stable operating cycles of 180 days and cash conversion cycles of 140 days over the past several years. Sisyphus' operating and cash conversion cycles remained at these levels in the most recent year, but Quixote's cash conversion cycle contracted to 120 days while its operating cycle remained at 180 days. Relative to Sisyphus, Quixote has *most likely* begun:
    A. taking more time to pay its suppliers.
    B. operating with less inventory on hand.
    C. offering easier credit terms to its customers.

77. A company prepares a chart with the net present value (NPV) profiles for two mutually exclusive projects with equal lives of five years. Project Jones and Project Smith have the same initial cash outflow and total undiscounted cash inflows, but 75% of the cash inflows for Project Jones occur in years 1 and 2, while 75% of the cash inflows for Project Smith occur in years 4 and 5. Which of the following statements is *most accurate* regarding these projects?
    A. Project Smith has a higher internal rate of return than Project Jones.
    B. There is a range of discount rates in which the optimal decision is to reject both projects.
    C. There is a range of discount rates in which the company should choose Project Jones and a range in which it should choose Project Smith.

78. Which of the following is a sign of a well-qualified board member?
    A. Major supplier to the firm.
    B. Has other board experience.
    C. Does not have a significant stock position.

Questions 79 through 84 relate to Portfolio Management. (9 minutes)

79. The investment needs of property and casualty insurers are characterized by a:
    A. short-term time horizon and low risk tolerance.
    B. long-term time horizon and high risk tolerance.
    C. short-term time horizon and high risk tolerance.

80. Using historical index returns for an equities market over a 20-year period, an analyst has calculated the average annual return as 5.60% and the holding period return as 170%. The compound annual index return over the period is *closest* to:
    A. 2.69%.
    B. 5.09%.
    C. 5.24%.

81. Which portion of an investment policy statement is *most likely* to state any restriction on portfolio leverage?
    A. Procedures.
    B. Investment guidelines.
    C. Duties and responsibilities.

82. Davis Samuel, CFA, is meeting with one of his portfolio management clients, Joseph Pope, to discuss Pope's investment constraints. Samuel has established that:
    - Pope plans to retire from his job as a bond salesman in 17 years, after which this portfolio will be his primary source of income.
    - Pope has sufficient cash available that he will not need this portfolio to generate cash outflows until he retires.
    - Pope, as a registered securities representative, is required to have Samuel send a copy of his account statements to the compliance officer at Pope's employer.
    - Pope opposes certain policies of the government of Lower Pannonia and does not wish to own any securities of companies that do business with its regime.

    To complete his assessment of Pope's investment constraints, Samuel still needs to inquire about Pope's:
    A. tax concerns.
    B. liquidity needs.
    C. unique needs and preferences.

83. When a risk-free asset is combined with a portfolio of risky assets, which of the following is *least accurate*?
    A. The standard deviation of the return for the newly created portfolio is the standard deviation of the returns of the risky asset portfolio multiplied by its portfolio weight.
    B. The expected return for the newly created portfolio is the weighted average of the return on the risk-free asset and the expected return on the risky asset portfolio.
    C. The variance of the resulting portfolio is a weighted average of the returns variances of the risk-free asset and of the portfolio of risky assets.

84. If a stock's beta is equal to 1.2, its standard deviation of returns is 28%, and the standard deviation of the returns on the market portfolio is 14%, the covariance of the stock's returns with the returns on the market portfolio is *closest* to:
    A. 0.168.
    B. 0.024.
    C. 0.600.

©2012 Kaplan, Inc.

Questions 85 through 96 relate to Equity Investments. (18 minutes)

85. An analyst classifies Mettler, Inc., an operator of retail grocery stores, in the same industry group as Powell Corporation, a manufacturer of industrial machinery. This analyst's classification system is *most likely* based on:
    A. statistical methods.
    B. products and services.
    C. sensitivity to the business cycle.

86. To ensure the continuity of a value-weighted index when one of the stocks in the index is split:
    A. no adjustment is necessary.
    B. only the denominator must be adjusted for the split.
    C. both the numerator and the denominator must be adjusted for the split.

87. Robert Higgins is estimating the price-earnings (P/E) ratio that will be appropriate for an index at the end of next year. He has estimated that:
    - Expected annual dividends will increase by 10% compared to this year.
    - Expected earnings per share will increase by 10% compared to this year.
    - The expected growth rate of dividends will be the same as the current estimate of 5%.
    - The required rate of return will rise from 8% to 11%.

    Compared to the current P/E, the end-of-the-year P/E will be:
    A. 50% lower.
    B. 2% higher.
    C. 10% higher.

88. An analyst gathered the following data about a stock:
    - The stock paid a $1 dividend last year.
    - Next year's dividend is projected to be 10% higher.
    - The stock is projected to sell for $25 at the end of the year.
    - The risk-free rate of interest is 8%.
    - The expected return on the market is 13%.
    - The stock's beta is 1.2.

    The value of the stock today is *closest* to:
    A. $19.45.
    B. $22.89.
    C. $26.74.

89. A contract that requires one party to pay $100,000 each quarter to another company that will make a variable quarterly payment based on the market value of an equities portfolio is referred to as:
    A. a swap.
    B. an index option.
    C. portfolio insurance.

90. Visser, Inc. is an unprofitable fishing enterprise. Visser rents most of its boats and equipment but owns valuable transferable fishing quotas. If a competitor is interested in acquiring Visser, the *most appropriate* equity valuation model to use is a(n):
    A. asset-based valuation model.
    B. earnings multiplier model.
    C. Gordon growth model.

91. A firm has a constant growth rate of 7% and just paid a dividend of $6.25. If the required rate of return is 12%, what will the stock sell for two years from now based on the dividend discount model?
    A. $133.75.
    B. $149.80.
    C. $153.13.

92. In a transaction referred to as a management buyout (MBO):
    A. management sells its shares to an investor group attempting to gain control of a company.
    B. management buys a controlling interest in a public company to gain control of the board of directors.
    C. an investor group that includes management buys all the shares of a company and they no longer trade on an exchange.

93. Archer Products is in an industry that has experienced low levels of price competition but recently excess capacity has led to aggressive price cutting. An analyst would be *least likely* to describe Archer's industry as:
    A. concentrated and with high barriers to exit.
    B. in the shakeout stage with low concentration.
    C. in the maturity stage with high barriers to entry.

94. Assume the Wansch Corporation is expected to pay a dividend of $2.25 per share this year. Sales and profit for Wansch are forecasted to grow at a rate of 20% for two years after that, then grow at 5% per year forever. Dividend and sales growth are expected to be equal. If Wansch's shareholders require a 15% return, the per-share value of Wansch's common stock based on the dividend discount model is *closest* to:
    A. $22.75.
    B. $26.00.
    C. $28.50.

95. Under which of the following conditions are market values of securities *most likely* to be persistently greater than their intrinsic values?
A. Short selling is restricted.
B. Transactions costs are high.
C. Arbitrage trading is restricted.

96. Moore Company stock is currently trading at $40 per share. An investor attempting to protect against losses of more than 10% on a short position in Moore should place a:
A. stop buy order at $44.
B. stop sell order at $36.
C. limit buy order at $44.

Questions 97 through 110 relate to Fixed Income. (21 minutes)

97. Compared to the underlying MBS, a collateralized mortgage obligation (CMO):
A. has lower duration.
B. may have more or less prepayment risk.
C. allows an investor to select an exact maturity.

98. An analyst collects the following spot rates, stated as annual BEYs:
- 6-month spot rate = 6%.
- 12-month spot rate = 6.5%.
- 18-month spot rate = 7%.
- 24-month spot rate = 7.5%.

Given only this information, the price of a 2-year, semiannual-pay, 10% coupon bond with a face value of $1,000 is *closest* to:
A. $918.30.
B. $1,000.00.
C. $1,046.77.

99. A bond has an effective duration of 7.5. If the bond yield changes by 100 basis points, the price of the bond will change by:
A. exactly 0.75%.
B. approximately 7.5%.
C. approximately 0.75%.

100. Which of the following *best* describes the motivation for a corporation to issue an asset-backed security? Securitization of specific assets by a corporation enables the corporation to:
A. improve the recovery rate in the event of default.
B. use the assets as collateral for additional borrowing.
C. get a credit rating on the ABS that will result in a lower cost of borrowing.

101. An analyst is considering two bonds: Bond A yields 7.5%, and Bond B yields 7.0%. Using Bond B as the reference bond, the yield ratio for Bond A is *closest* to:
   A. 0.93.
   B. 1.07.
   C. 7.14.

102. In contrast to the full valuation approach to measuring interest rate risk, the duration/convexity approach:
   A. accounts for the curvature of the price-yield relation.
   B. provides a more accurate assessment of interest rate risk.
   C. simplifies the process of estimating the value impact of changes in yield.

103. An analyst collects the following information regarding spot rates of interest:
   - 1-year rate = 4%.
   - 2-year rate = 5%.
   - 3-year rate = 6%.
   - 4-year rate = 7%.

   Utilizing the pure expectations theory of the term structure of interest rates, the expected annualized 2-year interest rate two years from today is *closest* to:
   A. 7.02%.
   B. 8.03%.
   C. 9.04%.

104. A credit analyst determines the following selected financial ratios for three firms in an industry after making all appropriate adjustments:

	Johnson	*Knight*	*Lawrence*
EBIT / revenue	0.25	0.30	0.35
EBIT / interest	12.5	14.0	10.5
Debt / capital	0.55	0.70	0.35
Revenue / assets	0.20	0.15	0.10

   In evaluating the creditworthiness of these firms, the analyst should conclude that:
   A. Knight has the most favorable leverage and Johnson has the most favorable coverage.
   B. Lawrence has the most favorable leverage and Knight has the most favorable coverage.
   C. Johnson has the most favorable leverage and Lawrence has the most favorable coverage.

105. An analyst is comparing two bonds and has collected the following data:
    - Bond P: Nominal spread of 125 basis points, zero-volatility spread of 125 basis points, and option-adjusted spread of 65 basis points.
    - Bond Q: Nominal spread of 95 basis points, zero-volatility spread of 95 basis points, and option-adjusted spread of 95 basis points.

    Each bond is similar in all respects except that Bond P is a mortgage passthrough security and Bond Q is a noncallable corporate bond. Based only on this information, which of the following statements is *most accurate*?
    A. The yield curve is flat.
    B. Bond P is preferred to Bond Q because its nominal spread is 30 basis points higher.
    C. Bond P is preferred to Bond Q because the embedded option in Bond P returns the investor an additional 65 basis points.

106. If a corporate bond is non-refundable, the issuer:
    A. must leave the bonds outstanding until their scheduled maturity.
    B. may call the bonds and issue common equity in their place.
    C. may issue zero coupon bonds and use the proceeds to call the bonds.

107. CureAll General Hospital has been forced to file for bankruptcy protection. The company managing the hospital has been allowed to reorganize under the name United Hospital of Hope. The courts have specified that a new indenture should be written to accompany a planned new bond issue. The issue would have ten years to maturity and carry a 10% coupon that would be paid annually. The new agreement would relieve the company of the obligation to make interest payments during the first five years after the bond is issued. For the remaining five years, regular interest payments would resume. Finally, at maturity, the principal ($1,000) plus the interest that was not paid during the first five years would be paid. However, no additional interest would be payable on the deferred interest. If the bond's YTM is 10%, its value is *closest* to:
    A. $778.
    B. $814.
    C. $856.

108. Which of the following statements regarding the term structure of interest rates is *least accurate*?
    A. Forward interest rates are the best estimates of future short-term interest rates under the pure expectations theory.
    B. The observed yield curve likely contains elements of liquidity preference, market segmentation, and expectations theories.
    C. Under the market segmentation theory, a flat yield curve is likely to become positively sloped if the demand for long-term bonds exceeds supply and if the supply of short-term bonds exceeds demand.

109. A floating-rate security is *most likely* to trade at a discount to its par value because the:
   A. next reset date is in three months.
   B. security's yield premium for credit risk decreases.
   C. floating rate includes a margin over LIBOR to compensate for the issue's liquidity risk.

110. The price value of a basis point (PVBP) for a bond is *most accurately* described as:
   A. the product of a bond's value and its duration.
   B. the change in the price of the bond when its yield changes by 0.01%.
   C. an estimate of the curvature of the price-yield relationship for a small change in yield.

Questions 111 through 116 relate to Derivatives. (9 minutes)

111. Which of the following statements about interest rate swaps and currency swaps is *least accurate*?
   A. A plain-vanilla interest rate swap involves trading fixed interest rate payments for floating-rate payments.
   B. A fixed-for-floating currency swap involves trading floating-rate interest payments on one currency for fixed-rate interest payments on another currency.
   C. In a currency swap, the net difference between the notional principal amounts is exchanged at the beginning and termination of the swap. Full interest rate payments are exchanged on each settlement date.

112. A borrower with a variable-rate loan who wants to protect herself from an increase in interest rates without sacrificing potential gains from an interest rate decrease should:
   A. sell an interest rate floor.
   B. buy an interest rate cap.
   C. buy an interest rate cap and sell an interest rate floor.

113. An investor has a call option on a stock that is currently selling for $35. The call option is in the money by $3. The call option's strike price is:
    A. $32.
    B. $35.
    C. $38.

114. An investor is short a portfolio of stocks that has volatility and return characteristics similar to that of the S&P 500. Which of the following strategies would *best* hedge the market risk of the short portfolio position?
    A. Buy a put option on the S&P 500.
    B. Write a call option on the S&P 500.
    C. Write a put option and buy a call option on the S&P 500.

115. A put on a stock with a strike price of $50 is priced at $4 per share, while a call with a strike price of $50 is priced at $6. What is the maximum per share loss to the writer of the put?
    A. $46.
    B. $50.
    C. Unlimited.

116. A major bank has entered into a 4-year, annual-pay, 6% plain-vanilla interest rate swap with a notional principal value of $10,000,000 as the fixed-rate payer. The following spot and forward rates are observed and expected:
    - 1-year LIBOR today = 5%.
    - Expected 1-year LIBOR in one year = 6%.
    - Expected 1-year LIBOR in two years = 7%.

    Based solely on this information, the expected net payment in 24 months (for the fixed-rate payer) will be:
    A. $100,000 inflow.
    B. $0.
    C. $100,000 outflow.

Questions 117 through 120 relate to Alternative Investments. (6 minutes)

117. Supplying capital to companies that are just moving into operation, but do not as yet have a product or service available to sell, is a description that *best* relates to which of the following stages of venture capital investing?
    A. Early stage.
    B. Mezzanine stage.
    C. Angel investing stage.

118. An equity hedge fund that uses technical analysis techniques to identify undervalued shares to buy and overvalued shares to sell short is *best* described as pursuing a(n):
    A. market neutral strategy.
    B. special situations strategy.
    C. quantitative directional strategy.

119. A hedge fund that requires incentive fees to be calculated only on the portion of returns above a benchmark return is said to have a:
    A. soft hurdle rate.
    B. hard hurdle rate.
    C. high water mark.

120. Compared to investing in commodities, investing in farmland is *most likely* to provide which of the following benefits?
    A. More liquidity.
    B. Higher income.
    C. Better inflation hedge.

Exam 3
Afternoon Session

Calculating Your Score

Topic	Maximum Score	Your Score
Ethical and Professional Standards	18	
Quantitative Methods	14	
Economics	12	
Financial Reporting and Analysis	24	
Corporate Finance	10	
Portfolio Management	6	
Equity Investments	12	
Fixed Income	14	
Derivatives	6	
Alternative Investments	4	
Total	120	

The morning and afternoon exams are identically weighted over the topics and readings. You can therefore treat the morning and afternoon exams as independent exams.

If you took more than three hours (180 minutes) to complete this portion of the exam, you should adjust your score downward by one point for each minute you ran over.

Remember: the real exam *will be more difficult* than these practice exams. The main reason for this is the general anxiety and stress that you will be feeling on exam day, coupled with the time pressure you will be under. Many of the questions on this practice exam and the real exam are not individually difficult, so if you take extra time to answer the questions on this practice exam, your score will go up significantly. However, if you want an accurate measure of your potential performance on the exam, adhere to the 3-hour time limit.

After you have finished grading your practice exam, you may find it useful to use the exam questions and recommended solutions for review. Many of these questions were specifically written for your use as study tools. Once again, I feel I should remind you not to rely on memorizing these questions; you are not likely to see them on the actual exam. What you will see on the exam, though, are the concepts, terms, and procedures presented in these questions.

Your actual exam will most likely look different than what you see in this book. Please remember, no study provider knows the content of the actual exam. These practice exams are our best guess as to the structure, content, and difficulty of an actual exam.

Test Answers

1.	(A)	(B)	(C)	41.	(A)	(B)	(C)	81.	(A)	(B)	(C)
2.	(A)	(B)	(C)	42.	(A)	(B)	(C)	82.	(A)	(B)	(C)
3.	(A)	(B)	(C)	43.	(A)	(B)	(C)	83.	(A)	(B)	(C)
4.	(A)	(B)	(C)	44.	(A)	(B)	(C)	84.	(A)	(B)	(C)
5.	(A)	(B)	(C)	45.	(A)	(B)	(C)	85.	(A)	(B)	(C)
6.	(A)	(B)	(C)	46.	(A)	(B)	(C)	86.	(A)	(B)	(C)
7.	(A)	(B)	(C)	47.	(A)	(B)	(C)	87.	(A)	(B)	(C)
8.	(A)	(B)	(C)	48.	(A)	(B)	(C)	88.	(A)	(B)	(C)
9.	(A)	(B)	(C)	49.	(A)	(B)	(C)	89.	(A)	(B)	(C)
10.	(A)	(B)	(C)	50.	(A)	(B)	(C)	90.	(A)	(B)	(C)
11.	(A)	(B)	(C)	51.	(A)	(B)	(C)	91.	(A)	(B)	(C)
12.	(A)	(B)	(C)	52.	(A)	(B)	(C)	92.	(A)	(B)	(C)
13.	(A)	(B)	(C)	53.	(A)	(B)	(C)	93.	(A)	(B)	(C)
14.	(A)	(B)	(C)	54.	(A)	(B)	(C)	94.	(A)	(B)	(C)
15.	(A)	(B)	(C)	55.	(A)	(B)	(C)	95.	(A)	(B)	(C)
16.	(A)	(B)	(C)	56.	(A)	(B)	(C)	96.	(A)	(B)	(C)
17.	(A)	(B)	(C)	57.	(A)	(B)	(C)	97.	(A)	(B)	(C)
18.	(A)	(B)	(C)	58.	(A)	(B)	(C)	98.	(A)	(B)	(C)
19.	(A)	(B)	(C)	59.	(A)	(B)	(C)	99.	(A)	(B)	(C)
20.	(A)	(B)	(C)	60.	(A)	(B)	(C)	100.	(A)	(B)	(C)
21.	(A)	(B)	(C)	61.	(A)	(B)	(C)	101.	(A)	(B)	(C)
22.	(A)	(B)	(C)	62.	(A)	(B)	(C)	102.	(A)	(B)	(C)
23.	(A)	(B)	(C)	63.	(A)	(B)	(C)	103.	(A)	(B)	(C)
24.	(A)	(B)	(C)	64.	(A)	(B)	(C)	104.	(A)	(B)	(C)
25.	(A)	(B)	(C)	65.	(A)	(B)	(C)	105.	(A)	(B)	(C)
26.	(A)	(B)	(C)	66.	(A)	(B)	(C)	106.	(A)	(B)	(C)
27.	(A)	(B)	(C)	67.	(A)	(B)	(C)	107.	(A)	(B)	(C)
28.	(A)	(B)	(C)	68.	(A)	(B)	(C)	108.	(A)	(B)	(C)
29.	(A)	(B)	(C)	69.	(A)	(B)	(C)	109.	(A)	(B)	(C)
30.	(A)	(B)	(C)	70.	(A)	(B)	(C)	110.	(A)	(B)	(C)
31.	(A)	(B)	(C)	71.	(A)	(B)	(C)	111.	(A)	(B)	(C)
32.	(A)	(B)	(C)	72.	(A)	(B)	(C)	112.	(A)	(B)	(C)
33.	(A)	(B)	(C)	73.	(A)	(B)	(C)	113.	(A)	(B)	(C)
34.	(A)	(B)	(C)	74.	(A)	(B)	(C)	114.	(A)	(B)	(C)
35.	(A)	(B)	(C)	75.	(A)	(B)	(C)	115.	(A)	(B)	(C)
36.	(A)	(B)	(C)	76.	(A)	(B)	(C)	116.	(A)	(B)	(C)
37.	(A)	(B)	(C)	77.	(A)	(B)	(C)	117.	(A)	(B)	(C)
38.	(A)	(B)	(C)	78.	(A)	(B)	(C)	118.	(A)	(B)	(C)
39.	(A)	(B)	(C)	79.	(A)	(B)	(C)	119.	(A)	(B)	(C)
40.	(A)	(B)	(C)	80.	(A)	(B)	(C)	120.	(A)	(B)	(C)

Exam 3
Afternoon Session

Questions 1 through 18 relate to Ethical and Professional Standards. (27 minutes)

1. Which of the following statements about the CFA Institute's Professional Conduct Program (PCP) is *least accurate*?
    A. Possible sanctions include condemnation by a member's peers or suspension of a candidate's participation in the CFA Program.
    B. If the Designated Officer determines that a sanction against a member is warranted, the member must either accept the sanction or lose the right to use the CFA designation.
    C. Members who cooperate with a PCP inquiry by providing confidential client information to PCP staff are not in violation of Standard III(E) Preservation of Confidentiality.

2. Robert Miguel, CFA, is a portfolio manager for a large investment advisory firm. In appreciation of his impressive portfolio returns last quarter, one of his clients, Kevin Goodman, has invited Miguel and his wife to be his guests at his luxury suite for a major league baseball playoff game. Miguel, a baseball fan, accepts the invitation and attends the game. The next day at work, Miguel doesn't mention to his supervisor that he attended the game as a guest of the client. According to the Standard concerning independence and objectivity and the Standard on knowledge of the law, Miguel's actions are in violation of:
    A. both of these Standards.
    B. neither of these Standards.
    C. only one of these Standards.

3. Ann Smith, CFA, calls Bill Jones, CFA, and tells him that her research shows that Biokem Company is underpriced and that earnings per share will exceed $3.00 this year. Jones had never heard of Biokem before her call but knows that Smith is widely considered to be the best analyst in her sector. Smith's research has been released publicly, and Smith tells Jones he's "welcome to it." After their conversation, Jones arranges a conference call with his firm's portfolio managers and announces that Biokem is underpriced and will likely earn over $3.00 per share this year. During the call with the portfolio managers, Jones does not reference his conversation with Smith. According to the Standards that concern misrepresentation and diligence and reasonable basis, Jones violated:
    A. both of these Standards.
    B. neither of these Standards.
    C. only one of these Standards.

4. Doug Watson, CFA, serves in a sales position at Sommerset Brokerage, a registered investment adviser. As part of his employment, he is expected to entertain clients. Frequently at these client outings, Watson drinks excessively. On one occasion, after dropping off a client, Watson was cited by local police for misdemeanor public intoxication. According to the Standard on knowledge of the law and the Standard on misconduct, Watson is in violation of:
    A. both of these Standards.
    B. neither of these Standards.
    C. only one of these Standards.

5. Kevin Richards is a performance analyst for Reliable Advisors, a retail investment advisory and consulting firm. Richards, who is a Level I CFA candidate, was hired as part of the firm's efforts to attract CFA candidates into critical areas of the firm, such as performance measurement and attribution. Richards' supervisor instructs him to reference the firm's compliance with GIPS in marketing materials to attract more clients. For Richards' reference to the firm's GIPS compliance to be accurate, Reliable is *least likely* required to:
    A. apply GIPS compliance firmwide and not only to the specific asset classes mentioned in the marketing materials.
    B. claim compliance with GIPS only if it has a compliant performance history of five years or more.
    C. include all discretionary fee-paying accounts in composites based on their investment objectives and/or strategies.

6. Peter Taylor, a CFA charterholder and a food industry analyst for a large investment firm, has been invited by Sweet Pineapple Co. to visit the firm's processing plants in Hawaii. The Standard concerning independence and objectivity recommends that Taylor:
   A. use and pay for commercial transportation, if available.
   B. obtain written permission from his employer before he accepts this invitation.
   C. decline this invitation if he issues recommendations on the firm's securities.

7. Ruth Brett, a Level I CFA candidate, is a research analyst for a large investment firm. Due to a demanding work schedule with long hours, Brett was unable to attend any sort of exam preparation class, and has only been able to study sporadically. Feeling nervous and unprepared the night before the exam, Brett writes a few key notes on the bottom of her shoe. At the exam, Brett sees the large number of proctors present and decides not to risk getting caught and does not look at her shoe. According to the CFA Institute Code of Ethics and Standards of Professional Conduct, Brett is:
   A. not in violation of any Standard or the Code of Ethics because she did not use the notes.
   B. in violation of the Code of Ethics for bringing the notes into the examination room but is not in violation of any Standard because she did not use the notes.
   C. in violation of both the Code of Ethics and the Standard governing conduct as Members and Candidates in the CFA Program for taking the notes into the examination room.

8. Which of the following is *least likely* included in the CFA Code of Ethics? Members of CFA Institute must:
   A. place their clients' interests before their employer's interests.
   B. strive to maintain and improve the competence of others in the profession.
   C. use reasonable care and exercise independent professional judgment.

9. In formulating her report on GammaCorp's common stock, Barb Kramer, CFA, did a complex series of statistical tests on the company's past sales and earnings. Based on this statistical study, Kramer stated in her report that, "GammaCorp's earnings growth for the next five years will average 15% per year." Her conclusion was based in part on a regression analysis with a high level of statistical significance. Has Kramer violated the Standard on communication with clients and prospective clients?
    A. Yes, because she didn't give complete details of the statistical model used.
    B. Yes, because she failed to indicate that 15% growth is an estimate.
    C. No, because her projections are within the generally accepted bounds of statistical accuracy.

10. Alpha Advisors Inc. is an investment management firm with a client base that ranges from individuals to large foundations. Which of the following firm policies is *least appropriate* if Alpha adopts the Code and Standards? Alpha:
    A. monitors the personal trading activity of firm personnel and requires them to pre-clear personal trades.
    B. regularly calls larger accounts first after changes in investment recommendations have been faxed to all clients.
    C. excludes client accounts of family members of employees from participating in IPOs.

11. Dudley Thompson is a bond salesman for a small broker/dealer in London. His firm is the lead underwriter on a new junk bond issue for the Ibex Corporation. In order to stimulate sales of the new issue, Thompson calls all of his accounts over £1,000,000, many of which belong to elderly clients with low risk tolerances, and tells them that the Ibex issue is a fantastic opportunity for high returns that is not to be missed. Thompson also posts overly optimistic projections for Ibex's performance on several Internet "chat rooms" in order to increase the price of the bond issue and enhance his clients' returns on the investment. According to the Standards concerning market manipulation and suitability, Watson is in violation of:
    A. both of these Standards.
    B. neither of these Standards.
    C. only one of these Standards.

©2012 Kaplan, Inc.

12. Rob Elliott, a CFA candidate, is an analyst with a large asset management firm. His personal portfolio includes a large amount of common stock of TECH Inc., a semiconductor company which his firm does not currently follow. The director of the research department has just asked Elliott to analyze TECH and write a report about its investment potential, which will be distributed to clients and prospective clients. Based on the CFA Institute Standards of Professional Conduct, the *most appropriate* course of action for Elliot to take would be to:
   A. sell his shares of TECH before completing the report.
   B. decline to write the report.
   C. disclose the ownership of the stock to his employer and in the report if he writes it.

13. Antonio Mendoza, CFA, is an investment manager in private practice under the name Mendoza Investments. Mendoza solicits new business by making brief presentations describing his investment performance record. At each presentation, he makes available a 1-page information sheet that outlines his performance history for the past ten years. His telephone number is on the sheet for prospective clients who wish to contact him for additional supporting information. At the bottom of the sheet the following is stated: "Mendoza Investments has prepared and presented this report in compliance with the Global Investment Performance Standards (GIPS®)." Mendoza's information sheet:
   A. does not comply with GIPS.
   B. violates the Standard that concerns performance presentation.
   C. complies with both GIPS and the Standard that concerns performance presentation.

14. Anne Franklin, CFA, is an analyst who covers technology stocks for Medallion Investments. Franklin frequently meets with company management and makes site visits to company facilities. Cynthia Lucas, chief technology officer for Level Tech, tells several analysts, including Franklin, during a conference call that overseas shipments of the company's important new product are going to be delayed due to manufacturing defects, which she expects are correctable. This information has not been released in any other format. Medallion manages discretionary accounts for Lucas and Franklin. Subsequent to her meeting, Franklin sends a note to Medallion's investment personnel telling them to "sell the stock in all client accounts," as the shipment information is significant and contrary to recent earnings guidance from the company. Franklin's use of the information received from Lucas:

A. violates the Code and Standards, as Franklin received material nonpublic information that should not have been acted upon.

B. violates the Code and Standards, since she directed the sale in all client accounts instead of acting in the best interests of her own clients.

C. does not violate the Code and Standards, as Franklin was adhering to her fiduciary duty to Medallion's clients by sharing the information and recommending a "Sell."

15. R. J. Young is meeting with a new client for the first time. At this meeting, he will be gathering information about the client in order to assess the client's investment objectives and constraints. As he does for all of his clients, Young will then prepare a written investment policy statement (IPS). According to the recommended procedures for complying with the Standard on suitability, which of the following statements regarding an IPS is *least accurate*?

A. An IPS should describe the roles and responsibilities of the adviser and client.

B. A member or candidate is not responsible for financial information withheld by the client.

C. A client's IPS must be updated at least quarterly to reflect any changes in their investment profile.

16. Sue Johnson, CFA, has an elderly client with a very large asset base. The client intends to start divesting her fortune to various charities. Johnson is on the Board of a local charitable foundation. Johnson *most* appropriately:
    A. must not discuss anything regarding her client and her client's intentions with the charitable foundation without permission.
    B. can discuss her client's situation with the charitable foundation as long as she informs other local charities of her client's intentions.
    C. can make this known to the charitable foundation so that they can solicit the client, since it is the client's wish to divest assets to charities in the future.

17. According to the Standard related to loyalty, prudence, and care, which of the following statements regarding the voting of proxies on client holdings is *least accurate*?
    A. Proxies have economic value to a client.
    B. An investment management firm should vote all proxies on client holdings unless the client reserves that right.
    C. Members and candidates should explicitly disclose the firm's proxy voting policies to clients.

18. Alvin Gold, CFA, resides in Country T and does business as an investment advisor primarily in Country U. Country T allows trading on non-public information and does not require disclosure of referral fees. Country U prohibits trading on non-public information only if it is gained by illegal means and requires disclosure of referral fees of over $100 (U.S. equivalent). Gold accepts a referral fee of $75, and in the course of a meeting with two other analysts and the firm's CFO, Gold receives material non-public information. To comply with the Code and Standards, Gold:
    A. need not disclose the referral fee but cannot trade on the non-public information.
    B. must disclose the referral fee and cannot trade on the non-public information.
    C. must disclose the referral fee but may trade on the non-public information.

Questions 19 through 32 relate to Quantitative Methods. (21 minutes)

19. Three years from now, an investor will deposit the first of eight $1,000 payments into a special fund. The fund will earn interest at the rate of 5% per year until the third deposit is made. Thereafter, the fund will return a reduced interest rate of 4% compounded annually until the final deposit is made. How much money will the investor have in the fund at the end of ten years assuming no withdrawals are made?
    A. $8,872.93.
    B. $9,251.82.
    C. $9,549.11.

20. An investor places $5,000 in an account. The stated annual interest rate is 6% compounded monthly. The value of the account at the end of three years is *closest* to:
    A. $5,970.
    B. $5,978.
    C. $5,983.

21. Compared to a *t*-distribution with 10 degrees of freedom, and compared to a normal distribution, a *t*-distribution with 20 degrees of freedom and the same variance has:

	Compared to df = 10	Compared to normal
A.	thinner tails	fatter tails
B.	fatter tails	thinner tails
C.	fatter tails	fatter tails

22. The initial market value of a portfolio was $100,000. One year later the portfolio was valued at $90,000 and two years later at $99,000. The geometric mean annual return excluding any dividend income is *closest* to:
    A. −0.5%.
    B. −0.4%.
    C. 0.0%.

23. A college endowment fund has $150 million. The fund manager intends to withdraw $2 million from the fund for operations, and she has a minimum year-end acceptable level of $151 million. The fund has two choices for the portfolio. The endowment manager can choose Portfolio X, which has an expected return of 10% and a standard deviation of 14%, or Portfolio Y, which has an expected return of 12% and a standard deviation of 20%. Given this scenario, which of the following statements regarding Roy's safety-first criterion is *most accurate*?
   A. The fund should choose Portfolio Y.
   B. The fund should choose Portfolio X.
   C. Portfolios X and Y are both acceptable because their safety-first ratios fall in the acceptable range.

24. An investor purchases 500 shares of Nevada Industries common stock for $22.00 per share today. At t = 1 year, this investor receives a $0.42 per share dividend (which is not reinvested) on the 500 shares and purchases an additional 500 shares for $24.75 per share. At t = 2 years, he receives another $0.42 (not reinvested) per share dividend on 1,000 shares and purchases 600 more shares for $31.25 per share. At t = 3 years, he sells 1,000 of the shares for $35.50 per share and the remaining 600 shares at $36.00 per share, but receives no dividends. Assuming no commissions or taxes, the money-weighted rate of return received on this investment is *closest* to:
   A. 14.3%.
   B. 17.6%.
   C. 18.5%.

25. The "up-move factor" in a binomial tree is *best* described as:
   A. the probability that the variable increases in any period.
   B. one minus the "down-move factor" for the binomial tree.
   C. one plus the percentage change in the variable when it increases.

26. Jane Acompora is calculating equivalent annualized yields based on the 1.3% holding period yield of a 90-day loan. The correct ordering of the annual money market yield (MMY), effective yield (EAY), and bond equivalent yield (BEY) is:
   A. MMY < EAY < BEY.
   B. MMY < BEY < EAY.
   C. BEY < EAY < MMY.

27. An analyst develops the following probability distribution for the states of the economy and market returns.

	Unconditional Probability P(A)		Conditional Probability P(B × A)
Good economy	60%	Bull market	50%
		Normal market	30%
		Bear market	20%
Poor economy	40%	Bull market	20%
		Normal market	30%
		Bear market	˙50%

Which of the following statements about this probability distribution is *least accurate*?
A. The unconditional probability of a normal market is 0.30.
B. The joint probability of having a good economy and a bear market is 0.20.
C. Given that the economy is poor, the probability of a normal or a bull market is 0.50.

28. An analyst estimates a stock has a 40% probability of earning a 10% return, a 40% probability of earning a 12.5% return, and a 20% probability of earning a 30% return. The stock's standard deviation of returns based on this returns model is *closest* to:
A. 3.74%.
B. 5.75%.
C. 7.58%.

29. An investment manager has a pool of five security analysts he can choose from to cover three different industries. In how many different ways can the manager assign one analyst to each industry?
A. 15.
B. 60.
C. 125.

30. Shortfall risk is *best* described as the probability:
A. of a credit rating downgrade due to possible earnings shortfalls.
B. of failing to make a contractually promised payment.
C. that portfolio value will fall below some minimum level at a future date.

31. If a two-tailed hypothesis test has a 5% probability of rejecting the null hypothesis when the null is true, it is *most likely* that the:
    A. power of the test is 95%.
    B. confidence level of the test is 95%.
    C. probability of a Type I error is 2.5%.

32. Which of the following statements about hypothesis testing is *most accurate*?
    A. Rejecting a true null hypothesis is a Type I error.
    B. The power of a test is the probability of failing to reject the null hypothesis when it is false.
    C. For a one-tailed test involving X, the null hypothesis would be $H_0: X = 0$, and the alternative hypothesis would be $H_A: X \neq 0$.

Questions 33 through 44 relate to Economics. (18 minutes)

33. A business cycle theory developed by applying utility theory and budget constraints to macroeconomic models is *most closely* associated with which school of economic thought?
    A. Austrian.
    B. New Classical.
    C. New Keynesian.

34. A loss of economic efficiency from price regulation is *least likely* to result from a:
    A. rent ceiling that effectively increases renters' search times for available units.
    B. minimum wage that is greater than the equilibrium wage for unskilled workers.
    C. maximum price for electricity set at a price level at which the quantity of electricity supplied is greater than the quantity demanded.

35. Consider the following foreign exchange and interest rate information:
    - Spot rate: 1.3382 USD/EUR.
    - One year riskless USD rate = 2.5%.
    - One year riskless EUR rate = 3.5%.

    The one-year arbitrage-free forward exchange rate is *closest* to:
    A. 1.2391 USD/EUR.
    B. 1.3253 USD/EUR.
    C. 1.3513 USD/EUR.

36. Monthly demand for gasoline at a particular location, as a function of the price of gasoline and the price of bus travel, is given (in hundreds of gallons) as $Q_D = 300 - 15\,P_{gas} + 2\,P_{bus}$. The slope of the demand curve for gasoline is *closest* to:
   A. −0.07.
   B. −0.13.
   C. −15.00.

37. Which of the following statements about monopolists is *most accurate*?
   A. Monopolists have imperfect information about demand.
   B. Without government intervention, monopolists will always earn economic profits.
   C. A monopolist maximizes total revenue where marginal revenue equals marginal cost.

38. A central bank's ability to achieve its policy goals is *most likely* to be limited by available resources when which of the following actual rates is below its target rate?
   A. Interest rate.
   B. Inflation rate.
   C. Exchange rate.

39. Which of the following statements regarding the money supply and determination of short-term interest rates is *least accurate*?
   A. On balance, growth in real GDP tends to increase the transactional demand for money.
   B. If the short-term interest rate is greater than the equilibrium rate, there will be excess supply of real money balances.
   C. An increase in the real money supply from an initial equilibrium situation will cause households and businesses to sell interest-bearing securities.

40. What are the *most likely* effects on aggregate demand in the current period of an increase in expected future incomes and of an increase in the money supply?
   A. Both increase aggregate demand.
   B. Both decrease aggregate demand.
   C. One increases aggregate demand and one decreases aggregate demand.

41. Incorrect production decisions are *most likely* to occur when the inflation rate is:
    A. lower than expected only.
    B. higher than expected only.
    C. either higher or lower than expected.

42. The source of comparative advantage, according to the Heckscher-Ohlin model of international trade, is each country's:
    A. labor productivity.
    B. available natural resources.
    C. relative amounts of labor and capital.

43. Under which market structure is the profit maximizing strategy to produce the quantity of output for which the price is equal to marginal cost?
    A. Monopoly.
    B. Perfect competition.
    C. Monopolistic competition.

44. Which of the following statements about elasticity is *least accurate*?
    A. Both demand and supply are more elastic in the long run than in the short run.
    B. When demand is inelastic, an increase in price will cause a decrease in the total expenditure on a good.
    C. When the price of a product increases, consumers will reduce their consumption by a larger amount in the long run than in the short run.

**Questions 45 through 68 relate to Financial Reporting and Analysis.
(36 minutes)**

45. Which of the following statements about nonrecurring items is *most accurate*?
    A. The correction of an accounting error is reported net of taxes below extraordinary items on the income statement.
    B. Discontinued operations are classified as unusual or infrequent and are reported as a component of net income from continuing operations.
    C. Uninsured losses from earthquakes and expropriations by foreign governments can be classified as extraordinary items under U.S. GAAP but not under IFRS.

46. On January 31, Dowling Inc. borrowed funds to purchase capital equipment for its business operations. On the same day, it also recorded the cost of salaries incurred to January 31, which will be paid on February 6. When these two transactions are recorded on January 31, the financial statement item that will increase the most is:
   A. assets.
   B. expenses.
   C. liabilities.

47. Under U.S. GAAP, which of the following statements about classifying cash flows is *most accurate*?
   A. Cash received from issuing long-term debt or stock is considered a financing cash flow.
   B. Income taxes paid are considered financing or investing cash flows if they arise from financing or investing activities.
   C. Dividend payments made are financing cash flows, while interest payments received are investing cash flows.

48. Kimberwick Technologies reported the following information for the year ending December 31.

Data	
Net sales	50,000
Cash expenses	3,250
Cash inputs	17,000
Cash taxes	7,000
Increase in receivables	500
Depreciation expense	1,000
Cash flow from investing	–5,000
Cash flow from financing	–4,250

If the cash balance increased $13,000 over the year, cash flow from operations (CFO) is *closest* to:
   A. $21,250.
   B. $21,750.
   C. $22,250.

49. A company has a cash conversion cycle of 80 days. If the company's average receivables turnover increases from 11 to 12, the company's cash conversion cycle:
   A. decreases by approximately 3 days.
   B. increases by approximately 3 days.
   C. decreases by approximately 1 day.

©2012 Kaplan, Inc.

50. Which of the following statements about a United States public corporation's annual reports, SEC filings, and press releases is *most accurate*?
    A. Annual and quarterly SEC filings must be audited.
    B. Interim SEC filings typically update the major financial statements and footnotes.
    C. Annual reports to shareholders are typically the most factual and objective source of information about a company.

51. A company had the following changes in its stock:
    - The company had 2 million shares outstanding on December 31, 20X6.
    - On March 31, 20X7, the company paid a 10% stock dividend.
    - On June 30, 20X7, the company sold $10 million face value of 7% convertible debentures, convertible into common at $5 per share.
    - On September 30, 20X7, the company issued and sold 100,000 shares of common stock.

    The company should compute its 20X7 basic earnings per share based on:
    A. 2,225,000 shares.
    B. 2,250,000 shares.
    C. 3,225,000 shares.

52. When a used delivery truck is sold, the gain or loss on disposal is *most accurately* stated as:
    A. original cost – accumulated depreciation + selling price.
    B. selling price – original cost – accumulated depreciation.
    C. selling price – original cost + accumulated depreciation.

53. Haltata Turf & Sod currently uses the first in, first out (FIFO) method to account for inventory. Due to significant tax-loss carryforwards, the company has an effective tax rate of zero. Prices are rising and inventory quantities are stable. If the company were to use last in, first out (LIFO) instead of FIFO:
    A. net income would be lower and cash flow would be higher.
    B. cash flow would remain the same and working capital would be lower.
    C. gross margin would be higher and stockholder's equity would be lower.

54. Which of the following effects is *most likely* to occur when using ratio screens for high dividend yield stocks and low P/E stocks, respectively?

High dividend yield	Low P/E ratios
A. Include too many financial services firms	Exclude too many growth firms
B. Exclude too many financial services firms	Include too many growth firms
C. Include too many financial services firms	Include too many growth firms

55. The ratio of operating cash flow to net income (the cash flow earnings index) is *least likely* be an "accounting red flag" when it is:
   A. less than one.
   B. declining over time.
   C. highly variable.

56. A firm that reports under IFRS is producing under a long-term contract for which it cannot measure the outcome reliably. In the first year of the contract, the firm has spent €300,000 and collected €200,000 in cash. What amounts related to this contract should the firm recognize on its income statement for the year?
   A. Revenue of €300,000, expenses of €300,000, and no profit.
   B. No revenue, expenses, or profit until the contract is completed.
   C. Revenue of €200,000, expenses of €300,000, and a loss of €100,000.

57. Which of the following statements about the role of depreciable lives and salvage values in the computation of depreciation expenses for financial reporting is *most accurate*?
   A. The estimated useful life of the same depreciable asset should be the same regardless of which company owns the asset.
   B. Companies are specifically required to disclose data about estimated salvage values in the footnotes to the financial statements.
   C. Depreciable lives and salvage values are chosen by management and allow for the possibility of income manipulation.

58. A company's investments in marketable securities include a 3-year tax-exempt bond classified as held-to-maturity and a 5-year Treasury note classified as available-for-sale. On its income statement, the company should report the coupon interest received from:
   A. both of these securities.
   B. neither of these securities.
   C. only one of these securities.

59. Acme Corp. purchased a new stamping machine for $100,000, paid $10,000 for shipping, and paid $5,000 to have it installed in their plant. Based on an estimated salvage value of $25,000 and an economic life of six years, the difference between straight-line depreciation and double-declining balance depreciation in the second year of the asset's life is *closest* to:
   A. $7,220.
   B. $10,556.
   C. $16,666.

60. How will a firm's operating cash flow be affected by a decrease in accounts receivable and by an increase in accounts payable?
   A. Both will increase operating cash flow.
   B. Both will decrease operating cash flow.
   C. One will increase operating cash flow and one will decrease operating cash flow.

61. From the point of view of a financial analyst, when evaluating companies that use different inventory cost assumptions, in a period of:
   A. stable prices, LIFO inventory is preferred to FIFO inventory.
   B. decreasing prices, FIFO inventory is preferred to LIFO inventory.
   C. increasing prices, FIFO cost of sales is preferred to LIFO cost of sales.

62. In general, as compared to companies with operating leases, companies with finance leases report:
   A. lower working capital and asset turnover.
   B. higher debt-to-equity ratios and return on equity in the early years.
   C. higher expenses in the early years and over the life of the lease.

63. Longboat, Inc. sold a luxury passenger boat from its inventory on December 31 for $2,000,000. It is estimated that Longboat will incur $100,000 in warranty expenses during its 5-year warranty period. Longboat's tax rate is 30%. To account for the tax implications of the warranty obligation prior to incurring warranty expenses, Longboat should:
   A. record a deferred tax asset of $30,000.
   B. record a deferred tax liability of $30,000.
   C. make no entry until actual warranty expenses are incurred.

64. During 20X3, Rory, Inc., reported net income of $15,000 and had 2,000 shares of common stock outstanding for the entire year. Rory also had 2,000 shares of 10%, $50 par value preferred stock outstanding during 20X3. During 20X1, Rory issued 100, $1,000 par, 6% bonds for $100,000. Each of these is convertible to 50 shares of common stock. Rory's tax rate is 40%. Assuming these bonds are dilutive, 20X3 diluted EPS for Rory is *closest* to:
    A. $0.71.
    B. $1.23.
    C. $2.50.

65. The category of items on the balance sheet that typically offers an analyst the best information on a non-financial firm's investing activities is:
    A. current assets.
    B. current liabilities.
    C. noncurrent assets.

66. A firm issues a 4-year semiannual-pay bond with a face value of $10 million and a coupon rate of 10%. The market interest rate is 11% when the bond is issued. The balance sheet liability at the end of the first semiannual period is *closest* to:
    A. $9,650,700.
    B. $9,683,250.
    C. $9,715,850.

67. The presentation format of balance sheet data that standardizes the first-year values to 1.0 and presents subsequent years' amounts relative to 1.0 is a(n):
    A. indexed balance sheet.
    B. vertical common-size balance sheet.
    C. horizontal common-size balance sheet.

68. Debt covenants to protect bondholders are *least likely* to:
    A. restrict the payment of dividends.
    B. require sinking fund redemptions.
    C. prohibit bond repurchases at a premium to par.

Questions 69 through 78 relate to Corporate Finance. (15 minutes)

69. At the beginning of the year, Breidel Company changes its inventory accounting method from first in first out to average cost. Assuming an environment of increasing prices, how will this accounting change affect Breidel's forecasts of its net cash position?
   A. No effect because this accounting change does not affect cash flows.
   B. Less net cash in both the short-term forecast and the long-term forecast.
   C. No effect on the short-term forecast but greater net cash in the long-term forecast.

70. A strong corporate code of ethics is *most likely* to permit:
   A. the company to award consulting contracts to board members.
   B. board members to simultaneously sit on the board of another firm.
   C. finder's fees for merger or acquisition targets to be paid to board members.

71. The greatest amount of detailed capital budgeting analysis is typically required when deciding whether to:
   A. expand production capacity.
   B. introduce a new product or develop a new market.
   C. replace a functioning machine with a newer model to reduce costs.

72. When using the CAPM to estimate the cost of common equity for a company in a developing country, an analyst should *most* appropriately:
   A. add a country risk premium to the market risk premium.
   B. add the sovereign yield spread to the CAPM cost of common equity.
   C. make no adjustments because country risk is reflected in the equity's beta.

73. The type of short-term financing for which the financing cost is *most closely* tied to the creditworthiness of a firm's customers is:
   A. factoring.
   B. issuing commercial paper.
   C. an uncommitted line of credit.

74. Smith Company's earnings per share are more sensitive to changes in operating income than are those of Jones Company. This implies that Smith Company has a higher degree of:
   A. total leverage.
   B. financial leverage.
   C. operating leverage.

75. If flotation costs are treated correctly in calculating the net present value of a project that will begin in the current period, the flotation costs are *most likely*:
    A. included in the initial outlay.
    B. reflected in the discount rate used for the project.
    C. included in the cost of the capital raised.

76. In a net present value (NPV) profile, the internal rate of return is represented as the:
    A. point where two NPV profiles intersect.
    B. intersection of the NPV profile with the vertical axis.
    C. intersection of the NPV profile with the horizontal axis.

77. Thompson Products has seen its marginal tax rate increase from 28% to 34% over the last two years and believes the change is permanent. The effects of this change on Thompson's current WACC and on its financial leverage over time are *most likely* a(n):
    A. increase in both.
    B. decrease in both.
    C. increase in one and a decrease in the other.

78. The payment of a stock dividend will *most likely* decrease:
    A. a firm's net income and earnings per share.
    B. the value of a firm's equity and increase its return on equity.
    C. a firm's earnings per share but not affect the value of its equity.

Questions 79 through 84 relate to Portfolio Management. (9 minutes)

79. In the market model, beta measures the sensitivity of an asset's rate of return to the market's:
    A. rate of return.
    B. excess return.
    C. risk-adjusted return.

80. A portfolio is invested 30% in Asset A with the remainder invested in Asset B. Asset A has an expected return of 6% and variance of returns of 0.031, while Asset B has an expected return of 7% and variance of returns of 0.045. The covariance between the returns of the two assets is 0.03735. The standard deviation of returns for the portfolio is *closest* to:
    A. 18%.
    B. 20%.
    C. 22%.

81. Open-end mutual funds differ from closed-end funds in that:
    A. open-end funds stand ready to redeem their shares, while closed-end funds do not.
    B. closed-end funds require active management, while open-end funds do not.
    C. open-end funds issue shares that are then traded in secondary markets, while closed-end funds do not.

82. An analyst determines that four stocks have the following characteristics:

Stock	Beta	Estimated Return
X	1.0	10%
Y	1.6	16%
Z	2.0	16%

    If the risk-free rate is 4% and the expected return on the market is 10%, which of the following statements is *least accurate*?
    A. Stock X is properly valued.
    B. Stock Y is undervalued.
    C. Stock Z is overvalued.

83. According to the CAPM, a rational, risk-averse investor would be *least likely* to choose as his optimal portfolio:
    A. a 100% allocation to the risk-free asset.
    B. the global minimum variance portfolio.
    C. a 130% allocation to the market portfolio.

84. The risk-free rate is 5% and the expected market risk premium is 10%. A portfolio manager is projecting a return of 20% on a portfolio with a beta of 1.5. After adjusting for its systematic risk, this portfolio is expected to:
    A. equal the market's performance.
    B. outperform the market.
    C. underperform the market.

Questions 85 through 96 relate to Equity Investments. (18 minutes)

85. An analyst determines that a company has a return on equity of 16% and pays 40% of its earnings in dividends. If the firm recently paid a $1.50 dividend and the stock is selling for $40, what is the required rate of return on the stock if it is priced according to the dividend discount model?
    A. 9.6%.
    B. 10.2%.
    C. 13.7%.

86. An investor buys a stock for $50. The initial margin requirement is 50%, and the maintenance margin requirement is 25%. The price below which the investor would receive a margin call would be:
    A. $25.00.
    B. $33.33.
    C. $37.50.

87. A securities market exhibits operational efficiency if it offers:
    A. low transaction costs.
    B. prices that respond rapidly to new information.
    C. rates of return that are proportional to risk on average.

88. A stock index consists of two stocks:
    - Company A has 50 shares outstanding valued at $2 each.
    - Company B has 10 shares outstanding valued at $10 each.
    - The price-weighted index is 6, and the value-weighted index is 100.

    If the price of Company A's stock increases to $4 per share, and Company B's stock splits two-for-one and is priced at $5, the value of the price-weighted index and the value-weighted index are:

	Price-weighted	Value-weighted
A.	7	150
B.	7	125
C.	4.5	150

89. Pam Robers, CFA, is performing a valuation analysis on the common stock of Allstare Inc. The stock's beta is 1.1, the risk-free rate is 5%, and the market risk premium is expected to be 8%. Allstare's ROE is expected to be constant at 18%, and its dividend payout ratio has been fairly constant over time at 40%. The forward-earnings multiplier that Robers should use to estimate the current value of the shares is *closest* to:
    A. 7.
    B. 13.
    C. 20.

©2012 Kaplan, Inc.

90. Other things equal, which of the following would be *most likely* to increase a firm's return on shareholders' equity?
    A. Payment of a large special dividend by the firm.
    B. Repurchase of common stock with the proceeds of a debt offering.
    C. Decrease in the market price of a firm's shares due to a sharp decrease in stock prices overall.

91. Over the past few years, the companies in an industry have experienced positive but decreasing profitability and growth rates. The companies have begun to compete intensely with each other and customers switch frequently among brands. This industry's life-cycle stage is *most accurately* described as:
    A. growth.
    B. maturity.
    C. shakeout.

92. An analyst gathered the following data about a company:
    - The historical earnings retention rate of 40% is projected to continue into the future.
    - The sustainable ROE is 12%.
    - The stock's beta is 1.2.
    - The nominal risk-free rate is 6%.
    - The expected market return is 11%.

    If the analyst believes next year's earnings will be $4 per share, what value should be placed on this stock?
    A. $22.24.
    B. $33.32.
    C. $45.45.

93. Which of the following classifications of firms is *least likely* to comprise cyclical firms?
    A. Housing.
    B. Technology.
    C. Telecommunications.

94. The assertion that investors, analysts, and portfolio managers exhibit psychological tendencies that cause them to make systematic errors is *most* consistent with:
    A. behavioral finance.
    B. weak-form market efficiency.
    C. fundamental analysis.

95. An investor purchases 1,000 shares of each of the stocks in a price-weighted index at their closing prices (ignore transactions costs). On a total return basis, if the index stocks remain the same, this portfolio will:
    A. perform exactly like the index over time.
    B. outperform the index over time.
    C. underperform the index over time.

96. Among valuation models, the difficulty of estimating a required rate of return is *most likely* to be a disadvantage of using a(n):
    A. Gordon growth model.
    B. asset-based valuation model.
    C. enterprise value multiplier model.

Questions 97 through 110 relate to Fixed Income. (21 minutes)

97. Which of the following statements about the risks associated with investing in bonds is *most accurate*?
    A. Corporate debentures are not subject to prepayment risk.
    B. Liquidity risk is not relevant if the portfolio manager intends to hold the bond to maturity.
    C. Event risk refers to the possibility that the issuer breaches one of its debt covenants and triggers a "credit event."

98. The type of credit risk that is most directly reflected in a bond's rating is:
    A. default risk.
    B. downgrade risk.
    C. credit spread risk.

99. What effects will an increase in yield volatility have on the values of a putable bond and a callable bond?
    A. Both bonds will increase in value.
    B. Both bonds will decrease in value.
    C. One bond will increase in value and the other will decrease.

100. Which of the following statements about debt securities is *least accurate*?
    A. Commercial paper is a short-term (less than nine months) vehicle for corporate borrowing.
    B. An asset-backed security is a security whose cash flows are linked to a pool of underlying loans or financial instruments.
    C. A medium-term note (MTN) differs from a corporate bond in that an MTN is sold to investors on a "firm commitment" basis wherein the investment banker guarantees a price to the issuer.

101. An inverse floating-rate bond:
    A. may, under certain circumstances, require the bondholder to make payments to the issuer.
    B. increases in principal value as market rates decrease and decreases in principal value as market rates increase.
    C. has an implicit cap on the maximum coupon rate and typically includes a floor on the minimum coupon rate.

102. Portfolio duration *most accurately* approximates the sensitivity of the value of a bond portfolio to:
    A. parallel shifts in the yield curve.
    B. increases in the slope of the yield curve.
    C. decreases in the slope of the yield curve.

103. A firm is said to have a top-heavy capital structure if a high percentage of its total capital is:
    A. senior debt.
    B. short-term debt.
    C. secured bank debt.

104. An 8%, semiannual pay, option-free corporate bond that is selling at par has ten years to maturity. What is the effective duration of the bond based on a 75 basis point change (up or down) in rates?
    A. 5.6.
    B. 6.8.
    C. 7.2.

105. The current 4-year spot rate is 4% and the current 5-year spot rate is 5.5%. What is the 1-year forward rate in four years?
    A. 9.58%.
    B. 10.14%.
    C. 11.72%.

106. An economic expansion has caused Treasury yields to increase and absolute credit spreads to narrow. Which of the following is *most likely* accurate?
    A. Relative corporate yield spreads to Treasuries will have increased.
    B. Even if absolute credit spreads had remained the same, the yield ratio and relative yield spread of BBB to AAA bonds could have decreased.
    C. Absolute spreads are generally considered a better indicator than relative yield spreads.

107. The face value of a $1,000,000 T-bill with 78 days to maturity is priced at $987,845. What is the bank discount yield (annualized) quote for the T-bill?
    A. 5.61%.
    B. 5.67%.
    C. 5.75%.

108. A decrease in mortgage interest rates will *most likely* have what effects on the prices of interest-only stripped mortgage-backed securities and principal-only stripped mortgage-backed securities?
    A. Both will increase.
    B. Both will decrease.
    C. One will increase and one will decrease.

109. For which of the following securities is estimating the future cash flows *least* difficult?
    A. 5-year, 6% bond with two years of call protection.
    B. 3-year note with a coupon of Libor + 100 basis points.
    C. 8% preferred stock with mandatory redemption in five years.

110. Which of the following yields *least likely* represents a spot rate?
    A. 91-day Treasury bill holding period yield.
    B. 2-year Treasury inflation protected security yield.
    C. 7-year Treasury coupon strip yield.

Questions 111 through 116 relate to Derivatives. (9 minutes)

111. An investor writes a covered call with a strike price of $44 on a stock selling at $40 for a $3 premium. The range of possible payoffs to the writer of this covered call on the combined position is:
    A. –$40 to $47.
    B. –$37 to $7.
    C. $7 to infinity.

112. The payoff diagram of portfolio insurance (owning a stock and a put) has the same shape as the payoff diagram for:
    A. writing a put option.
    B. buying a call option.
    C. writing a call option.

113. Which of the following statements about interest rate swaps is *most accurate*?
    A. The parties agreeing to a swap typically make a margin deposit with a clearinghouse.
    B. A plain vanilla interest rate swap exchanges fixed rate payments for variable rate payments.
    C. The counterparties exchange the notional principal at initiation and termination, while only net interest rate payments are exchanged on the settlement dates.

114. A European call and a European put on the same underlying asset each have an exercise price of $45. The two options have six months to expiration and are both selling for $4. The underlying asset is selling for $43 and the rate of return on a 1-year Treasury bill is 6%. According to put-call parity it is *most likely* that:
    A. the call option is overvalued.
    B. the put option is overvalued.
    C. the underlying asset is overvalued.

115. A company wants to hedge against a possible interest rate increase by entering into a forward rate agreement. The following quotes are obtained from a dealer for 30-day FRAs:

Dealer Quotes
60-Day LIBOR = 0.0480
90-Day LIBOR = 0.0500
180-Day LIBOR = 0.0525

The contract covers a notional principal of $50 million. The company hedges its risk of an increase in 60-day LIBOR with an FRA, and 30 days later when the contract expires, the 60-day LIBOR rate is 5%. What does the company collect from, or pay to, the dealer? The company:
    A. collects $16,529.
    B. pays $29,691.
    C. neither collects nor pays since the rate on 60-day LIBOR at expiration is the same as the rate on 90-day LIBOR initially.

116. Which of the following statements about futures margins is *least accurate*?
    A. The initial margin is set by the clearinghouse based on the volatility of the price of the underlying asset.
    B. If the balance of the margin account exceeds the initial margin requirement, the trader can remove the excess funds from the account.
    C. If the margin account balance falls below the maintenance margin level, the account balance must be brought back up to the maintenance level.

Questions 117 through 120 relate to Alternative Investments. (6 minutes)

117. Which of the following statements with respect to hedge fund investing is *least accurate*?
    A. Hedge funds only publicly disclose performance information on a voluntary basis.
    B. Hedge funds are not typically registered with the SEC in the United States.
    C. Survivorship bias in hedge fund data causes risk to be overstated because funds that take on more risk tend to have higher returns.

118. An investor who wants to hedge against inflation by allocating a portion of a portfolio to alternative investments should *most appropriately* invest in:
    A. real estate and commodities.
    B. private equity and real estate.
    C. commodities and private equity.

119. A leveraged buyout firm that carries out a secondary sale has:
    A. offered additional shares to the public.
    B. exited an investment in a portfolio company.
    C. received new capital from its general or limited partners.

120. The notice period for a hedge fund is *best* described as the period following:
    A. the opening of the fund to investors, before the fund is closed to new investors.
    B. a request for redemption of shares, within which the fund must fulfill the request.
    C. an investment in the fund, during which the investor is not permitted to redeem shares.

EXAM 1
MORNING SESSION ANSWER KEY

To get valuable feedback on how your score compares to those of other Level I candidates, use your Username and Password to gain Online Access at schweser.com and choose the left-hand menu item "Practice Exams Vol. 1."

1. B	31. C	61. B	91. C
2. C	32. A	62. A	92. C
3. A	33. A	63. C	93. C
4. A	34. C	64. B	94. B
5. A	35. A	65. A	95. B
6. B	36. B	66. A	96. B
7. C	37. A	67. A	97. B
8. A	38. B	68. B	98. B
9. B	39. B	69. B	99. C
10. B	40. C	70. C	100. C
11. B	41. B	71. A	101. A
12. A	42. C	72. C	102. B
13. A	43. C	73. C	103. B
14. C	44. B	74. C	104. B
15. A	45. A	75. B	105. B
16. B	46. C	76. B	106. B
17. C	47. C	77. C	107. C
18. A	48. B	78. C	108. A
19. C	49. C	79. C	109. A
20. B	50. A	80. B	110. A
21. C	51. B	81. A	111. A
22. B	52. C	82. B	112. A
23. B	53. A	83. A	113. C
24. A	54. A	84. A	114. C
25. C	55. A	85. A	115. B
26. C	56. B	86. B	116. A
27. C	57. C	87. B	117. B
28. C	58. C	88. A	118. A
29. B	59. B	89. A	119. A
30. B	60. B	90. C	120. B

Exam 1
Morning Session Answers

Answers referencing the Standards of Practice address Study Session 1, LOS 1.b, c and LOS 2.a, b, c, except where noted.

1. **B** According to Standard VII(B) Reference to the CFA Institute, the CFA Designation, and CFA Program, citing an expected date for completing a level of the CFA Program is a misuse of the CFA designation.

2. **C** All investment personnel in this example are subject to the CFA Institute Code and Standards as part of the firm's established policies. The candidate's reference to her Level III status and the inclusion of such information in her biographical information is not in violation of the CFA Institute Code and Standards. Candidates may clearly reference their participation in the CFA program, provided such reference does not imply the achievement of any type of partial designation. The analyst is considered a candidate since she is registered to take the next scheduled examination. The Code and Standards prohibit using material nonpublic information. Since the Code and Standards are *stricter* than the local law, they must be followed by the analyst. The junior analyst failed to exercise diligence and thoroughness in making investment recommendations and failed to have a reasonable and adequate basis for such recommendations.

3. **A** Standard VI(B) Priority of Transactions recommends, but does not require, that a member or candidate obtain pre-clearance from his or her supervisor before participating in an equity IPO. Guidance for Standard III(B) Fair Dealing states that members and candidates distributing IPO shares must distribute shares in an oversubscribed IPO to clients and may not withhold shares for themselves.

4. **A** To comply with Standard IV(B) Additional Compensation Arrangements, Bryant must obtain written consent from her employer before undertaking the independent consulting project. Bryant must also provide a description of the types of services being provided, the length of time the arrangement will last, and the compensation she expects to receive for her services.

5. **A** Standard V(C) Record Retention requires members to maintain records of the data and analysis they use to develop their research recommendations. Recommendations may be brief, in capsule form, or simply a list of buy/sell recommendations. A list of recommendations may be sent without regard to suitability, including both safe income stocks and aggressive growth stocks, for example.

6. **B** Standard IV(C) Responsibilities of Supervisors indicates that a member should decline supervisory responsibility in writing until the firm adopts reasonable compliance procedures. Otherwise, Brooks cannot adequately exercise her responsibility.

7. **C** Standard III(D) Performance Presentation recommends that terminated accounts be *included* in historical performance calculations.

8. **A** Standard V(B) Communication with Clients and Prospective Clients requires that Toma separate opinion from fact. Toma's statement that excess demand will persist into the foreseeable future is an opinion, not a fact.

9. **B** Under Standard III(A) Loyalty, Prudence, and Care, the fiduciary duty in this case is to plan participants and beneficiaries, not shareholders or plan trustees.

10. **B** According to Standard III(B) Fair Dealing, if a client places an order that goes against the firm's recommendation for that security, members and candidates should inform the client of the discrepancy between the order and the firm's recommendation before accepting the order.

11. **B** Private equity is one of the nine major sections of the GIPS standards; the others are not. (Study Session 1, LOS 4.d)

12. **A** The trader has carried out an arbitrage transaction. Because she did not exhibit any intent to distort prices or trading volume, the member did not violate Standard II(B) Market Manipulation. Standard III(B) Fair Dealing is concerned with fair treatment of clients and is not relevant to this transaction.

13. **A** Hoffman has violated both Standard I(B) Independence and Objectivity, which specifically addresses the requirement of disclosure of the nature of any compensation from the subject company, and Standard VI(A) Disclosure of Conflicts, which, more generally, requires disclosure of any potential conflict of interest in research reports and investment recommendations.

14. **C** Both market-making activities by her firm and the directorship held by a principal in the firm must be disclosed according to Standard VI(A) Disclosure of Conflicts.

15. **A** According to Standard II(A) Material Nonpublic Information, Farr is free to act under the mosaic theory because nonmaterial nonpublic information does not fall within the prohibition on trading based on material nonpublic information. He should keep detailed documentation of his analysis to prove that he did not advise or act based upon material nonpublic information.

16. **B** GIPS require firms that claim compliance to maintain written documentation of their policies and procedures for complying with GIPS. Verification of GIPS compliance is optional. In order to initially claim compliance with GIPS, a firm must have a minimum of five years (or since firm inception) of GIPS-compliant data. After the first compliant presentation, another year of compliant performance must be added each year until the compliant performance history reaches at least ten years. (Study Session 1, LOS 3.c, 4.b)

17. **C** Standard VI(C) Referral Fees states that members and candidates must disclose to employers and to affected clients, before entering into any formal agreement for services, any benefits received for the recommendation of services provided by the member.

18. **A** Michaelson has violated Standard II(A) Material Nonpublic Information. Members who possess material nonpublic information are prohibited from acting or causing others to act on that information. Since the information Michaelson received during her flight involved Collective's proposed tender offer for the shares of Network, she was in possession of material nonpublic information and should not have shared the information with others in her firm who might act on it.

19. **C** If p is the probability that an event occurs, then the odds for the event occurring are expressed as $p / (1 - p)$, or the probability that the event occurs divided by the probability that the event does not occur. The odds against the event are expressed as the reciprocal of the odds for the event. (Study Session 2, LOS 8.c)

20. **B** The investor has to ensure that the amount deposited now will grow into the amount needed to fund the perpetuity. With semiannual compounding, the effective annual rate (EAR) earned on funds in the account is:

$$EAR = \left(1 + \frac{\text{annual rate}}{2}\right)^2 - 1 = \left(1 + \frac{0.04}{2}\right)^2 - 1 = 0.0404 = 4.04\%$$

The present value of the perpetuity = $25,000/0.0404 = $618,811.88.

Note that since the first scholarship award is paid out in four years, the present value of the perpetuity represents the amount that must be in the account at time t = 3. We can find the required deposit from:

FV = –618,811.88; N = 3; I = 4.04; CPT → PV = $549,487.24 or $\dfrac{618,811.88}{1.0404^3}$

(Study Session 2, LOS 5.c, d, e)

21. **C** If a return distribution has positive excess kurtosis, statistical models that do not account for the fatter tails will underestimate the likelihood of very bad or very good outcomes. A distribution with positive skewness will have a mean greater than the median and larger average positive deviations than average negative deviations. (Study Session 2, LOS 7.j, k, l)

22. **B** When testing hypotheses about the population mean, the sample standard deviation must be used in the denominator of the test statistic when the population standard deviation is unknown, the population is normal, and/or the sample is large. The statistic is a *t*-stat with n – 1 degrees of freedom. The numerator is the sampling error for the population mean if the true mean is μ_0 and the denominator is the standard error of the sample mean around the true mean. (Study Session 3, LOS 11.f)

23. **B** Dividing the covariance between returns of two assets by the individual *standard deviations* of returns of the two assets yields the correlation coefficient. (Study Session 2, LOS 8.k)

24. **A** The data are cross-sectional, which means that it is a sample of observations taken at a single point in time. Time-series data are observations taken at specific and equally spaced points in time (for example, the monthly returns on a specific stock for the period January 1 through December 31 of a given year. The sampling error is the difference between a sample statistic (here, the mean) and the corresponding population parameter, or 10.5 – 9.7 = 0.8. The sample statistic (here, the mean) is itself a random variable and has its own probability distribution. (Study Session 3, LOS 10.d)

25. **C** Relative strength charts display the price of an asset relative to the price of another asset or benchmark over time. This type of chart is useful for demonstrating whether one asset class or market has outperformed or underperformed another. Candlestick charts and point-and-figure charts are generally used to display price patterns for a single asset or market over time. (Study Session 3, LOS 12.b,h)

26. **C** The standard deviation of two stocks that are perfectly positively correlated is the weighted average of the standard deviations: $0.5(18.9) + 0.5(14.73) = 16.82\%$. This relationship is true only when the correlation is one. Otherwise, you must use the formula:

$$\sigma_p = \sqrt{w_1^2\sigma_1^2 + w_2^2\sigma_2^2 + 2w_1w_2\sigma_1\sigma_2\rho_{1,2}}$$

(Study Session 2, LOS 8.l)

27. **C** The Sharpe measure for a portfolio is calculated as the (mean portfolio return – mean return on the risk-free asset)/portfolio standard deviation. The Sharpe measures for the three mutual funds are:

mutual fund P = (13 – 5) / 18 = 0.44
mutual fund Q = (15 – 5) / 20 = 0.50
mutual fund R = (18 – 5) / 24 = 0.54

Assuming that investors prefer return and dislike risk, they should prefer portfolios with large Sharpe ratios to those with smaller ratios. Thus, the investor should prefer mutual fund R. (Study Session 2, LOS 7.i)

28. **C** When order of selection matters, as it does here, use the permutation formula:

$$_nP_r = \frac{n!}{(n-r)!}$$

$_nP_r = 6! / (6 - 3)! = (6 \times 5 \times 4 \times 3 \times 2 \times 1) / (3 \times 2 \times 1) = (6 \times 5 \times 4) = 120$

(Study Session 2, LOS 8.o)

29. **B** The standard error of the sample mean can be estimated by dividing the population standard deviation by $\sqrt{n}$. (Study Session 3, LOS 10.e, f)

30. **B** Given that the population variance is unknown and the sample size is large, the 95% confidence interval for the population mean is:

$$\overline{x} \pm z_{\alpha/2} \frac{s}{\sqrt{n}}$$

The confidence interval is:

$$1.7 \pm 1.96\left(\frac{0.4}{\sqrt{100}}\right) = 1.7 \pm 1.96(0.04) = 1.7 \pm 0.0784 = 1.622 \text{ to } 1.778.$$

(Study Session 3, LOS 10.j)

31. **C** This is a test of the value of a single variance and is based on a test statistic with a performed via the chi-square distribution. (Study Session 3, LOS 11.i)

32. **A** The forecast resistance levels are one-half, five-eighths, and two-thirds of the price decrease from $180 to $100. All of these are Fibonacci ratios. Projecting from the breakout of an inverse head and shoulders pattern would more likely suggest a single price target or range than three different specific targets. Moving average convergence/divergence lines are unlikely to be used for price targeting because they are not on the same scale as prices. (Study Session 3, LOS 12.d, e, g)

33. **A**   Price discrimination involves a single product, not two alternatives. As long as the company faces a downward-sloping demand curve, can identify at least two groups of customers with different price elasticities of demand, and can prevent reselling between groups, the company can profit from price discrimination. (Study Session 4, LOS 16.b, d)

34. **C**   Automatic stabilizers are built-in features that tend to automatically promote a budget deficit during a recession and a budget surplus during an inflationary boom, without a change in policy. (Study Session 5, LOS 19.n)

35. **A**   Short-run equilibrium may occur above full employment, for example as a result of an increase in aggregate demand caused by a decrease in taxes. Both employment and the price level increase in the short run. Above-full employment causes upward pressure on wages that will reduce short-run aggregate supply until, in the long run, output returns to its full-employment level with a still-higher equilibrium price level. (Study Session 5, LOS 17.j)

36. **B**   A firm will increase production if its marginal revenue is greater than its marginal cost, until it reaches the profit-maximizing output level at which marginal revenue equals marginal cost. Under perfect competition, marginal revenue equals price. (Study Session 4, LOS 15.g, 16.d)

37. **A**   For the base period, three years ago, the real exchange rate is the same as the nominal exchange rate, 1.32 USD/EUR. The real exchange rate over the period has changed from 1.32 to 1.40 × (112 / 118) = 1.3288. This increase in the real USD/EUR exchange rate indicates that the base currency (EUR) has appreciated in real terms, so that eurozone goods are now more expensive in real terms to U.S. consumers. (Study Session 6, LOS 21.a)

38. **B**   There is a market equilibrium at a price of 250, where Q_S = 750 and Q_D = 750. Although the supply curve is downward sloping, the equilibrium is stable because the supply curve intersects the demand curve from above—the slope of the supply curve (−1/3) is steeper than the slope of the demand curve (−1/5). (Study Session 4, LOS 13.e)

39. **B**   Differentiated products are a feature of monopolistic competition markets. Interdependence is a characteristic of oligopoly markets. Horizontal demand curves facing producers are a feature of perfect competition. (Study Session 4, LOS 16.a)

40. **C**   The Fisher effect states that a nominal interest rate is the sum of a real interest rate and the expected inflation rate. (Study Session 5, LOS 19.e)

41. **B**   Falling money wages would cause businesses to increase (profit-maximizing) output levels at each price level for final goods and services. Changes in the price level of goods and services are represented by a movement along a short-run aggregate supply curve, not a shift in the curve. A rise in resource prices will decrease aggregate supply. An increase in government spending will shift the aggregate demand curve but not the aggregate supply curve. (Study Session 5, LOS 17.h)

42. **C**   Declines in real personal income and industrial production, which are coincident indicators, and the increase in inventories relative to sales, a lagging indicator, suggest the economy is most likely in a contraction phase. Inventory-to-sales ratios tend to increase when sales decrease unexpectedly. (Study Session 5, LOS 18.b, j)

43. **C** In a descending price or Dutch auction, the government will sell bonds to the bidders who bid the lowest yields (highest prices) until all the bonds are sold. Bidder 1 receives 200 bonds at a yield of 5.25%, Bidder 2 receives 100 bonds at a yield of 5.30%, and Bidder 3 receives the remaining 200 bonds at a yield of 5.40%. (Study Session 4, LOS 13.h)

44. **B** In the short run, the average product of labor curve is first increasing and then decreasing as diminishing marginal returns to that factor take effect. In the short run, the marginal product of labor is first increasing and then decreasing when diminishing marginal returns take effect. The marginal product of labor curve will be above the average product of labor curve initially, and, at some point, will intersect the average product curve at its maximum. When the total product of labor begins to increase at a decreasing rate, the average product of labor will be decreasing. (Study Session 4, LOS 15.j)

45. **A** The $478,000 is unearned revenue, a liability. The $2.3 million owed to the government but not yet paid is income tax payable, also a liability. Deferred tax accounts arise from temporary differences between tax reporting and financial reporting. (Study Session 7, LOS 23.a, d)

46. **C** The installment method should be used when future cash collection cannot be reasonably estimated. For long-term projects, a firm should use percentage of completion when payment is reasonably assured and the firm can reliably estimate the project's outcome, and completed contract when the firm cannot estimate the outcome reliably. (Study Session 8, LOS 25.b)

47. **C** Use the direct method.

Collections from customers	$5,000
Cash expenses	−$2,000
Cash flow from operations	$3,000

Cash expenses are given. If you had been given COGS, you would need to adjust that for inventory changes to get cash expenses for inputs. Depreciation is a non-cash change.

Changes in depreciation are used with the indirect method. Net change in cash will reflect CFI and CFF, not just CFO. (Study Session 8, LOS 27.f)

48. **B** Using the indirect method requires adjusting for change in working capital accounts such as accounts receivable, inventory, and accounts payable. (Study Session 8, LOS 27.f)

49. **C** In a period of rising prices, LIFO results in higher COGS, lower inventory balances, and lower gross profit, as compared to FIFO. In a falling price environment, these effects are the opposite. Working capital (current assets minus current liabilities) is higher under FIFO in a rising price environment because inventories are higher. (Study Session 9, LOS 29.c, e)

50. **A** Promised retirement payments from a defined benefit pension plan are an obligation of the sponsoring firm. A defined contribution plan does not promise a specific periodic payment after retirement and the firm's obligations are limited to its promised contributions to current employees' accounts. (Study Session 9, LOS 32.j)

51. **B** Operating profit margin can be read directly from a common-size income statement. Asset turnover and return on equity mix balance sheet and income statement items. (Study Session 8, LOS 25.i, j, 28.b)

52. **C** Use the Treasury stock method:

    Step 1: Determine the number of common shares created if the warrants are exercised = 100,000.

    Step 2: Calculate the cash inflow if the warrants are exercised: (100,000)($50 per share) = $5,000,000.

    Step 3: Calculate the number of shares that can be purchased with these funds using the average market price ($60 per share): 5,000,000 / 60 = 83,333 shares.

    Step 4: Calculate the net increase in common shares outstanding from the exercise of the warrants: 100,000 − 83,333 = 16,667.

    Step 5: Add the net increase in common shares from the exercise of the warrants to the number of common shares outstanding for the entire year: 1,000,000 + 16,667 = 1,016,667.

    (Study Session 8, LOS 25.g)

53. **A** Unless impairment has been recognized, land is reported at historical cost and is not subject to depreciation. Increases in value are not reflected in balance sheet values under U.S. GAAP. (Study Session 8, LOS 26.e)

54. **A** The income statement reports the amounts for each of the major line items within the general categories of revenues and expenses. The various accruals, adjustments, and management assumptions are implicit in the reported amounts but are not specifically explained in the income statement. Much of the detail contained in various accruals, adjustments, and management assumptions that go into the financial statements can be found in the footnotes to the statements and Management's Discussion and Analysis. Supplementary schedules contain additional information, including a more detailed breakdown of certain large account balances. (Study Session 7, LOS 22.c)

55. **A** The income statement shows an extraordinary item, which is permitted under U.S. GAAP but not under IFRS. From this we can conclude that the firm reports under U.S. GAAP. U.S. GAAP requires dividends received to be classified as CFO, while IFRS allows them to be classified as either CFO or CFI. A firm reporting under U.S. GAAP may not revalue assets upward but may use LIFO. (Study Session 8, LOS 25.e, 26.e, 27.c)

56. **B** The installment sales method of revenue recognition does not result in permanent differences between pretax and taxable income. Premium payments on life insurance of key employees is an expense on the financial statements, but is not deducted on tax returns. Tax exempt interest is recognized as revenue on the financial statements. These items result in permanent differences between pretax income and taxable income. (Study Session 9, LOS 31.f)

57. **C** The IASB Conceptual Framework for Financial Reporting describes the two fundamental qualitative characteristics of financial statements as relevance and faithful representation. The Conceptual Framework lists timeliness, comparability, verifiability, and understandability as characteristics that enhance relevance and faithful representation. (Study Session 7, LOS 24.d)

58. **C** For a firm using FIFO, gross profit is the same whether the firm uses a periodic or perpetual inventory system. For a firm using LIFO or average cost, gross profit can be different depending on the choice of inventory system. (Study Session 9, LOS 29.d)

59. **B**   Operating leases are not recognized as liabilities and therefore the debt-to-equity ratio will be lower than a similar finance lease. Capitalizing a lease will increase the asset base and decrease asset turnover. Lease capitalization decreases the operating cash outflow and therefore increases operating cash flows (all else equal). (Study Session 9, LOS 32.g)

60. **B**   "Pretax income" denotes earnings before taxes for financial reporting. "Taxable income" is earnings before taxes for computing taxes payable, where taxes payable refers to the actual tax liability to the government. Since taxable income is $80,000, the difference in taxes payable is ($80,000)(0.5) – ($80,000)(0.4) = $8,000. (Study Session 9, LOS 31.d)

61. **B**   A mindset that allows rationalization or justification of the fraud is the third important condition underlying accounting fraud. Poor financial controls are an example of opportunity for fraud and pressure to meet earnings expectations is a possible motive. (Study Session 10, LOS 33.c)

62. **A**   Banks often present liquidity-based balance sheets, which list all assets and liabilities in order of liquidity, because for banks this format is typically more relevant and reliable than a classified balance sheet. Firms in most other industries typically present classified balance sheets. (Study Session 8, LOS 26.c)

63. **C**   When stated on a per-share basis, different companies' financial data cannot be compared meaningfully because these ratios depend on the number of shares outstanding, which is unrelated to the companies' operating performance or profitability. A company with a $200 share price should have much higher valuation measures than a company with a $2 share price. (Study Session 8, LOS 28.e)

64. **B**   Under IFRS, when an asset is permanently impaired, it must be written down to its recoverable amount (greater of value in use or fair value less selling costs) in the period in which the impairment is recognized. (Study Session 9, LOS 30.h)

65. **A**   This is a discount bond since the market interest rate at issuance exceeds the coupon rate. The initial liability is equal to the proceeds received when the bond was issued. We can find this amount from the following calculation: FV = 50,000,000; N = 10; I = 3.5; PMT = 1,500,000; CPT → PV = $47,920,848.67. Change N to 8 and calculate PV to get liability value at the beginning of the second year of the bond's life, 48,281,511. Interest expense for the next semiannual period is 48,281,511(0.035) = $1,689,853. The subsequent change in the market rate has no effect on the amortization of the discount. (Study Session 9, LOS 32.a, b)

66. **A**   For firms that revalue assets upward, IFRS requires disclosure of the date the asset was revalued, how management determined its fair value, the asset's carrying value using the historical cost model, and (for intangible assets) whether the asset's useful life is finite or indefinite. Although assets and shareholders' equity will increase as a result of the revaluation, net income will not increase. The increase in the value of the asset is reported as a revaluation surplus in shareholders' equity. Amortization expense will not increase because indefinite-lived intangible assets are not amortized. (Study Session 9, LOS 30.e, g, j)

67. **A**   Goodwill has an indefinite life and is not amortized. A trademark or other intangible asset that has an expiration date but is renewable at minimal cost is treated as having an indefinite life and is not amortized. The patent has a finite life and its cost will be amortized at the rate of $1 million each year over ten years under the straight-line method. (Study Session 9, LOS 30.f)

68. **B** Reducing the numerator and denominator by the same amount will increase a ratio that is greater than one and decrease a ratio that is less than one. (Study Session 8, LOS 28.b)

69. **B** Selecting an external auditor (subject to shareholder approval) is a responsibility of the Board's audit committee. (Study Session 11, LOS 41.e)

70. **C** $k_{ce} = D_1/P_0 + g = (3)(1.05)/(31.50) + 0.05 = 0.15$ or 15%

$k_d(1 - t) = 10\%(1 - 0.4) = 6\%$

If the company has a debt-to-equity ratio of 0.5, it will have $0.50 in debt for each $1.00 in equity. V = debt + equity = 0.5 + 1 = 1.5. Therefore, the weight is 33.3% (0.5 / 1.5) for the debt component and 66.7% (1.0 / 1.5) for the equity component.

$$WACC = \frac{D}{V}(k_{debt})(1-t) + \left(\frac{E}{V}\right)k_s = 0.333(6.0\%) + 0.677(15\%) = 2\% + 10\% = 12\%.$$

(Study Session 11, LOS 37.h)

71. **A** The 19th space is neither an incremental cost, nor an opportunity cost or a type of cannibalization. It is a sunk cost since the firm has already committed to parking for 20 taxis. The cost of the 19th parking space is not directly relevant to the capital budgeting decision. (Study Session 11, LOS 36.b)

72. **C** Risky projects will seem relatively more attractive than they actually are, causing them to be undertaken a disproportionately high percentage of the times they are considered. (Study Session 11, LOS 37.a)

73. **C** When companies that require shareholder attendance to vote hold their meetings on the same day but in different locations, it prevents shareholders from attending all the meetings and therefore exercising their full voting rights. (Study Session 11, LOS 41.g)

74. **C** The firm should reject both projects.

	0	1	2	3	4	5	6
Project J:	−$12,000	$4,000	$5,000	$6,000			
Project K:	−$20,000	$3,000	$3,000	$3,000	$5,000	$8,000	$8,000

Project J: I/Y = 12; CF_0 = (12,000); CF_1 = 4,000; CF_2 = 5,000; CF_3 = 6,000; CPT → NPV = −172.

Project K: same process. NPV = −1,025. (Study Session 11, LOS 36.d)

75. **B** The recommended method is to treat flotation costs as a cash outflow at project initiation rather than as a component of the cost of equity. (Study Session 11, LOS 37.l)

76. **B** Given that they have the same amount of sales and Acme's receivables turnover (sales/average accounts receivable) is higher, Acme must have lower average accounts receivable than Butler. Given that they have equal quick ratios, subtracting accounts receivable from the numerators of the quick ratios of both firms will produce a cash ratio for Butler that is lower than the cash ratio for Acme. (Study Session 11, LOS 40.b)

77. **C** The book value of Daker shares is (£140 million – £85 million) / 11 million = £5 per share. Repurchasing its shares at a price equal to book value will not change the book value of Daker shares. (Study Session 11, LOS 39.e)

78. **C** The firm would not want to exhaust its capital budget on "bad" projects, (i.e., projects with IRR < cost of capital [NPV < 0]). They should continue to invest as long as the project's return is greater than the marginal cost of capital of the firm. When the project's IRR = cost of capital, the NPV = 0. This project will only make the firm larger; it will add nothing to the stock price. The investment opportunity schedule plots expected project returns from highest to lowest IRR. (Study Session 11, LOS 37.d)

79. **C** In descending order of standard deviation of returns the major U.S. asset classes over the period are small-cap stocks, large-cap stocks, long-term government bonds, long-term corporate bonds, T-bills. (Study Session 12, LOS 43.c)

80. **B** Although the risk measure on the capital market line diagram is total risk, all portfolios that lie on the CML are well diversified and have only systematic risk. This is because portfolios on the CML are all constructed from the risk-free asset and the (well-diversified) market portfolio. Any portfolio, including single securities, will plot along the SML in equilibrium. Their unsystematic risk can be significant, but it is not measured on the SML diagram because unsystematic risk is not related to expected return. Both the CML and the SML reflect relations that hold when prices are in equilibrium. (Study Session 12, LOS 44.f)

81. **A** Portfolio X has a lower expected return and a higher standard deviation than Portfolio Y. X must be inefficient. (Study Session 12, LOS 43.g)

82. **B** In addition to the three factors of the Fama and French model, market-to-book, firm size, and excess returns on the market, Carhart added a momentum factor based on prior relative price performance. (Study Session 12, LOS 44.d)

83. **A** An IPS requires an investor to consider and articulate his objectives and constraints. It also provides an objective standard by which the portfolio's performance will be judged by specifying a benchmark portfolio. Guidance for Standard III(C) Suitability requires members to prepare IPS when beginning advisory relationships with clients. Asset allocation is determined after strategy is developed and capital market conditions are assessed. (Study Session 12, LOS 42.c, 45.a)

84. **A** Stock A: k_A = 8% + 1.5(7%) = 18.5%. Because the estimated return of 18.1% is less than the required return of 18.5%, Stock A is *overvalued*.

    Stock B: k_B = 8% + 1.1(7%) = 15.7%. Because the estimated return of 15.7% equals the required return of 15.7%, Stock B is *properly valued*.

    Stock C: k_C = 8% + 0.6(7%) = 12.2%. Because the estimated return of 12.5% is greater than the required return of 12.2%, Stock C is *undervalued*. (Study Session 12, LOS 44.h)

85. **A** The price return on the index does not include cash dividends. Since the reinvested dividends will add to the number of shares of those stocks that pay dividends, Gomez's portfolio return (total return) will be higher than the price return on the index. The relative performance of high-priced and low-priced stocks does not affect this result. (Study Session 13, LOS 47.b)

86. **B** Good-till-cancelled is a validity instruction, which indicates when an order may be filled. Execution instructions include limit orders and market orders, as well as instructions regarding trade size and visibility. A clearing instruction indicates how to arrange final settlement of the trade. (Study Session 13, LOS 46.g)

87. **B** The owner of a sponsored DR share has the same voting rights and receives the same dividends as the owner of a common share of the firm. With an unsponsored DR, the depository bank retains the voting rights. A global depository receipt may be sponsored or unsponsored. (Study Session 14, LOS 49.d)

88. **A** Peer groups should include comparable companies with similar business activities. An analyst can appropriately include a company in multiple peer groups if the company's business activities are comparable to firms in more than one peer group. (Study Session 14, LOS 50.d)

89. **A** dividend payout = 1 − earnings retention rate = 1 − 0.6 = 0.4

    $$R_S = R_f + \beta(R_{mkt} - RFR) = 0.05 + 1.0(0.10 - 0.05) = 0.10$$

    g = (retention rate)(ROE) = (0.6)(0.10) = 0.06

    $$P/E = \frac{\text{dividend payout}}{k - g} = \frac{0.4}{0.10 - 0.06} = 10$$

    price = (E)(P/E) = (2)(10) = $20

    Alternatively, dividend will be 40% of $2 earnings or $0.80, and $\dfrac{0.80}{0.10 - 0.06} = \$20$

    (Study Session 8, LOS 28.e, and Study Session 14, LOS 51.e)

90. **C** g = (retention rate)(ROE); retention rate = 1 − payout ratio = 1 − 0.55 = 0.45

    $$P/E = \frac{\text{dividend payout}}{k - g} = \frac{0.55}{0.12 - (0.45)(0.15)} = \frac{0.55}{0.12 - 0.0675} = 10.48$$

    price = (E)(P/E) = $4.00(10.48) = $41.92

    (Study Session 8, LOS 28.e, Study Session 14, LOS 51.e)

91. **C** Security market indexes may be used as benchmarks for the performance of active managers, but the index chosen should represent the universe of securities from which the manager is choosing. Here, an index of high yield bonds would be a more appropriate benchmark. (Study Session 13, LOS 47.g)

92. **C** While an increase in a firm's ROE due to a sharp increase in earnings will, if unexpected, lead to an increase in the intrinsic value of its shares, an increase in a firm's ROE due to the repurchase of stock with debt will not necessarily increase the intrinsic value of the firm's shares, as any increase in ROE may be offset by an increase in the risk inherent in the firm's shares. (Study Session 14, LOS 49.h)

93. **C** The short seller loses if the stock price increases. The other choices are accurate statements. (Study Session 13, LOS 46.e)

94. **B** Bond indexes are more difficult to build and maintain than stock indexes for several reasons. Bonds in an index have to be replaced as they mature, so turnover is likely to be greater in a bond index than in a stock index. Many bonds lack the continuous trade data that exists for exchange-traded equities. (Study Session 13, LOS 47.i)

95. **B** You can select the correct answer without calculating the share values. Royal is using a shorter period of supernormal growth and a higher required rate of return on the stock. Both of these factors will contribute to a lower value using the multistage DDM.

    Knight: $\dfrac{\$1(1.10)}{1.09} + \dfrac{\$1(1.10)^2}{1.09^2} + \dfrac{\$1(1.10)^3 / (0.09 - 0.04)}{1.09^2} = \$24.43$

    Royal: $\dfrac{\$1(1.10)}{1.10} + \dfrac{\$1(1.10)^2 / (0.10 - 0.04)}{1.10} = \$19.33$

    Royal's valuation is $5.10 less that Knight's valuation. (Study Session 14, LOS 51.e)

96. **B** An industry in the growth stage is usually characterized by increasing profitability, decreasing prices, and a low degree of competition among competitors. (Study Session 14, LOS 50.h)

97. **B** The market value of the Treasury note is the present value of the remaining coupons plus the present value of the principal, discounted at the semiannual rates available from dividing each annual spot rate in the table by two.

    value of T-note = $\dfrac{\$25}{(1.015)} + \dfrac{\$25}{(1.0175)^2} + \dfrac{\$25}{(1.02)^3} + \dfrac{\$1,025}{(1.0225)^4} = \$1,010.05$

    At $1,008, the T-note is priced below the present value of its cash flows ($1,010) and is therefore underpriced. (Study Session 16, LOS 56.f)

98. **B** An issuer of a callable bond must compensate the bondholder when the issue is sold by offering a higher coupon rate or accepting a lower price than if the call feature was not included. Convexity will typically be much less than for an option-free bond, and reinvestment risk is greater for callable bonds. (Study Session 15, LOS 53.h)

99. **C** The bond equivalent yield rate on the par bond (Z) is 6% or a 3% semiannual rate. The equivalent quarterly rate, $1.03^{1/2} - 1 = 0.014889$. Security X makes 20 quarterly payments of $15 and 20 quarterly payments of $20. We need to use the cash flow function as follows: $CF_0 = 0$; $CF_1 = 15$; $F_1 = 20$; $CF_2 = 20$; $F_2 = 19$; $CF_3 = 1,020$; $F_3 = 1$; $I = 1.4889$; CPT $\rightarrow$ NPV = $1,067.27. Note that CF_3 contains the final quarterly payment of $20 along with the $1,000 face value payment. (Study Session 16, LOS 56.c)

100. **C** Yield spreads reflect the credit quality of bond issuers and the liquidity of the market for their bonds. Narrowing (decreasing) yield spreads reflect improving credit quality or more liquidity. Widening (increasing) yield spreads reflect deteriorating credit quality or less liquidity. Increased estimates of the recovery rate in the event of default represent an improvement in investors' assessment of the issuer's credit quality and are likely to narrow yield spreads on the issuer's bonds. (Study Session 16, LOS 59.a)

101. **A** The full price is clean price plus accrued interest. (Study Session 15, LOS 52.c)

102. **B** The issuer may deliver either cash or bonds to the trustee. Specific bonds to be redeemed are not typically identified in advance. Companies would retire through the delivery of securities if yields have increased. (Study Session 15, LOS 52.d,e)

103. **B** Restricted subsidiaries are those whose cash flows and assets are designated to service the debt of their holding company. Classifying a subsidiary as restricted alleviates structural subordination by making holding company debt rank pari passu with the subsidiary's debt. (Study Session 16, LOS 59.j)

104. **B** Calculate the new bond prices at the 50 basis point change in rates both up or down and then plug into the effective duration equation:

current price: N = 50; FV = 1,000; PMT = (0.075/2)1,000 = 37.50; I/Y = 4.625; CPT → PV = $830.54

+50 basis pts: N = 50; FV = 1,000; PMT = (0.075/2)1,000 = 37.50; I/Y = 4.875; CPT → PV = $790.59

−50 basis pts: N = 50; FV = 1,000; PMT = (0.075/2)1,000 = 37.50; I/Y = 4.375; CPT → PV = $873.93.

$$D_{effective} = \frac{V_- - V_+}{2V_0 \Delta y} = \frac{\$873.93 - \$790.59}{2(830.54)(0.005)} = 10.03$$

(Study Session 16, LOS 58.d)

105. **B** [1 + 7.48 (0.0075)] 1,018 = $1,075 (Study Session 15, LOS 53.f)

106. **B** Inflation adjustments to principal are made semiannually. The coupon rate is fixed. Inflation adjustments make the yields on TIPS good estimates of their real returns. (Study Session 15, LOS 54.b)

107. **C** With YTM = 10.45% (I/Y = 5.225), PMT = 40, N = 24, FV = 1,000, PV = $834.61. With YTM = 10.07% (I/Y = 5.035), PV = $857.67, an increase of $23.06. (Study Session 15, LOS 53.f)

108. **A** If we want the 3-year forward rate in three years, the appropriate formula is:

$$_3f_3 = \left[\frac{(1+z_6)^6}{(1+z_3)^3} \right]^{1/3} - 1$$

z_6 = 6-year spot rate and z_3 = 3-year spot rate. (Study Session 16, LOS 57.g)

109. **A** The call benefits the issuer, so a bondholder will require a higher yield on a callable bond, while the put option has value to the bondholder. Therefore a callable bond will have a higher yield spread to Treasuries than an otherwise identical putable bond. Other things equal, a bond with less liquidity will have a higher spread to Treasuries than a bond with more liquidity. Smaller issue size is associated with less liquidity. (Study Session 15, LOS 55.g, h)

110. **A** This question does not require calculations. Because the return on reinvested coupon interest is less than the note's yield to maturity, the investor's realized yield on the note must be less than the YTM. Only Choice A can be correct. (Study Session 16, LOS 57.c)

111. **A** Powers is betting that the stock's price will not rise above $50. If she's right, she will pocket the $3.50 and lose nothing. If the stock rises above the strike price, she is losing all of the upside potential. Once the stock price rises above $53.50, the benefit of the strategy (i.e., the income generated by the option premium) is offset by the gain she has foregone on the stock. (Study Session 17, LOS 65.b)

112. **A** The forward contract price is $\left[1-\left(0.0185\times\dfrac{81}{360}\right)\right]\times\$20,000,000 = \$19,916,750$.

The market price at settlement is $\left[1-\left(0.0195\times\dfrac{81}{360}\right)\right]\times\$20,000,000 = \$19,912,250$.

The long will pay $19,916,750 – $19,912,250 = $4,500.

Alternatively, $0.001\left(\dfrac{81}{360}\right)\times\$20,000,000 = \$4,500$.

(Study Session 17, LOS 61.d)

113. **C** For most options with values greater than zero, a longer time to expiration makes an option more valuable than an otherwise identical option with a shorter time to expiration. One exception is an in-the-money European style put, which under certain conditions (low volatility, high interest rate) can have a lower value than an otherwise identical put with a shorter time to expiration. For both American and European style options, a call with a lower exercise price will be more valuable than an otherwise identical call with a higher exercise price, and a put with a higher exercise price will have more value than a put with a lower exercise price. (Study Session 17, LOS 63.l)

114. **C** Over-the-counter derivatives are customized private contracts between counterparties. (Study Session 17, LOS 60.a)

115. **B** The price (or premium) of an option is its intrinsic value plus its time value. An out-of-the-money option has an intrinsic value of zero, so its entire premium consists of time value. Time value is zero at an option's expiration date. Time value is the amount by which an option's premium exceeds its intrinsic value. (Study Session 17, LOS 63.i)

116. **A** While Treasury securities are never at risk to default, forward contracts have default risk because the counterparty may default. The short has delivery options with T-bond futures, not a T-bill forward contract. The forward contract locks in a purchase price, which will not change regardless of the bill's performance. (Study Session 17, LOS 61.a)

117. **B** Macro strategy funds invest based on expected shifts of global economies, primarily in currency and interest rate derivatives. Quantitative directional funds take long and short positions in equities based on technical analysis. Event-driven funds seek to profit from investment strategies based on specific corporate events and one-time transactions. (Study Session 18, LOS 66.d)

118. **A** One of the ways to invest in real estate is by purchasing residential or commercial mortgage-backed securities. (Study Session 18, LOS 66.b)

119. **A** If a fund calculates a trading NAV, it will adjust market prices downward for securities in which it holds positions that are large relative to trading volume or total value outstanding and thus are less liquid. (Study Session 18, LOS 66.e)

120. **B** In the context of an LBO, mezzanine financing refers to debt that carries warrants or equity conversion features. This debt is typically subordinated to other bonds that are issued to finance the LBO. Committed capital is the investment of limited partners in a private equity fund and does not include debt that the fund issues to finance a particular LBO. (Study Session 18, LOS 66.d)

EXAM 1
AFTERNOON SESSION ANSWER KEY

To get valuable feedback on how your score compares to those of other Level I candidates, use your Username and Password to gain Online Access at schweser.com and choose the left-hand menu item "Practice Exams Vol. 1."

1. C	31. B	61. C	91. C
2. A	32. B	62. C	92. B
3. A	33. C	63. A	93. B
4. C	34. C	64. B	94. A
5. A	35. A	65. C	95. B
6. B	36. B	66. A	96. C
7. B	37. A	67. C	97. B
8. A	38. B	68. B	98. A
9. B	39. B	69. A	99. A
10. B	40. C	70. B	100. B
11. A	41. A	71. B	101. B
12. A	42. C	72. C	102. B
13. C	43. B	73. B	103. C
14. C	44. B	74. A	104. C
15. C	45. C	75. A	105. C
16. B	46. C	76. A	106. B
17. C	47. B	77. C	107. B
18. B	48. C	78. C	108. C
19. B	49. C	79. C	109. B
20. C	50. B	80. C	110. C
21. B	51. A	81. A	111. B
22. A	52. A	82. B	112. A
23. A	53. B	83. B	113. C
24. B	54. A	84. B	114. A
25. A	55. B	85. B	115. B
26. A	56. C	86. A	116. C
27. B	57. C	87. C	117. B
28. C	58. A	88. A	118. A
29. C	59. A	89. A	119. A
30. A	60. B	90. A	120. C

EXAM 1
AFTERNOON SESSION ANSWERS

Answers referencing the Standards of Practice address Study Session 1, LOS 1.b, c and LOS 2.a, b, c, except where noted.

1. **C** Standard VI(C) Referral Fees requires members and candidates to disclose to clients and prospects any consideration or benefit received by the member or delivered to others for the recommendation of any service to the client or prospect. This allows the client to evaluate possible bias in referrals.

2. **A** Standard IV(C) Responsibilities of Supervisors explicitly states that speaking to the employee to determine the extent of the violations and receiving assurances that it will not be repeated is not enough. Finley must take positive steps to insure that the violation will not be repeated, including promptly launching an investigation and limiting the employee's activities and/or increasing supervision of the employee until the results of the investigation are known.

3. **A** Stein violated Standard I(C) Misrepresentation by presenting material developed by another to her supervisor without disclosing that the work was not her own.

4. **C** Standard V(A) Diligence and Reasonable Basis. The recommendation reflects the consensus of the group and not necessarily the opinion of the member or candidate. If the consensus opinion has a reasonable basis, the member does not have to dissociate from the report but should document the difference of opinion.

5. **A** Under Standard IV(C) Responsibilities of Supervisors, if Klein clearly cannot discharge supervisory responsibilities because of an inadequate compliance system, he should decline in writing to accept the supervisory responsibility until the firm adopts reasonable procedures to allow him to adequately exercise such responsibility.

6. **B** Standard III(A) Loyalty, Prudence, and Care. Crocker is essentially using a soft-dollar arrangement to pay for research used in managing her clients' accounts. Crocker may pay higher fees without violating her fiduciary duty as long as (1) the commission paid is reasonable in relation to the research and execution of services received and (2) the research benefits the firm's clients.

7. **B** Standard IV(A) Loyalty does not prohibit former employees from contacting clients of their pervious firm so long as the contact information does not come from the records of the previous employer or violate a non-compete agreement.

8. **A** Houser has not violated the Code and Standards. Guidance for Standard II(A) Material Nonpublic Information states that an analyst does not need to make his recommendations public just because investors would want to know about them, and is free to issue recommendations only to his clients. The guideline about what makes information material (i.e., investors would want to have the information before making an investment decision) applies to nonpublic information from the issuer of a security. An analyst covering the security, however, is not an insider with the issuing firm.

9. **B** To comply with Standard VI(A) Disclosure of Conflicts, members and candidates must make full disclosure of all matters that could impair their independence. Sell-side members and candidates should disclose to their clients any ownership in a security that they are recommending.

10. **B** According to Standard IV(B) Additional Compensation Arrangements, members and candidates must obtain written permission from their employer before accepting an offer of compensation (for the performance of work done for their employer) in addition to what they receive from their employer and that is contingent on future performance. Payment to investment bankers to complete an underwriting is standard business practice.

11. **A** Compliance requires that the firm follow local law and disclose the conflict between local law and GIPS. (Study Session 1, LOS 4.c)

12. **A** Standard III(D) Performance Presentation requires that statements about performance be not only accurate but also fair and complete. While Vance's statement may be accurate in a technical sense, it is neither fair nor complete, and it seems intended to mislead prospects about Vance's track record in managing equities accounts and/or selecting equity securities. While compliance with GIPS and its methods of composite construction are recommended, they are not required by the Standards.

13. **C** Drake is in violation of Standard V(B) Communication with Clients and Prospective Clients. Brief communications must be supported by background reports or data that can be made available to the client if requested. Drake should have given the client a more detailed analysis of the investment when the client called to request such information. Drake did not violate Standard III(C) Suitability because he thoroughly read and evaluated the analysis and determined that the structured product was in line with his client's objectives before recommending the product to his client.

14. **C** Farley is in violation of Standard VI(B) Priority of Transactions. Client transactions must take precedence over members' or candidates' trades. He should have submitted his personal trade order only after trading for his client. Standard III(B) Fair Dealing requires that Farley deal fairly with all clients when recommending securities or taking investment action. Since the endowment fund is Farley's only account, he has not disadvantaged any other client by only taking action on the behalf of the endowment.

15. **C** Under Standard III(A) Loyalty, Prudence, and Care, members and candidates must comply with their fiduciary duty to those persons and interests by whom the duty is owed. Specifically, members must always act for the benefit of their clients and place clients' interests before their own. Murphy's actions in directing trades to Casanova violate the fiduciary duty owed to Wellington & Worrel's clients, as he appears to be selecting Casanova for the discounts received on personal securities transactions. Casanova charges higher commission rates and delivers poorer execution than other brokers used by the firm. By using Casanova, Murphy violates his fiduciary duty by failing to act in the clients' best interest. Alternatively, the arrangement with Cedrock appears to comply with Murphy's fiduciary duty, as the firm receives investment research used in managing client portfolios (a soft-dollar arrangement) and achieves better execution for client trades. Because the trading arrangement with Cedrock benefits clients, it does not violate Standard III(A).

16. **B**   Dodd has most likely violated Standard III(B) Fair Dealing by giving Phillips an overgenerous allocation of the oversubscribed ("hot") new issue. The issue is not that he is offering compensation to a client to resolve a dispute, but that by overallocating the IPO shares to Phillips he is not treating his other clients fairly. Standard III(B) Fair Dealing requires that candidates and members not use shares of "hot issues" as an incentive to achieve a reward or benefit. The benefit in this case is that the dispute will "go away."

17. **C**   The nine major sections of the CFA Institute Global Investment Performance Standards are Fundamentals of Compliance, Input Data, Calculation Methodology, Composite Construction, Disclosures, Presentation and Reporting, Real Estate, Private Equity, and Wrap Fee/Separately Managed Account (SMA) Portfolios. (Study Session 1, LOS 4.d)

18. **B**   Standard III(C) Suitability requires that the client portfolio fit the client risk and return objectives as stated in the investment policy statement, and that seems to be the case here. The proper focus of risk analysis is on the entire portfolio and need not be applied on an issue-by-issue basis. There appears to be no violation of V(A) Diligence and Reasonable Basis since his previous analysis indicated the portfolio was suitable and his records supported that conclusion.

19. **B**   With no interest paid on the original $5,000 loan, at 6% in five years the loan balance will be:

New loan balance = $5,000(1.06)^5 = $6,691.13$ or PV = 5,000; I/Y = 6; N = 5; PMT = 0; CPT $\rightarrow$ FV = $-$6,691.13.

$6,691.13 is the loan that has to be retired over the next five years. The financial calculator solution is:

PV = 6,691.13; I/Y = 6; N = 5; FV = 0; CPT $\rightarrow$ PMT. You obtain PMT = $-$1,588.45. (Study Session 2, LOS 5.e)

20. **C**   N = 4; PMT = 0; PV = $-$4,000; FV = 6,520; CPT $\rightarrow$ I/Y = 12.99%,

or $\left(\dfrac{6{,}520}{4{,}000}\right)^{1/4} - 1 = 12.99\%$.

The question asks for the *effective* annual rate and gives the beginning and ending values. That the ending value was arrived at by monthly compounding is not relevant. (Study Session 2, LOS 5.c)

21. **B**   Choice A describes a histogram, and Choice C describes a frequency polygon. (Study Session 2, LOS 7.d)

22. **A**   holding period return (HPR) = $\dfrac{\text{ending value} + \text{dividends}}{\text{beginning value}} - 1$

$HPR = \dfrac{10 + 50 + 105 + 2 + 4}{20 + 40 + 100} - 1 = 0.06875 = 6.875\%$

(Study Session 2, LOS 6.c, 7.e)

23. **A**   Calculate the mean: $\dfrac{25+15+35+45+55}{5}=35$. To get the mean absolute deviation,

   sum the deviations around the mean (ignoring the sign), and divide by the number of

   observations $=\dfrac{10+20+0+10+20}{5}=12$. (Study Session 2, LOS 7.g)

24. **B** $\text{mean}=\dfrac{5+10+15}{3}=10$

   $\text{population standard deviation}=\sqrt{\dfrac{(5-10)^2+(10-10)^2+(15-10)^2}{3}}=4.0825$

   $\text{CV}=\dfrac{\text{standard deviation}}{\text{mean}}=\dfrac{4.0825}{10}=0.408$

   (Study Session 2, LOS 7.i)

25. **A**   For the positively skewed distribution, the mode is less than the median, which is less than the mean. (Study Session 2, LOS 7.k)

26. **A**   The probability of surviving to the end of the fifth year is the product of the probabilities of surviving in each year, or one minus the probability of failure. Therefore, the 5-year survival probability is $(1 - 0.25) (1 - 0.20) (1 - 0.20) (1 - 0.15) (1 - 0.10)$ $= 0.3672$.

   The present value of the expected payoff is $\dfrac{\$20,000(0.3672)}{1.25^5}=\$2,407$.

   (Study Session 2, LOS 8.i)

27. **B**   The first year account return was $\dfrac{55}{42}-1=31\%$. The second year return was

   $\dfrac{54}{55}-1=-1.8\%$. The geometric mean is $(1.31\times0.982)^{\frac{1}{2}}-1=13.4\%$, which is the

   time-weighted return. Since only one asset was involved, $\left(\dfrac{54}{42}\right)^{\frac{1}{2}}-1=13.4\%$ also gives

   the time-weighted return. To calculate the money-weighted return, use the cash flow function with Cf0 = −42,000, Cf1 = −55,000, and Cf2 = 54,000 × 2 = 108,000, and compute IRR, which is 7.73%. The money-weighted return is lower because the amount in the account was greater in the second period, when the return was poor. (Study Session 2, LOS 6.d)

28. **C**   The binomial distribution is a discrete distribution, while the normal distribution is an example of a continuous distribution. Univariate distributions can be discrete or continuous. (Study Session 3, LOS 9.a)

29. **C**   About 68% of all observations fall within ±1 standard deviation of the mean. Thus, about 68% of the values fall between 5 and 25. (Study Session 3, LOS 9.m)

30. **A**   The central limit theorem holds for any distribution as long as the sample size is large (i.e., n > 30). (Study Session 3, LOS 10.e)

31. **B**   The population variance is known (in this case 100), so the standard error of the sample

   mean is $\dfrac{\sigma}{\sqrt{n}}=\dfrac{\sqrt{100}}{\sqrt{225}}=\dfrac{10}{15}=0.67$. (Study Session 3, LOS 10.f)

32. **B** The *t*-test must be used when the sample size is small, the population is normal, and the population variance is unknown. If the population is non-normal and the variance is unknown, there is no valid test statistic when the sample is small. (Study Session 3, LOS 11.c, e, f)

33. **C** Increased government borrowing would decrease, not increase, the profitability of corporate investment projects since it will tend to increase interest rates and required rates of return in general. (Study Session 5, LOS 19.p)

34. **C** If the domestic government collects the full value of the import license, a quota can have the same economic result as a tariff. Quota rents are the gains to those foreign exporters who receive import licenses under a quota if the domestic government does not charge for the import licenses. With respect to the importing country, import quotas, tariffs, and voluntary export restraints all decrease consumer surplus and increase producer surplus. (Study Session 6, LOS 20.e)

35. **A** The price coefficient of a complement in a demand function is negative. This means a decrease in the price of a complement to a good will increase the quantity demanded of that good. (Study Session 4, LOS 13.b)

36. **B** The manager's investment decisions are most consistent with expectations of a recessionary gap. In a recession, commodity prices and interest rates are likely to decrease. Decreasing interest rates should increase the prices of high-quality bonds. An inflationary gap would likely cause interest rates to increase, which would decrease bond prices. An inflationary gap or stagflation conditions would likely result in increasing commodity prices. (Study Session 5, LOS 17.i)

37. **A** The long-run production decision differs from the short-run production decision in that fixed costs can be changed in the long run but not the short run. Thus, short-run cost curves apply for a given size of a plant, and long-run cost curves can show costs for different size plants. (Study Session 4, LOS 15.h)

38. **B** To calculate the cross price elasticity of the quantity demanded of gasoline with respect to the price of bus travel, we must first calculate the quantity of gas demanded:

    $300 - 14(1.5) + 2(12) = 303$

    The cross elasticity is:

    $$\frac{\Delta Q_D}{\Delta P_{bus}} \times \frac{P_{bus}}{Q_D} = 2 \times \left(\frac{12}{303} \right) = 0.0792 \text{ or } 0.08$$

    (Study Session 4, LOS 13.l)

39. **B** In some cases, a monopolist may be unable to sell for a profit. Price may be insufficient to cover the per-unit cost of the monopolist, even when operating at the MR = MC rate of output. The monopolist faces a downward-sloping demand curve. (Study Session 4, LOS 16.a, b, d)

40. **C** These conditions characterize *monopolistic competition*. By contrast, monopolies and oligopolies have high barriers to entry and involve either a single seller (monopoly) or a small number of interdependent sellers (oligopoly). Similar to monopolistic competition, pure competition involves a large number of independent sellers. With pure competition, products are homogeneous (not differentiated), no barriers to entry exist (not low barriers to entry), and the demand schedule is horizontal (not downward sloping) and perfectly elastic (not highly elastic). (Study Session 4, LOS 16.h)

41. **A**   Both processes require repeated expansionary policy actions to result in inflation. The demand-pull inflation process originates with an increase in aggregate demand from either expansion of the money supply or an increase in the federal deficit when the economy is already at its full-employment level. Persistent increases in the price level (inflation) will only result if policy makers repeatedly attempt to increase real GDP above the full-employment level through monetary or fiscal expansion. Although cost-push inflation originates with an increase in the price of an important productive resource, it only results in inflation if the monetary authorities repeatedly increase the money supply to counteract the (short-term) reductions in real GDP that result from further increases in the price of the productive input. (Study Session 5, LOS 18.h)

42. **C**   Accounting profit is often an unsatisfactory performance measure from an economic point of view because accounting costs generally do not include the opportunity costs of equity capital. Accounting costs do reflect the cost of depreciation. (Study Session 4, LOS 15.a)

43. **B**   Arbitrage-free forward = 2.875 WSC/BDR × [(1 + 0.015 / 2) / (1 + 0.03 / 2)] = 2.8538 WSC/BDR. (Study Session 6, LOS 21.g)

44. **B**   At a minimum wage above the equilibrium wage, there will be an excess supply of workers. Firms substitute other productive resources for labor and use more than the economically efficient amount of capital. The result is increased unemployment and a decrease in economic efficiency. Firms may decrease the quality or quantity of the non-monetary benefits they previously offered to workers. (Study Session 4, LOS 13.j, k)

45. **C**   Paying off accounts payable from cash lowers current assets and current liabilities by the same amount. Because the current ratio started off above 1, the current ratio will increase. Because the quick ratio started off less than 1, it will decrease further. The other choices are incorrect. Buying fixed assets on credit decreases both ratios because the denominator increases, with no change to the numerator. Using cash to purchase inventory would result in no change in the current ratio but would decrease the quick ratio by decreasing the numerator. (Study Session 8, LOS 26.g, 28.b)

46. **C**   cash conversion cycle (CCC) = days of sales outstanding + days of inventory on hand – number of days of payables

$$\text{number of days of payables} = \frac{365}{\text{payables turnover}} = \frac{365}{11} = 33.18 \text{ days}; \quad \frac{365}{10} = 36.5 \text{ days}$$

Since the payables payment period increases by 3.32 days and receivables days increases by 5, CCC increases by 1.68 days. (Study Session 8, LOS 28.b)

47. **B**   Inventory turnover is cost of goods sold divided by average inventory. A manager who wishes to manipulate earnings or the balance sheet to show improvement in this ratio can either understate inventories, which would understate working capital and total assets, or overstate cost of goods sold, which would understate earnings. (Study Session 9, LOS 29.h; Study Session 10, LOS 33.a)

48. **C**   The three objectives of financial market regulation according to IOSCO are to (1) protect investors; (2) ensure the fairness, efficiency, and transparency of markets; and (3) reduce systemic risk. Because of the increasing globalization of securities markets, IOSCO seeks to attain uniform financial regulations across countries. (Study Session 7, LOS 24.b)

49. **C**   Sales revenue for which the product or service has yet to be delivered gives rise to a liability account, unearned revenue. This liability will be reduced as the product or service is actually delivered. (Study Session 8, LOS 26.e)

50. **B**

Sales	+$4,000		
Cash received from customers		+$4,000	(since no change in AR)
Cost of goods sold	−2,000		
Increase in inventory	−100		
Increase in accounts payable	+300		
Other cash input expenses	−500		
Cash paid for inputs		−2,300	
Cash paid for taxes		−200	
Cash flow from operations		+1,500	

(Study Session 8, LOS 27.f)

51. **A**   The analyst should add the U.S. GAAP firm's LIFO reserve to its balance sheet inventory and subtract the change in the LIFO reserve from its cost of goods sold. This adjustment will increase the firm's total assets and change its pretax income, income taxes, net income, and retained earnings (increasing them if the LIFO reserve increased, or decreasing them if the LIFO reserve decreased). These adjustments will change the firm's debt-to-equity ratio by changing total equity, and change the cash conversion cycle by changing inventories. The adjustments do not change current liabilities or current assets other than inventories, so the quick ratio is not affected. (Study Session 8, LOS 28.b, c and Study Session 10, LOS 35.e)

52. **A**   The required disclosures for long-lived assets under IFRS are more extensive than they are under U.S. GAAP. IFRS requires a reconciliation of beginning and ending carrying values for classes of long-lived tangible assets, while U.S. GAAP does not. (Study Session 9, LOS 30.j)

53. **B** $\text{ROE} = \dfrac{\text{net income}}{\text{equity}} = \dfrac{0.16(1,500)}{(1-0.40)(2,000)} = 0.20$, or 20%

   If the debt ratio (TD/TA) is equal to 40% and the firm has no preferred stock, the percentage of equity is $1 - 0.40$, or 60%. (Study Session 8, LOS 28.b)

54. **A**   Shares issued post-split need not be adjusted for the split as they are already "new" shares. Options with an exercise price greater than the average share price do not affect diluted EPS. (Study Session 8, LOS 25.g)

55. **B**   Diluted EPS uses average price. Since the average price is greater than the exercise price, the warrants are dilutive.

   $$\frac{60-50}{60} \times 1,000,000 = 166,667$$

   (Study Session 8, LOS 25.g, h)

56. **C** The cash conversion cycle is (365/6) + (365/9) − (365/12) = 60.8 + 40.6 − 30.4 = 71 days. ROA is lower than ROE when net income is positive and debt is present. Just the fact that a company has a high gross profit margin does not necessarily mean it will have a high net profit margin. For example, the company could have very high operating expenses and end up with a low net profit margin. (Study Session 8, LOS 28.b)

57. **C** Prior service costs arise when changes in the terms of a defined benefit pension plan increase the future benefits due to employees based on their prior employment with the company. (Study Session 9, LOS 32.k)

58. **A** FIFO COGS:

100 @ $210	= $21,000
70 @ $225	= $15,750
	$36,750

LIFO ending inventory:

Purchases	190
Sales	170
Balance	20 @ $210 = $4,200 (Study Session 9, LOS 29.c)

59. **A** Straight-line depreciation: $14 million / 7 = $2.0 million

Accelerated depreciation: $14 million × 0.333 = $4.662 million

Difference in depreciation: $4.662 million − $2.0 million =	$2.662 million
× Tax rate	0.35
Increase in deferred tax liability	$931,700

(Study Session 9, LOS 31.d)

60. **B** Depreciation methods are an example of a difference that may require an analyst to adjust financial statements to make them comparable. Acquisition goodwill is treated the same way under IFRS and U.S. GAAP: it is not amortized but is tested for impairment at least annually. Securities held for trading are reported at fair value with unrealized gains and losses reported on the income statement. (Study Session 10, LOS 35.e)

61. **C** Unrealized gains and losses on securities held for trading are included in net income. Unrealized gains and losses on securities available for sale are not reported in net income but are included in comprehensive income. Net income will show a $2 million loss from the securities held for trading. Shareholders' equity will reflect this loss as well as the $3 million unrealized gain from securities available for sale, for a net increase of $1 million. (Study Session 8, LOS 25.l)

62. **C** This transaction results in a reduction of debt and an increase in equity. However, since no cash is involved, it is not reported as a financing activity in the cash flow statement, but will be disclosed in the notes to the cash flow statement. (Study Session 8, LOS 27.b)

63. **A** Operating lease payments distinguish the fixed charge coverage ratio from the interest coverage ratio. The fixed charge coverage ratio is decreasing at the same time the interest coverage ratio is increasing, which means the company's operating lease payments are increasing. (Note that the years are presented right-to-left.) The increasing interest coverage ratio suggests earnings before interest and taxes are increasing more (or decreasing less) than the interest payments on the company's debt. The debt-to-capital ratio is essentially unchanged in the period shown, which implies that the company has not changed its capital structure significantly. (Study Session 8, LOS 28.b, c and Study Session 9, LOS 32.l)

64. **B** Cash flows are no different under the percentage-of-completion method compared with the completed-contract method. Income statement and balance sheet accounts will differ between the two firms. (Study Session 8, LOS 25.b)

65. **C** A specific explanatory paragraph that makes reference to (questions) the going concern assumption may be a signal of serious problems and call for close examination by the analyst. Therefore, in the absence of such a paragraph, there is no need for a close examination of the going concern assumption by the analyst. The objective of an audit is to enable the auditor to provide an opinion on the fairness and reliability of the financial statements. This is not the same as numerical accuracy. The auditor generally only provides reasonable assurance that there are no material errors in the financial statements, not an opinion about their numerical accuracy. An independent certified public accounting firm must be appointed by the audit committee of the company's board of directors, not by its management. Appointment of the auditors by management would reduce the level of perceived independence. (Study Session 7, LOS 22.d and Study Session 11, LOS 41.e)

66. **A** For growing firms, capitalizing results in higher net income compared to expensing. A capitalizing company classifies the costs of the capitalized assets as CFI outflows, while a company that expenses these costs classifies them as CFO outflows. Thus, Alfred's CFO will be higher and CFI lower than Canute's. Working capital is unaffected by the decision to capitalize or expense because the decision does not affect current assets or current liabilities. (Study Session 9, LOS 30.a)

67. **C** Accrued wages should be recorded as a liability (wages payable). Failing to record a liability for accrued wages will understate wage expense, which leads to an overstatement of net income. Since net income is overstated, retained earnings and owners' equity are both overstated. Assets are unaffected. (Study Session 7, LOS 23.e)

68. **B** When the PV of the lease payments is greater than the carrying value of an asset, the lessor records an immediate gross profit on sale equal to the excess of the PV over the carrying value, and the lease is termed a sales-type lease, not a direct financing lease. (Study Session 9, LOS 32.g)

69. **A** Since at breakeven sales, fixed costs + variable costs = revenue, variable costs for Rodgers at sales of $5 million must be $5 million – $2 million = $3 million, or 60% of sales. With sales of $7 million, variable costs are 0.6 × 7 million = 4.2 million. Operating income is then 7 million – 4.2 million – 2 million = $800,000.

    By assuming some arbitrary price for the product such as $1,000, this problem can be solved in units as well. Variable costs would be $600 per unit and operating income would be 7,000 (1,000 – 600) – 2 million = $800,000. (Study Session 11, LOS 38.e)

©2012 Kaplan, Inc.

70. **B**   The weights used to calculate WACC should be based on the firm's target capital structure. If the company does not provide information about its target capital structure, an analyst can use the company's current capital structure or the average capital structure weights for the industry. Similar size is not enough for the average weights for other companies to be relevant if those companies are not in the same industry. (Study Session 11, LOS 37.c)

71. **B**   Information is typically not available to compare the aging of receivables between companies, among groups of companies, or within an industry. Receivables turnover can be calculated from the balance sheet. An aging schedule shows either the absolute or percentage amount of accounts receivable that are current and that are past due by various lengths of time. (Study Session 11, LOS 40.f)

72. **C**   Klepp is incorrect about both consulting contracts for Board members and Board members' use of company assets. Either practice is likely to compromise the independence of Board members and their incentive to act in shareholders' best interests. A strong corporate code of ethics should discourage such forms of compensation to Board members. (Study Session 11, LOS 41.f)

73. **B**   No calculation is necessary. Assuming the tax treatment of the two alternatives is the same, a share repurchase results in the same shareholder wealth as a cash dividend payment of an equal amount. (Study Session 11, LOS 39.f)

74. **A**   Since the net present value of the five projects is the expected increase in firm value from undertaking the projects, maximizing the NPV of the projects chosen will result in the selection of the optimal group of five projects. Since the profitability index is the ratio of the present value of the expected after-tax cash flows to the initial outlay, choosing the five projects with the greatest profitability indexes will identify the five projects with the greatest total present values and the projects with the greatest total net present values. (Study Session 11, LOS 36.c)

75. **A**   The policy statement is inappropriate because it is too restrictive. A policy statement should focus on meeting the specific safety and liquidity needs of the firm but should also allow the flexibility to increase yield within these constraints. There are many other securities potentially suitable for cash management that would provide equivalent or better liquidity and safety of principal at least equivalent to that of the securities issued by A+ rated banks. (Study Session 11, LOS 40.e)

76. **A**   Sunk costs are not to be included in investment analysis. Opportunity costs and the project's impact on taxes are relevant variables in determining project cash flow for a capital investment. (Study Session 11, LOS 36.b)

77. **C**   An increase in the number of days of payables suggests a company is taking longer to pay its vendors. This reduces the cash conversion cycle and represents effective working capital management, a source of liquidity for a company. A decrease in days of payables would be a drag on liquidity because the company is paying its vendors more quickly, which uses cash. (Study Session 11, LOS 40.a, c)

78. **C**   Regularly reviewing performance, independence, skills, and experience of existing board members is a responsibility of the Nominations Committee, not the Audit Committee. The other choices are positive characteristics of the Audit Committee. (Study Session 11, LOS 41.e)

79. **C**   The important points in the determination of asset classes are that assets included in a class have similar performance characteristics and a relatively high correlation of returns between assets, and that returns of asset classes have relatively low correlations to realize the benefits of diversification across asset classes. Some asset classes, such as real estate and hedge funds, may be illiquid. The asset classes in the strategic allocation should be mutually exclusive and cover the universe of investable assets available to the fund manager(s) based on the client's objectives and constraints, not the broadest possible universe of asset classes. (Study Session 12, LOS 45.f)

80. **C**   The Standards of Practice have very little to do with investment constraints. (Study Session 12, LOS 45.e)

81. **A**   A risk-averse investor prefers less risk to more risk. The lower the correlation, the greater the risk reduction. Thus, a risk-averse investor would most prefer the portfolio with the lowest correlation coefficient and least prefer the one with the highest. Of the choices given, W and Y's correlation coefficient of +0.6 is the highest. (Study Session 12, LOS 43.d, f)

82. **B**   The CAPM concludes that expected returns are a positive (linear) function of systematic risk. (Study Session 12, LOS 44.c)

83. **B**   The SML and CML both intersect the vertical axis at the risk-free rate. The SML describes the risk/return tradeoff for individual securities or portfolios, whereas the CML describes the risk/return tradeoff of various combinations of the market portfolio and a riskless asset. (Study Session 12, LOS 44.b, f)

84. **B**   Even risk-averse investors will prefer leveraged risky portfolios if the increase in expected return is enough to offset the increase in portfolio risk. Scott's portfolio selection implies that she is more risk averse than Fiona, has steeper indifference curves, and is willing to take on less additional risk for an incremental increase in expected returns than Fiona. (Study Session 12, LOS 43.h)

85. **B**   A price-weighted index will put the most weight on Stock X, which had the worst performance. A price-weighted index will have a beginning value of $(160 + 80 + 60) / 3 = 100$ and an ending value of $(136 + 100 + 66) / 3 = 100.67$, for an increase of 0.67%. The percent change for a value-weighted index is $(13,600 + 10,000 + 66,000) / (16,000 + 8,000 + 60,000) - 1 = 6.7\%$. The percent change for an equal-weighted index using the geometric mean is $[(1 - 0.15)(1 + 0.25)(1 + 0.1)]^{1/3} - 1 = 5.3\%$. (Study Session 13, LOS 47.d)

86. **A**   High industry concentration refers to an industry that has a small number of firms, which often leads to less price competition, higher pricing power, and higher return on invested capital. High barriers to entry refer to industries where it is costly for new competitors to enter the industry, which allows companies already in the industry to maintain high profitability and prices. Low industry capacity refers to a situation where demand is greater than supply at current prices, which allows companies to maintain high prices and profits. (Study Session 14, LOS 50.g)

87. **C**   Consumer discretionary goods purchases are very sensitive to economic cycles, while consumer staples are a non-cyclical industry. (Study Session 14, LOS 50.c, j)

88. **A** An investor cannot achieve positive abnormal returns on average by using technical analysis if prices fully reflect all available security market (price and volume) information. The weak form of the EMH assumes prices reflect this information, and the semistrong and strong forms assume prices reflect additional (non-market) information as well. (Study Session 13, LOS 48.e)

89. **A** First solve for D_5: $D_5 = (D_1)(1 + g)^n = \$1(1.05)^4 = \$1.216$

$$P_4 = \frac{D_5}{(k-g)} = \frac{\$1.216}{(0.15-0.05)} = \$12.16$$

or

$$P_0 = \frac{1}{0.15-0.05} = 10$$

$$P_4 = 10(1.05)^4 = \$12.16$$

(Study Session 14, LOS 51.e)

90. **A** By taking a short position in a put option, the investor has long exposure to the risk in the underlying asset. Because the value of a put option decreases when the price of the underlying asset increases, the value of a short position in a put increases when the price of the underlying increases. Both a short position in a call option and a long position in a put option increase in value when the price of the underlying asset decreases; that is, these option positions have short exposure to the risk of the underlying asset. (Study Session 13, LOS 46.e)

91. **C** $$P/E = \frac{\text{dividend payout ratio}}{k-g}$$

$$g = ROE \times \text{retention rate}$$

Increases in k reduce P/E. Increases in g or the dividend payout ratio increase P/E. (Study Session 14, LOS 51.e, h)

92. **B** Sales of newly issued securities take place in the primary market. Registration of shares sold in private placements of securities is not required. The secondary market refers to the markets in which previously issued securities are traded. (Study Session 13, LOS 46.i)

93. **B** Callable shares typically pay a higher dividend than noncallable shares because investors demand compensation for the fact that the call option limits investors' potential return. Callable shares are riskier than noncallable shares because the issuer has the option to buy back the shares at a fixed price. (Study Session 14, LOS 49.e)

94. **A** A stop buy order is an order to buy a security if the price increases to the specified stop price. This type of order is often used to limit losses on a short position. A limit buy order specifies a maximum price and is executed if the market price is less than or equal to that price. (Study Session 13, LOS 46.g, h)

95. **B** This is a supernormal growth stock valuation problem.

Step 1: Find the dividends in the supernormal growth period.

$D_1 = 1.00(1.20) = \$1.20$; $D_2 = 1.2(1.2) = \$1.44$; $D_3 = 1.44(1.15) = \$1.656$

Step 2: Use the constant growth model to find the price at the end of period 2.

$$P_2 = \frac{D_3}{k-g} = \frac{1.656}{0.10 - 0.06} = \$41.40$$

Step 3: Discount all of the cash flows back to time zero.

$$P_0 = \frac{D_1}{(1+k)} + \frac{D_2}{(1+k)^2} + \frac{P_2}{(1+k)^2} = \frac{1.20}{1.10} + \frac{1.44}{(1.10)^2} + \frac{41.40}{(1.10)^2} = \$36.50$$

(Study Session 14, LOS 51.e)

96. **C** Semistrong-form market efficiency implies that fundamental analysis of publicly available information will not generate abnormal returns on average. Portfolio managers should help quantify a client's risk tolerances and return needs, offer portfolio policies and strategies to meet these needs, and construct a portfolio by allocating funds to appropriate asset classes. Portfolio managers can also create value by diversifying their clients' portfolios globally to reduce risk, monitoring and evaluating changing capital market conditions, monitoring their clients' needs and circumstances, and rebalancing their clients' portfolios when necessary. (Study Session 13, LOS 48.e)

97. **B** To calculate a Treasury bond's arbitrage-free value, each cash flow is discounted using the Treasury spot rate that is specific to the maturity of the cash flow. (Study Session 16, LOS 56.f)

98. **A** Option-free bonds have positive convexity and the effect of (positive) convexity is to increase the magnitude of the price increase when yields fall and to decrease the magnitude of the price decrease when yields rise. (Study Session 16, LOS 58.h)

99. **A** Municipal bonds are traded in the over-the-counter market supported by municipal bond dealers across the country. (Study Session 15, LOS 54.d, g)

100. **B** The bond is sold at a premium. As time passes, the bond's price will move toward par. Thus, the price will fall.

N = 10; FV = 1,000; PMT = 100; I = 8; CPT → PV = $1,134

N = 9; FV = 1,000; PMT = 100; I = 8; CPT → PV = $1,125

(Study Session 16, LOS 56.d)

101. **B** The bond is an inverse floater because the coupon rate will move opposite to any move in the reference rate. (Study Session 15, LOS 52.b)

102. **B** The two investments combine to form a 10-year, $1,000 face value, 8.0% semiannual coupon bond that would sell at par because the YTM (expressed as a BEY) equals the coupon rate. Thus the combined value is $1,000. The zero-coupon bond is worth $\frac{1,000}{1.04^{20}} = \$456.39$, and the annuity payments are worth $543.61 (N = 10 × 2 = 20, PMT = 40, I/Y = 8/2 = 4, FV = 0, PV = –543.61).

(Study Session 16, LOS 56.c)

103. **C** $\Delta P/P = -D_{effective}\Delta i$

$\Delta P/P = -7.6(+0.0075) = -0.057, \text{ or } -5.7\%$

(Study Session 16, LOS 58.d)

104. **C** The nominal yield (another term for the coupon yield) is less than the yield to maturity for a discount bond. (Study Session 16, LOS 57.b)

105. **C** The key term here is *coupon bond*. While an investor in a fixed-coupon bond can usually eliminate interest rate risk by holding a bond until maturity, the same is not true for reinvestment risk. The receipt of periodic coupon payments exposes the investor to reinvestment risk. A noncallable bond reduces reinvestment risk by reducing the risk of repayment. Thus, an investor most concerned with reinvestment risk would prefer a noncallable bond to a callable bond. Since lower coupon bonds have lower reinvestment risk, this same investor would prefer a lower coupon bond to a higher coupon bond. (Study Session 15, LOS 53.i)

106. **B** A special purpose vehicle is a legal entity to which the assets used as collateral in an ABS issue are sold. This transaction separates the assets backing the ABS from the other assets of the company that creates the SPV. (Study Session 15, LOS 54.i)

107. **B** $_2f_1 = \left[\frac{(1+z_3)^{1+2}}{(1+z_1)^1}\right]^{1/2} - 1 = \left[\frac{(1.12)^3}{(1.10)}\right]^{1/2} - 1 = 13.01\%$

Note: $\frac{(3 \times 12) - (1 \times 10)}{2} = 13$ (Study Session 16, LOS 57.g)

108. **C** A flat term structure could be explained according to the liquidity preference theory as a case where investors expect short-term rates to decline slightly, coupled with a maturity premium that exactly offsets the downward pressure contained in investor expectations. The pure expectations theory makes no specific mention of the fact that an upward-sloping term structure is a consequence of investors expecting short-term rates to remain unchanged for a period of time followed by investors expecting short-term rates to rise for a period of time. All this theory says is that an upward-sloping term structure can be explained by investors believing that future short-term rates will rise. Finally, the liquidity preference theory attempts to explain the term structure according to two factors. These are expectations about future interest rates and a maturity premium to compensate for interest rate risk. If the term structure is declining, this could be explained simply by investor expectations of declining future short-term rates coupled with a maturity premium that is not large enough to offset the downward pressure on interest rates due to investor expectations. (Study Session 15, LOS 55.c)

109. **B** Secured creditors have priority of claims over unsecured creditors in a bankruptcy, rather than ranking pari passu with unsecured creditors. However, the priority of claims might not always be followed, either because the creditors have negotiated a different outcome or because a bankruptcy court has ordered one. (Study Session 16, LOS 59.b)

110. **C** The OAS is a measure of the yield spread over Treasury spot rates *without* the option. (Study Session 15, LOS 52.e, 55.e and Study Session 16, LOS 57.f)

111. **B** The holder of a long position in an FRA receives cash if the reference rate is greater than the rate specified in the contract on the expiration date, or pays cash if the reference rate is less than the contract rate. Combining a long interest rate call with a short interest rate put results in the same payoff pattern. A long interest rate call option has a positive value (receives cash) if the reference rate is greater than the strike rate at expiration. The holder of a short interest rate put option must pay cash if the reference rate is less than the strike rate at expiration. (Study Session 17, LOS 63.f)

112. **A** The variability of prices in general is significantly larger than the variability of (uncertainty about) dividend yields, and hence managing price risk is of primary importance, while the uncertainty about dividend yields is of secondary importance. The remaining statements are correct. (Study Session 17, LOS 61.d)

113. **C** This is an out-of-the-money covered call. The net cost is $37 (40 − 3) and the maximum payoff on the position is the exercise price, $42. Thus, the maximum profit is $5. (Study Session 17, LOS 65.b)

114. **A** A long position in an FRA gains value when future interest rates increase, while a short position gains if interest rates decrease. A short position in a Eurodollar future decreases in value if future interest rates decrease. A swap would have exposure to several future interest rates, not just the rate three months out. (Study Session 17, LOS 61.f, 62.f)

115. **B** Money is lost on a short futures position when the price of the underlying rises. With a maintenance margin of $1,312.50 per contract, a margin call will be issued when the margin account balance drops below 4 × $1,312.50 = $5,250. From the table below, we can see that this occurs on day 3. The variation margin is the amount that has to be deposited to bring the margin account balance back up to the initial margin level. The initial margin was 4 × $1,750 = $7,000. Therefore the variation margin is = $7,000 − $4,800 = $2,200.

Day	Closing Futures Price ($)	Gain (loss) ($)	Margin Account Balance ($)	Variation Margin ($)
1	345.50	1,800	8,800	
2	348.75	(1,300)	7,500	
3	355.50	(2,700)	4,800	2,200
4	356.25	(300)	6,700	

(Study Session 17, LOS 62.c, d)

Professor's Note: On futures margins problems, start by calculating the per-contract change in margin for a 1-unit change in the futures price. Here, a $1 change in the price of gold is $100 per contract. To reach minimum margin we need a change of 1,750 − 1,312.50 = 437.50, so a price change of 437.50 / 100 = $4.375 does it. Since we're short, an increase of 5.50 results in a 5.5(100)(4) = $2,200 decrease in the margin balance.

116. **C** An American-style call option must be worth at least as much as an otherwise identical European-style call option and has the same minimum value. This fact alone eliminates choice B. Since the American-style call is in the money and therefore must be worth more than the $6 difference between the strike price and the exercise price, you can eliminate response A and select response C without calculating the exact minimum value, which is given by:

$$\max[0, S_t - X / (1 + RFR)^{T-t}] = \max[0, 86 - 80 / (1.03)^{3/12}] = \$6.59$$

(Study Session 17, LOS 63.k)

117. **B** Gains and losses that result from entering into a new, longer-dated futures contract as previous contracts expire or are closed out depend on whether the contract is in contango (futures price greater than spot price) or backwardation (futures price less than spot price). Collateral yield depends on the yield on T-bills posted as collateral (margin). Contract yield is not defined as any particular yield measure. (Study Session 18, LOS 67.b)

118. **A** Mezzanine-stage venture capital financing provides capital during the period prior to an initial public offering. (Study Session 18, LOS 66.d)

119. **A** Historical mean and standard deviation of returns for hedge fund indexes are likely to overestimate expected return and underestimate risk due to survivorship and backfill biases. As a result, determining a portfolio asset allocation to hedge funds based on these measures is likely to overestimate the diversification benefits. (Study Session 18, LOS 66.c, g)

120. **C** Recapitalization is when the company issues debt to fund a dividend distribution to equity holders (the fund). It is not an exit, in that the fund still controls the company, but often is a intermediate step toward an exit. (Study Session 18, LOS 66.d)

Exam 2
Morning Session Answer Key

To get valuable feedback on how your score compares to those of other Level I candidates, use your Username and Password to gain Online Access at schweser.com and choose the left-hand menu item "Practice Exams Vol. 1."

1. B	31. A	61. C	91. C
2. A	32. C	62. B	92. C
3. A	33. C	63. B	93. A
4. C	34. B	64. B	94. C
5. C	35. C	65. A	95. B
6. A	36. B	66. B	96. C
7. C	37. B	67. A	97. B
8. A	38. A	68. A	98. C
9. A	39. B	69. B	99. C
10. B	40. B	70. A	100. C
11. A	41. C	71. C	101. B
12. A	42. B	72. A	102. A
13. C	43. B	73. A	103. A
14. B	44. A	74. B	104. B
15. A	45. B	75. B	105. C
16. B	46. C	76. B	106. B
17. A	47. A	77. C	107. C
18. B	48. A	78. B	108. A
19. B	49. B	79. B	109. C
20. B	50. B	80. C	110. C
21. B	51. A	81. C	111. A
22. A	52. C	82. A	112. B
23. C	53. A	83. B	113. A
24. B	54. C	84. B	114. A
25. B	55. A	85. C	115. C
26. A	56. C	86. C	116. B
27. A	57. A	87. C	117. B
28. C	58. C	88. C	118. C
29. A	59. A	89. A	119. C
30. B	60. B	90. B	120. B

Exam 2
Morning Session Answers

Answers referencing the Standards of Practice address Study Session 1, LOS 1.b, c and LOS 2.a, b, c, except where noted.

1. **B** Standard I(A) Knowledge of the Law requires candidates and members comply with all applicable rules and regulations, including the CFA Standards of Practice. Further, Standard I(A) requires that members and candidates must not *knowingly* participate in violations of applicable laws and Standards. Even though local law permits purchasing shares for personal accounts before purchasing IPO shares for client accounts, Standard VI(B) Priority of Transactions does not. The analyst *knowingly* violated the Code and Standards and, thus, violated Standard I(A). Since the analyst was unaware of the deceit in the valuation of the IPO stock [a violation of Standard I(D) Misconduct], her participation in publishing the research did not constitute a violation.

2. **A** Ray and the portfolio manager are in violation of Standard VII(B) Reference to CFA Institute, the CFA Designation, and the CFA Program because they have improperly referenced the CFA designation or exaggerated its meaning (e.g., "elite group of the most qualified"). The marketing brochure is only stating factual information regarding the portfolio managers' successful attempts at passing the CFA exams on their first attempts.

3. **A** Standard V(B) Communication with Clients and Prospective Clients requires prompt disclosure of any change that might significantly affect the manager's investment processes. The disclosure need not be in writing.

4. **C** Standard III(C) Suitability requires that members and candidates carefully consider the needs, circumstances, and objectives of clients before taking investment action. However, some members and candidates are merely executing specific instructions for retail clients. In this case, since Wells believes the trade is unsuitable, Wells should confirm that the client is aware the action is unsuitable before executing the trade or refrain from making the trade.

5. **C** According to Standard II(A) Material Nonpublic Information, information is considered material if the information is likely to affect the price of a security when disclosed, or if a reasonable investor would want to have the information before making an investment decision.

6. **A** According to Standard II(B) Market Manipulation, members and candidates should not engage in any practice that would artificially inflate trading volume or distort prices. However, this Standard does not prohibit transactions done for tax purposes. In this case, there was no intent to mislead market participants as to the stock price of Safety Airlines, and the trades were undertaken to take advantage of a legitimate tax strategy. Thus, there has been no violation of Standard II(B) or any other Standard.

7. **C** Standard I(B) Independence and Objectivity allows investor-paid research but requires that members and candidates limit the type of compensation they accept for writing a research report so that it is not dependent on the conclusions of the research report. Best practice is for analysts to only accept a flat fee for such company-paid research reports. Such research should also include complete disclosure of the nature of the compensation received for writing such a report so that investors will not be misled as to the relationship between the analyst and the company. Paying for one's own transportation and lodging when the analyst is not employed by the subject firm is a recommended procedure for complying with Standard I(B), but it is not a requirement.

8. **A** In the absence of regulatory requirements, Standard V(C) Record Retention recommends maintaining records supporting investment recommendations and actions and records of investment-related communications with clients for at least seven years. Here, there is regulatory guidance and seven years is a recommendation, not a requirement, in any case. Records can be maintained in electronic or hard copy format.

9. **A** Total firm assets must include all accounts whether discretionary or not and whether fee-paying or not. (Study Session 1, LOS 4.a)

10. **B** Under Standard III(B) Fair Dealing, changes from "Buy" to "Sell" should be disseminated, at a minimum, to clients the broker knows have purchased and held the security based on the earlier recommendation and to persons placing orders contrary to the firm's current recommendation.

11. **A** James is not in violation of the Standards. To comply with Standard VI(B) Priority of Transactions, members and candidates must give transactions for clients and employers priority over their personal transactions. In this instance, James did not adversely affect the client's interest because the client's trades were executed before James copied them. He has not acted fraudulently or deceitfully.

12. **A** The circumstances of the bankruptcy did not involve fraudulent or deceitful business conduct; therefore, there is no violation of Standard I(D) Misconduct. Hart's bankruptcy does not compromise his professional reputation.

13. **C** Marshall has an obligation to disclose that she receives special compensation based on the amount of client trading volume. Standard VI(A) Disclosure of Conflicts requires members to disclose to clients and prospects all matters that could potentially impair the member's ability to make investment decisions that are (and to give investment advice that is) objective and unbiased.

14. **B** Lunar can claim compliance as long as it has met the reporting requirements necessary and is held out to clients (advertised) as a distinct business entity. Claiming partial compliance is not allowed. (Study Session 1, LOS 4.b)

15. **A** Under Standard III(E) Preservation of Confidentiality, members and candidates should maintain the confidentiality of information received in the course of their professional service relating to both current and former clients. In the case of illegal activity, however, Reilly may have a legal obligation to report the activity. Ideally, he should consult with his employer first about what actions he may be required to take. Of the choices given, seeking the advice of outside counsel as to whether he has such an obligation under local law and whether the activity is indeed illegal is the one permitted under the Standard.

16. **B** Standard II(A) Material Nonpublic Information requires that members and candidates who possess material nonpublic information not act or cause others to act on the information. Putting the stock on a restricted list or refusing the trade are violations of this Standard since they involve acting or causing others to act on the nonpublic information he possesses. Dean should seek to have East Street make the information public. If East Street does not do so, Dean is not allowed to act on the information. Refusing to make the trade he was instructed to make would be "acting" on the information in this case. The obligation here is to the integrity of financial markets.

17. **A** Members and candidates should consider the knowledge and sophistication of those receiving the performance information. If only a brief presentation is given, members and candidates must make detailed information supporting the presentation available upon request. Individual account performance is permitted and no minimum number of years is recommended (these refer to GIPS, with which the Code and Standards do not require compliance). The primary requirement of Standard III(D) Performance Presentation is to not present false or misleading information.

18. **B** GIPS require that, to claim compliance, firms must present GIPS-compliant performance information for a minimum of five years or since inception if in existence less than five years. (Study Session 1, LOS 3.a)

19. **B** This problem involves determining the present value of an annuity followed by finding the present value of a lump sum. Enter PMT = 10,000, N = 10, and I = 14. Compute PV = 52,161.16. That is the present value of the 10-year annuity, four years from today. Next, we need to discount that back to present for four years to find the amount of the investment today. Enter FV = –52,161.16, N = 4, I = 14, PMT = 0. Compute PV = 30,883.59. (Study Session 2, LOS 5.e)

20. **B** The cumulative absolute frequency of the fourth interval is 80, which is the sum of the absolute frequencies from the first to the fourth intervals. (Study Session 2, LOS 7.b)

21. **B** High levels of the VIX indicate that the outlook of investors is bearish. A contrarian interprets this as a bullish sign. Low mutual fund cash balances indicate that mutual fund managers are bullish, and, as a result, contrarians are bearish. A low put-call ratio indicates bullish investor sentiment, which a contrarian interprets as a bearish sign. (Study Session 3, LOS 12.e)

22. **A** The average annual compound growth rate is calculated as:

$$[(1 + 0.25)(1 - 0.25)(1 + 0.30)(1 - 0.30)]^{0.25} - 1 = 0.9611 - 1 = -0.0389 \text{ or } -3.89\%$$

(Study Session 2, LOS 7.e)

23. **C** Mean = 120 / 10 = 12, median = 10, and mode = 10. The distribution is skewed to the right, so the mean is greater than the median and mode. Generally, for positively skewed distributions, the mode is less than the median, which is less than the mean. In this case, the mode and median are equal because the number of observations is small. (Study Session 2, LOS 7.e, k)

24. **B** The coefficient of variation, CV = standard deviation / arithmetic mean, is a common measure of relative dispersion (risk). $CV_X = 0.7 / 0.9 = 0.78$; $CV_Y = 4.7 / 1.2 = 3.92$; and $CV_Z = 5.2 / 1.5 = 3.47$. Because a higher CV means higher relative risk, Security Y has the highest relative risk. (Study Session 2, LOS 7.i)

25. **B**   The median is the midpoint of a distribution, such that 50% of the observations are greater than the median and 50% are less than the median. This is equivalent to the second quartile (4 groups) and the fifth decile (10 groups). If a distribution is divided into quintiles (5 groups), 60% of the observations are less than the third quintile. (Study Session 2, LOS 7.f)

26. **A**   *Subjective probability* is based on personal judgement. A *joint probability* is a probability that two or more events happen concurrently. An *a priori probability* is one based on logical analysis rather than on observation or personal judgment. An *empirical probability* is calculated using historical data. A *conditional probability* is the probability of one event happening on the condition that another event is certain to occur. (Study Session 2, LOS 8.a, b, d)

27. **A**   Technical analysis assumes that supply and demand are governed by many factors, both rational and irrational. (Study Session 3, LOS 12.a)

28. **C**

	Selected by the Previous Portfolio Manager	Selected by the Current Portfolio Manager	Total
Value stocks	28 (28%)	12 (12%)	40
Growth stocks	48 (48%)	12 (12%)	60
Total	76	24	100

This problem involves the addition rule for probabilities, P(A or B) = P(A) + P(B) − P(AB).

P(A) is the probability that a randomly selected stock is a value stock, which is given as 40%.

P(B) is the probability that a stock was picked by the previous manager. That probability is (0.7)(0.4) + (0.8)(1 − 0.4) = 0.76. The previous manager selected 76% of the stocks in the portfolio.

P(AB) is the probability that a randomly selected stock is a value stock picked by the previous manager. Since the previous manager picked 70% of the 40% of the stocks that are value stocks, the probability that a randomly selected stock is a value stock picked by the previous manager is 40% × 70% = 28%.

From this, we have P(A or B) = 40% + 76% − 28% = 88%. (Study Session 2, LOS 8.f)

29. **A**   The *standard* normal distribution has a mean of 0 and a standard deviation of 1. (Study Session 2, LOS 8.g and Study Session 3, LOS 9.j)

30. **B**   The 95% confidence interval is 10% ± 1.96(4%) or from 2.16% to 17.84%. The 90% confidence interval is 10% ± 1.65(4%) or from 3.4% to 16.6%. The probability of a return ± 1 standard deviation from the mean, between 6% and 14%, is approximately 68%. (Study Session 3, LOS 9.l)

31. **A** Using the standard normal probability distribution,

$$z = \frac{observation - mean}{standard\ deviation} = \frac{0 - 10}{5} = -2.0 \text{, the chance of getting zero or less return}$$

(losing money) is 1 – 0.9772 = 0.0228% or 2.28%. An alternative explanation: the expected return is 10%. To lose money means the return must fall below zero. Zero is about two standard deviations to the left of the mean. 50% of the time, a return will be below the mean, and 2.5% of the observations are below two standard deviations down. About 97.5% of the time, the return will be above zero. Thus, only about a 2.5% chance exists of having a value below zero. (Study Session 3, LOS 9.m)

32. **C** According to the central limit theorem, the sample mean for large sample sizes will be distributed normally regardless of the distribution of the underlying population. (Study Session 3, LOS 10.c, d, e)

33. **C** The crowding-out effect refers to a reduction in private borrowing and investment as a result of higher interest rates generated by budget deficits that are financed by borrowing in the private loanable funds market. (Study Session 5, LOS 19.p)

34. **B** Under the elasticities approach, a currency depreciation will lead to a greater reduction in a trade deficit when export demand and/or import demand are more elastic. The demand for luxury goods is relatively elastic, while the demand for goods without good substitutes or for goods that represent only a small portion of consumer expenditures is relatively inelastic. (Study Session 6, LOS 21.i)

35. **C** At competitive equilibrium, the sum of consumer and producer surplus is at its maximum level. Neither consumer nor producer surplus is necessarily at a maximum at the equilibrium output and price. Which surplus is larger or smaller depends on the elasticities of supply and demand. (Study Session 4, LOS 13.i)

36. **B** Open market operations are the U.S. Federal Reserve's most often used tool for changing the money supply. (Study Session 5, LOS 19.h)

37. **B** If quantity supplied does not respond to a change in price, supply is perfectly inelastic. For perfectly inelastic supply, elasticity equals zero. (Study Session 4, LOS 13.l)

38. **A** In the short run, an increase in the money supply will increase aggregate demand. The new short-run equilibrium will be at a higher price level and a greater level of real output (GDP). (Study Session 5, LOS 17.i)

39. **B** The law of diminishing returns states that at some point, as more of a resource is used in a production process, holding other inputs constant, output increases at a decreasing rate. This accounts for the upward slope of the SRMC curve beyond that point. Returns to scale determine the shape of the long-run cost curves. (Study Session 4, LOS 15.d)

40. **B** Under perfect competition, each firm faces a flat demand curve. This means the price is constant and the marginal revenue line is flat. A company will continue to produce as long as MR > MC, so the competitive company will produce as long as P > MC. It will stop when MC = MR = P. (Study Session 4, LOS 15.g, 16.d)

41. **C** Customs unions adopt uniform trade restrictions with non-members. Customs union members do not adopt a single currency. Both free trade areas and customs unions remove trade barriers among their members. (Study Session 6, LOS 20.f)

42. **B** Based on utility analysis, the optimum bundle of goods lies on the consumer's highest attainable indifference curve, at the point where this indifference curve is tangent to the consumer's budget line. The point of tangency is the only point at which this indifference curve intersects the consumer's opportunity set of attainable bundles. The consumer would prefer bundles that lie on higher indifference curves, but those bundles are unaffordable given the consumer's budget constraint. (Study Session 4, LOS 14.b, d)

43. **B** Unemployment insurance is an example of an automatic stabilizer that is not subject to the action lag of discretionary fiscal policy tools. One reason why the unemployment rate is a lagging indicator is the fact that employers are slow to lay off employees early in recessions and slow to add employees early in expansions, because frequent hiring and firing has high costs. Another reason is that early in expansions, more discouraged workers (who are not counted as unemployed because they are out of the labor force) may begin seeking work (thereby re-entering the labor force) than the number of new jobs that are available, which increases the unemployment rate. (Study Session 5, LOS 18.b, d, i, 19.o)

44. **A** A natural monopoly may exist when economies of scale are great. The large economies of scale mean that a single producer results in the lowest production costs. (Study Session 4, LOS 16.a, b)

45. **B** Extraordinary items are unusual and infrequent items that are reported separately, net of tax, after net income from continuing operations. (Study Session 8, LOS 25.e)

46. **C**

original shares of common stock	= 1,000,000(12)	= 12,000,000
stock dividend	= 100,000(12)	= 1,200,000
new shares of common stock	= 400,000(3)	= 1,200,000
total shares of common stock	$= \dfrac{14,400,000}{12}$	= 1,200,000

Stock dividends are assumed to have been outstanding since the beginning of the year. (Study Session 8, LOS 25.g)

47. **A** Cash conversion cycle is days in inventory + days in receivables – days in payables. Financing payables reduces accounts payable, decreases days' payables, and lengthens the cash conversion cycle. Stretching out payables increases accounts payable, increases days' payables, and decreases the cash conversion cycle. Securitization of receivables decreases receivables and days' receivables, which decreases the cash conversion cycle. (Study Session 8, LOS 28.b and Study Session 10, LOS 34.a)

48. **A** The debt ratio is total debt to total assets. Because common-size balance sheet data are stated as percentages of total assets, the debt ratio can be determined from the data given.

20X3: 10% + 24% = 34%
20X4: 11% + 21% = 32%
20X5: 12% + 18% = 30%

The debt ratio is decreasing over the period shown. Neither the inventory/sales ratio nor the quick ratio can be determined from the data given because the data do not include sales or current liabilities. (Study Session 8, LOS 26.h, i)

49. **B**   When using the direct method of calculating operating cash flows, depreciation and amortization are not "added back" (to net income) because we don't begin with net income under the direct method. Depreciation and amortization are noncash changes and are not used under the direct method. The other statements are true. Interest payments on debt affect cash flow from operations. When using the indirect method, an analyst should add any losses on sales of fixed assets to net income since they are not operating cash flows. (Study Session 8, LOS 27.c, f)

50. **B**   Under U.S. GAAP, a change to LIFO from another inventory cost method is an exception to the requirement of retrospective application of changes in an accounting principle. Instead of restating prior years' data, the firm uses the carrying value of inventory at the time of the change as the first LIFO layer. U.S. GAAP requires a company that is changing its inventory cost assumption to explain, in its financial statement disclosures, why the new method is preferable to the old method. (Study Session 9, LOS 29.g)

51. **A**   ROE 20X6 = (0.7)(0.85)(0.15)(1.5)(1.5) = 0.2008

ROE 20X7 = (0.7)(0.85)(0.10)(1.8)(1.6) = 0.1714

Profit margin fell, and the increase in the total asset turnover ratio and the leverage multiplier were not enough to offset the decline, so ROE decreased. (Study Session 8, LOS 28.d)

52. **C**   Options are derivatives, which are reported at fair value on the balance sheet with unrealized gains and losses recognized on the income statement. Available-for-sale securities are marked to market on the balance sheet, but unrealized gains and losses are reported in owners' equity as other comprehensive income. Bonds purchased in a private placement cannot be resold to the public and therefore are likely to be classified as held-to-maturity, in which case the firm does not recognize unrealized gains or losses. (Study Session 8, LOS 26.e; Study Session 13, LOS 46.i; Study Session 17, LOS 60.a)

53. **A**   If equity equals 45% of assets and current liabilities equal 20%, long-term debt must be 35%.

$$\text{long-term debt-to-equity ratio} = \frac{\text{long-term debt}}{\text{total equity}} = \frac{0.35}{0.45} = 0.778 = 77.8\%$$

CA = 0.1 + 0.15 + 0.20 = 0.45

$$\text{current ratio} = \frac{\text{CA}}{\text{CL}} = \frac{45}{20} = 2.25\text{x}$$

(Study Session 8, LOS 26.g, 28.b)

54. **C**   Interest expense is shown as a non-operating component of net income for a manufacturing company but would typically be classified as an operating expense for a financial services company. (Study Session 8, LOS 25.f)

55. **A**   In the IFRS framework, the two assumptions that underlie the preparation of financial statements are the accrual basis and the going concern assumption. (Study Session 7, LOS 24.d)

56. **C**   With an operating lease, the entire lease payment (rent expense) is subtracted from operating income. With a capital lease, only depreciation is subtracted from operating income, so operating income is higher with a capital lease. Net income in the first year is lower with a capital lease because the sum of depreciation (operating expense) and interest (non-operating expense) is greater than the lease payment. (Study Session 9, LOS 32.g)

57. **A**   The warrants are dilutive because their exercise price is less than the average market price.

shares issued to warrant holders = 100

warrants generate cash of 100(50) = $5,000

$$\text{repurchased shares} = \frac{5,000}{60} = 83$$

net new shares created = 100 − 83 = 17

Alternatively, $\dfrac{60-50}{60} \times 100 \approx 17$

$$\text{diluted EPS} = \frac{\text{NI} - \text{preferred dividends}}{\text{weighted average \# shares} + \text{warrant adjust}}$$

$$\text{diluted EPS} = \frac{5,000-500}{1,017} = \$4.42$$

(Study Session 8, LOS 25.g, h)

58. **C**   Corporate press releases are written by management and are often viewed as public relations or sales materials because of the great possibility of inherent management bias in such documents. Often, little or none of the material is independently reviewed by outside auditors. Such documents are not mandated by the securities regulators. Form 10-Q (quarterly financial statements) and proxy statements are mandatory SEC filings in the United States, which inherently increases their reliability given the penalties that can be imposed by the SEC if any serious irregularities are subsequently found. (Study Session 7, LOS 22.e)

59. **A**   The impairment writedown in 20X3 will reduce depreciation expense in 20X4, which will increase 20X4 EBIT and net income. Operating cash flow and taxes payable are not affected because an impairment cannot be deducted from income for tax reporting purposes until the asset is sold or otherwise disposed of. (Study Session 9, LOS 30.h)

60. **B**   There is a 20% reduction in the tax rate [(40% − 50%) / 50% = −0.2]. Hence, the deferred tax asset will be $800 = $1,000(1 − 0.2), the deferred tax liability will be $4,000 = $5,000(1 − 0.2), and the income tax expense will fall by the net amount of the decline in the asset and liability balances ($1,000 − $200 = $800). (Study Session 9, LOS 31.d)

61. **C**   Under U.S. GAAP, costs incurred to establish technological feasibility of software for sale are expensed, but software development costs incurred after technological feasibility has been established must be capitalized. Under IFRS, research costs are expensed as incurred and development costs are capitalized. Thus, both East and West will capitalize $90,000 of development costs. (Study Session 9, LOS 30.b)

62. **B** Capitalizing costs tends to smooth earnings and reduces investment cash flows. It will also increase cash flows from operations and increase profitability in the early years. (Study Session 9, LOS 30.a)

63. **B** When cash is paid before the expense is recognized in the income statement, a prepaid asset for this expense is increased and cash is decreased by the amount paid. A prepaid liability account would not be set up unless the expense is recorded before the cash payment is made. (Study Session 7, LOS 23.d)

64. **B** Based on the data given, use the basic DuPont equation and solve for expected net income.

    ROE = (net income / revenues) × (revenues / total assets) × (total assets / total equity)

    0.15 = (net income / $3 billion) × ($3 billion / $5 billion) × 2.5

    net income / $3 billion = 0.1

    net income = $300 million

    Alternatively, A/E = 2.5 and assets = $5 billion, so equity = $2 billion.

    net income / equity = 15%, so net income = 0.15($2 Billion) = $300 million
    (Study Session 10, LOS 35.b)

65. **A** PMT = 800,000; FV = 10,000,000; N = 5; I/Y = 8.25; CPT → PV = $9,900,837

    interest expense = 9,900,836.51 × 0.0825 = $816,819.01

    year-end adjustment = 816,819.01 − 800,000 = $16,819.01

    year-end debt = $9,900,836.51 + $16,819.01 = $9,917,655.52

    Note: Since this is a discount bond, we know the initial liability will be less than the face value, so we really didn't have to do any calculations to answer this question.
    (Study Session 9, LOS 32.a, b)

66. **B** Unrealized gains and losses from trading securities are reflected in the income statement and affect owners' equity. However, unrealized gains and losses from available-for-sale securities are included in other comprehensive income. Transactions included in other comprehensive income affect equity but not net income. Dividends paid to shareholders reduce owners' equity but not net income. (Study Session 8, LOS 25.l)

67. **A** Conversion of bonds into common stock is a non-cash transaction, but the conversion should be disclosed in a footnote to the statement of cash flows.
    (Study Session 8, LOS 27.f)

68. **A** With LIFO, more recent, lower costs would be used for COGS. A reduction in COGS will increase gross profits and net income, other things equal. (Study Session 9, LOS 29.b)

69. **B**

Year	0	1	2	3	4
Net cash flow	−$5,000.00	$1,900.00	$1,900.00	$2,500.00	$2,000.00
Net cash flow discounted at 12%	−$5,000.00	$1,696.43	$1,514.67	$1,779.45	$1,271.04
Cumulative discounted net cash flows	−$5,000.00	−$3,303.57	−$1,788.90	−$9.45	$1,261.59

$$\text{discounted payback period} = 3 + \frac{9.45}{1,271.04} = 3.01 \text{ years.}$$

(Study Session 11, LOS 36.d)

70. **A**   To compare these short-term securities, state the return on each as a bond-equivalent yield. For the commercial paper, the BEY is given as 5.10%. The BEY for the certificate of deposit is 2.5% × 365 / 180 = 5.07%. For the Treasury bill, the BEY is [(100 − 97.5) / 97.5] × 365 / 180 = 5.20%. Miller should purchase the Treasury bill. (Study Session 11, LOS 40.e)

71. **C**   Current market yields, not the coupon rate, should be used to estimate the cost of debt capital. (Study Session 11, LOS 37.f)

72. **A**   Surveys indicate that European companies and private companies tend to use the payback period criterion more than other types of companies. (Study Session 11, LOS 36.f)

73. **A**   Investors should take steps to discourage the use of the corporate funds to pay "greenmail." (Study Session 11, LOS 41.g)

74. **B** $K_e = \dfrac{0.93(1.07)}{16} + 0.07 = 13.2\%$

(Study Session 11, LOS 37.h)

75. **B**   Good corporate governance practices will discourage or prohibit both the payment of finder's fees to board members for identifying attractive merger or acquisition targets and the use of corporate assets by board members or their families. (Study Session 11, LOS 41.f)

76. **B**   IRR and NPV lead to the same decision when choosing independent projects but may lead to different decisions when choosing between projects. (Study Session 11, LOS 36.e)

77. **C**   Break points in the marginal cost of capital structure occur at the levels where the cost of one of the components of the company's capital structure increases, increasing its weighted average cost of capital. (Study Session 11, LOS 37.k)

78. **B**   Neither statement is accurate. The stock should decline in value by the amount of the dividend on the ex-dividend date, not the payment date. The holder-of-record date occurs two business days *after* the ex-dividend date. (Study Session 11, LOS 39.b)

79. **B**   In a situation where the client's expressed willingness to bear investment risk is significantly greater than the client's ability to bear investment risk, the advisor's assessment of the client's risk tolerance in the IPS should reflect the client's ability to bear investment risk. (Study Session 12, LOS 45.d)

80. **C** The capital market line plots expected return against standard deviation of returns for efficient portfolios. The efficient frontier plots expected return against the standard deviation of return, a measure of total risk. (Study Session 12, LOS 43.g, 44.b, f)

81. **C** As randomly selected securities are added to a portfolio, the diversifiable (unsystematic) risk decreases, and the expected level of nondiversifiable (systematic) risk remains the same. (Study Session 12, LOS 44.c)

82. **A** Based on the CAPM, the portfolio should earn: E(R) = 0.05 + 1.5(0.15 – 0.05) = 0.20 or 20%. On a risk-adjusted basis, this portfolio lies on the SML and is, thus, properly valued. (Study Session 12, LOS 44.h)

83. **B** These ethical issues fall under the heading of unique needs and preferences. Some investors would exclude these types of investments due to their own personal preferences. Legal restrictions and regulatory factors have to do with the type of account and its supporting legal documents. (Study Session 12, LOS 45.e)

84. **B** Since the portfolio manager is not directing the flow of cash into and out of the account, the time-weighted annual rate of return is the appropriate performance measure. Calculate the 2-year holding period return +1, then take the square root and subtract 1 to get the annual time-weighted rate of return:
$[(11.2 / 10)(12.5 / 12.4)(15 / 11.9)]^{1/2} – 1 = 19.29\%$. (Study Session 12, LOS 43.a)

85. **C** A *stop buy order* is a conditional market order by which an investor directs the purchase of a stock if it rises to a certain price. Stop buys are placed above the current market price. Limit orders can have market price as the limit, used when lack of liquidity is a concern. (Study Session 13, LOS 46.g, h)

86. **C** $P/E = \dfrac{\text{dividend payout ratio}}{k - g}$

dividend payout ratio = 1 – retention ratio = 1 – 0.4 = 0.6

growth rate (g) = retention rate × ROE = 0.4 × 15% = 6%

$P/E = \dfrac{0.6}{0.14 - 0.06} = 7.5$

(Study Session 14, LOS 51.h)

87. **C** The expected growth rate in dividends is an input into the dividend discount model, but the real risk-free rate, the expected inflation rate, and the risk premium are the components of the required rate of return. (Study Session 14, LOS 51.c)

88. **C** High return on invested capital and high pricing power are associated with high industry concentration (i.e., small number of firms), high barriers to entry, and low industry capacity. (Study Session 14, LOS 50.g)

89. **A** If capital markets are weak-form efficient and semistrong-form efficient, no publicly available information can be used to earn abnormal (risk-adjusted) returns. (Study Session 13, LOS 48.e)

90. **B** Time line = $0 now; $0 in year 1; $0 in year 2; $1 in year 3.

$$P_2 = \frac{D_3}{(k-g)} = \frac{1}{(0.17 - 0.07)} = \$10$$

Note that the price is always one year before the dividend date. Solve for the PV of $10 to be received in two years.

FV = 10; N = 2; I = 17; CPT → PV = $7.31. (Study Session 14, LOS 51.e)

91. **C** The forecast year-end price, *P*, is:

$$P = EPS \times \left(\frac{P}{E}\right) = 10(12) = 120$$

$$\text{expected return} = \frac{\text{dividend} + (\text{ending price} - \text{beginning price})}{\text{beginning price}} = \frac{\$5 + \$120 - \$100}{\$100} = 0.25 \text{ or } 25\%$$

(Study Session 14, LOS 51.e, h)

92. **C** There is no maximum time for which a security can be borrowed. It must be returned whenever the lender requires it to be. (Study Session 13, LOS 46.e)

93. **A** Consumers buy fewer durable goods, such as furniture, during recessions and buy more during expansions. As a result, producers of these goods tend to have cyclical demand, revenues, and earnings. Operating leverage (high fixed costs as a proportion of total costs) also contributes to cyclicality of earnings. (Study Session 14, LOS 50.c)

94. **C** Under cumulative voting, shareholders receive one vote per share for each board position election but can vote them for any board candidate or spread them over multiple candidates. This allows, for example, a holder of 20% of the shares to elect one of five board members. Under statutory voting, a minority shareholder could not elect any board members based only on their share voting rights. (Study Session 14, LOS 49.b)

95. **B** Equal-weighted indexes require regular and frequent rebalancing, because price changes of their component securities will cause component weights to drift away from their target weights. Price-weighted indexes and market-capitalization weighted indexes generally do not require regular rebalancing, because both the target weight and actual weight of each security varies with the price of that security. (Study Session 13, LOS 47.f)

96. **C** The shakeout phase of the industry life cycle is characterized by slowing growth, intense competition, and declining profitability. The mature phase is characterized by industry consolidation and little or no growth. In the decline phase of the industry lifecycle, growth is negative and excess capacity results. (Study Session 14, LOS 50.h)

97. **B** Long-term, low-coupon bonds are more sensitive than short-term and high-coupon bonds. Prices are more sensitive to rate decreases than to rate increases (duration rises as yields fall). (Study Session 15, LOS 53.c)

98. **C** Resetting interest rates makes the bond less, not more, susceptible to interest rate changes. (Study Session 15, LOS 53.e)

99. **C** $$\text{taxable-equivalent yield} = \frac{\text{tax-exempt yield}}{1 - \text{marginal tax rate}} = \frac{0.04}{1 - 0.28} = 0.0556 \text{ or } 5.56\%$$

(Study Session 15, LOS 55.i)

100. **C** *Prefunded municipal bonds* are bonds collateralized by an escrow of securities guaranteed by the U.S. government. *Revenue bonds* are supported through revenues generated from projects that are funded with the proceeds of the original bond issue.
(Study Session 15, LOS 54.b, f, g)

101. **B** A BEY of 8% is equivalent to a 6-month discount rate of 8 / 2 = 4%.

$$1,025 = \frac{50}{1.04} + \frac{1,050}{(1+r)^2}$$

$$1,025 - 48.08 = \frac{1,050}{(1+r)^2}$$

$$(1+r)^2 = \frac{1,050}{976.92} = 1.0748$$

$$r = (1.0748)^{0.50} - 1$$

r = 0.0367 or 7.34% on a bond equivalent basis

(Study Session 16, LOS 57.e)

102. **A** "Notching" refers to the credit rating agency practice of assigning ratings to debt issues that differ from the issuer's credit rating. An issuer credit rating applies to a firm's senior unsecured debt. Debt issues with different seniority or covenants may be notched to a higher or lower issue credit rating. (Study Session 16, LOS 59.c)

103. **A** $\frac{\Delta P}{P} = -D_{mod}\Delta i + C(\Delta i)^2$

$\frac{\Delta P}{P} = (-)(8)(-0.005) + (50)(-0.005)^2 = +0.0400 + 0.00125 = +0.04125$, or up 4.125%

The price would thus be $1,000 × 1.04125 = $1,041.25. (Study Session 16, LOS 58.h)

104. **B** Creating a CMO can redistribute the prepayment risk among the tranches, but it does not alter the overall prepayment risk of a mortgage passthrough security. CMOs are created from MBS. The prepayment option benefits the issuer, or homeowner, not the investor. (Study Session 15, LOS 54.e, f)

105. **C** A put option may be exercised by the holder, not the issuer. The other statements are true. Interest rate floors benefit the holder by providing a lower limit (or minimum) on the interest rate the bondholder will receive. To understand why the prepayment right granted to a mortgage holder benefits the issuer, remember that the issuer here is the homeowner. The bank acts as a passthrough from the homeowner to the owner of a bond collateralized by the loan. The right to prepay if interest rates decrease is a benefit to the homeowner. If the homeowner prepays, the holder of the bond has reinvestment risk. (Study Session 15, LOS 52.e)

106. **B** The clean price of the bond is the quoted price, 89.14% of par value, which is $891.40. (Study Session 15, LOS 52.c)

107. **C** The friend is incorrect about TIPS (the coupon rate is fixed, the par value is adjusted for inflation) and is correct about the bid-ask spread for on-the-run issues (on-the-run issues are more liquid and, thus, have a narrower bid-ask spread). (Study Session 15, LOS 54.b)

108. **A** When the foreign currency appreciates, each foreign currency-denominated cash flow buys more domestic currency units—increasing the domestic currency return from the investment. The appreciation of the foreign asset benefits the investor as well. (Study Session 15, LOS 53.l)

109. **C** Reinvestment risk becomes more problematic when the current coupons being reinvested are relatively large. (Study Session 15, LOS 53.i)

110. **C** The zero-volatility spread is the constant spread that is added to each Treasury spot rate to equate the present value of a bond's cash flows to its actual market price. (Study Session 16, LOS 57.f)

111. **A** Call options represent an obligation to perform in the case of the seller. The owner of the option (buy) has the right, but not an obligation, to purchase an underlying good at a specified price for a specified time from the seller. (Study Session 17, LOS 63.a, b, c)

112. **B** Exchange-traded options are available on many individual stocks. Options on currencies and government bonds trade primarily over the counter. (Study Session 17, LOS 63.d)

113. **A** In a foreign currency swap, both parties exchange full interest payments. The New Zealand company pays 6% variable on USD (USD 60,000). The U.S. company pays 7% fixed on NZD (NZD 140,000). (Study Session 17, LOS 64.b)

114. **A** The dealer pays the fixed rate for 91 days. Dealer payment = (5.50%)(91 / 365)($50M) = $685,616.44.

The fund pays the return on the Midcap Index: $\left(\dfrac{1{,}052.5}{1{,}038.4}-1\right)\$50M = \$678{,}929.12$

The dealer is the net payer: $685,616.44 − $678,929.12 = $6,687.32

(Study Session 17, LOS 64.b)

115. **C** *Forwards* are subject to default risk, but *futures* are not. *Forwards* are individualized contracts, but *futures* are standardized. (Study Session 17, LOS 62.b)

116. **B** A futures exchange sets the minimum price fluctuation, or "tick size," for the contracts that trade on that exchange. Speculators enter the futures market in pursuit of profit, accepting risk in the endeavor. Hedgers trade futures to reduce some pre-existing risk exposure. The clearinghouse takes no active position in the market but interposes itself between both parties to every transaction. Thus, the clearinghouse guarantees that traders in the future market will honor their obligations. (Study Session 17, LOS 62.a)

117. **B** By investing in a mortgage-backed security, an investor gains exposure to real estate, a category of alternative investments. Emerging markets are not classified as alternative investments. Neither convertible bonds nor high-yield bonds in general are classified as alternative investments, although some hedge funds (a class of alternative investments) invest in these assets. (Study Session 18, LOS 66.a, b)

118. **C** The fee may actually be substantial since, in addition to paying the manager of the FOF, a fee must be paid to each hedge fund within the FOF. (Study Session 18, LOS 66.d)

119. **C** Private investment in public equities refers to a private equity firm providing equity financing to publicly traded companies. Angel investing refers to financing the formation of a business. Mezzanine financing refers to subordinated equity-linked debt or preferred shares issued to finance a leveraged buyout. (Study Session 18, LOS 66.d)

120. **B** If a hedge fund has a high water mark, incentive fees are based on increases in investors' accounts above their highest previous values. As a result, fund managers do not receive incentive fees on returns that reverse previous losses. A hurdle rate is a minimum return a fund must achieve in a given period before fund managers receive incentive fees. A 2-and-20 structure means fund managers receive a 2% management fee and a 20% incentive fee; other provisions determine the base amounts on which these fees are calculated. (Study Session 18, LOS 66.f)

Exam 2
Afternoon Session Answer Key

To get valuable feedback on how your score compares to those of other Level I candidates, use your Username and Password to gain Online Access at schweser.com and choose the left-hand menu item "Practice Exams Vol. 1."

1. B	31. B	61. A	91. B
2. A	32. A	62. C	92. C
3. C	33. A	63. B	93. C
4. C	34. A	64. C	94. A
5. A	35. C	65. A	95. C
6. A	36. A	66. B	96. A
7. A	37. A	67. C	97. C
8. C	38. C	68. B	98. B
9. A	39. A	69. B	99. C
10. C	40. C	70. A	100. B
11. C	41. B	71. A	101. C
12. A	42. A	72. C	102. C
13. B	43. B	73. B	103. C
14. C	44. A	74. C	104. A
15. C	45. C	75. A	105. C
16. B	46. B	76. B	106. C
17. B	47. A	77. C	107. B
18. A	48. C	78. A	108. B
19. B	49. A	79. A	109. A
20. A	50. C	80. A	110. B
21. C	51. C	81. B	111. B
22. C	52. A	82. B	112. C
23. B	53. A	83. A	113. C
24. B	54. B	84. C	114. A
25. A	55. C	85. A	115. C
26. A	56. B	86. C	116. A
27. B	57. A	87. B	117. A
28. C	58. B	88. A	118. C
29. C	59. A	89. C	119. A
30. B	60. B	90. B	120. B

Exam 2
Afternoon Session Answers

Answers referencing the Standards of Practice address Study Session 1, LOS 1.b, c and LOS 2.a, b, c, except where noted.

1. **B** Standard VI(B) Priority of Transactions. Front-running is the purchase or sale of securities in advance of client trades to take advantage of knowledge of client activity and should be completely prohibited, not simply limited. Blackout periods and pre-clearance of employee trades are ways of accomplishing this.

2. **A** Perez violated Standard V(A) Diligence and Reasonable Basis. Perez is responsible for performing diligent and thorough research on the companies he recommends to clients. Overhearing a conversation among analysts who are recommending PharmCo does not constitute a reasonable basis for changing his recommendation and certainly does not suggest independence of thought in his investment recommendation.

3. **C** Under Standard I(C) Misrepresentation, Winkler must identify Thompson as having developed the original model to avoid the prohibition against plagiarism. The only permitted exception is using factual information published by recognized financial and statistical reporting services such as S&P.

4. **C** According to Standard VI(A) Disclosure of Conflicts, Smith should disclose to clients, prospects, and his employer all matters that could reasonably be expected to interfere with his ability to make unbiased and objective recommendations. All actual and potential conflicts of interest need to be disclosed. Clearly the potential exists for Smith to receive a monetary benefit from favorable reports on Braden. Smith may be tempted to issue overly positive recommendations in order to increase the value of his options and maintain a favorable relationship with Braden to ensure his income from the consulting arrangement. These potential influences must be disclosed so that clients, prospects, and his employer can evaluate the objectivity of his recommendations.

5. **A** Standard I(A) Knowledge of the Law requires members and candidates to comply with the strictest requirement among the law where they reside, the law in the area where they do business, and the Code and Standards. In this case, the Code and Standards is the strictest. Standard III(B) Fair Dealing prohibits members and candidates from withholding shares in oversubscribed IPOs from clients for their own benefit.

6. **A** Standard IV(B) Additional Compensation Arrangements requires that members and candidates obtain written consent from their employers to enter into the agreement for additional contingent compensation from a client. Harris only received verbal consent. The concern is that such an arrangement might create partiality to Cline's portfolio over those of her other clients.

7. **A** Once a firm has met all the required elements of the GIPS, the firm may only use the statement in answer choice A to indicate compliance. Any deviation in the compliance statement constitutes a violation of GIPS. (Study Session 1, LOS 3.c)

8. **C** Standard V(A) Diligence and Reasonable Basis. Cantor did not have a reasonable and adequate basis for recommending a "Buy." Watson's enthusiasm and claim that everyone knows that the stock will perform well are not Cantor's conclusions. She must perform her own analysis before changing her investment recommendation. She has also violated Standard I(B) Independence and Objectivity since she has not exhibited the independence of analysis and thought that is required by the Standard.

9. **A** The actions are not in violation of the Standards. Under Standard IV(A) Loyalty, the use in new employment, of knowledge and experience gained in previous employment, is not prohibited. He recreated the records from public sources as required by Standard V(C) Record Retention.

10. **C** The first requirement of the Code of Ethics is that members and candidates "act with integrity, competence, diligence, respect, and in an ethical manner with the public, clients, prospective clients, employers, employees, colleagues in the investment profession, and other participants in the global capital markets." Knowing the applicable laws and regulations is required by Standard I(A) Knowledge of the Law. Standard VII(A) Conduct as Members and Candidates in the CFA Program requires members and candidates not to compromise the integrity of CFA Institute.

11. **C** According to Standard IV(A) Loyalty, the interests of a member or candidate's employer are secondary to protecting the interests of the clients. In this circumstance, whistle blowing is justified. As long as his motivation is clearly not for personal gain, he may, according to the Standards, violate employer policies in this case. While he is only required to dissociate from the suspect activity, he is not prohibited from reporting it.

12. **A** The simplest, most conservative, and most effective way to comply with Standard III(E) Preservation of Confidentiality is to avoid disclosing any information received from a client, except to authorized fellow employees who are also working for the client.

13. **B** This statement conforms to the Code and Standards, as it is a factual statement related to a benefit of earning the CFA designation. The other answers violate Standard VII(B) reference to CFA Institute, the CFA Designation, and the CFA Program because they make promises that are tied to the CFA designation or suggest that holding the CFA designation implies superior investment performance.

14. **C** Standard VI(C) Referral Fees requires that members and candidates should disclose any referral arrangement in which the member or candidate receives some form of benefit from the referral. Such disclosure will allow the clients and employer to evaluate any impartiality that the referral arrangement may cause.

15. **C** The information received by Jenkins is covered by Standard II(A) Material Nonpublic Information, under which members who possess material nonpublic information related to the value of a security are prohibited from trading, or causing others to trade in, that security. Jenkins received material nonpublic information about the impending closure of the investment bank which was a large subsidiary of the parent company. For purposes of compliance with Standard II(A), Jenkins may attempt to achieve public dissemination of the information, and in the event that this is not possible, inform his compliance officer of the information. However, under no circumstances should Jenkins share material nonpublic information with other investment personnel for informational purposes or otherwise. Sharing such information may cause others to trade on the information in violation of Standard II(A).

16. **B** Woods' marketing activities for LAM's new international equity product violate Standard I(C) Misrepresentation by misrepresenting the services LAM could provide and the firm's qualifications in international equity. Members and candidates shall not make or imply any assurances or guarantees regarding the performance of any investment. The marketing presentation created by Woods regarding LAM's international equity product misrepresents the qualifications of the firm and provides assurances of performance in violation of the Standard. Although the new portfolio managers hired by LAM have investment experience in managing international equity, the firm clearly does not have a proven track record, nor overall experience in handling international equity mandates.

17. **B** According to Standard II(A) Material Nonpublic Information, the use of security analysis combined with nonmaterial nonpublic information to arrive at significant conclusions is allowable under the mosaic theory.

18. **A** All fee-paying discretionary accounts must be included in composites, but including non-fee-paying accounts is not required. The other statements are requirements for compliance. (Study Session 1, LOS 4.a)

19. **B** With monthly payments, we need a monthly rate:

    6% / 12 = 0.5%. Next, solve for the monthly payment. The calculator keystrokes are:

    PV = 200,000; FV = 0; N = 360; I/Y = 0.5; CPT → PMT = –$1,199.10. The balance at any time on an amortizing loan is the present value of the remaining payments. There are 312 payments remaining after the 48th payment is made. The loan balance at this point is: PMT = –1,199.10; FV = 0; N = 312; I/Y = 0.5; CPT → PV = $189,228.90.

    Note that only N has to be changed to calculate this new present value; the other inputs are unchanged. (Study Session 2, LOS 5.f)

20. **A** What is a bond question doing here? CFA Institute examiners can and will insert material from other topics as they see fit. This is just a reminder to be on your guard!

    First, find the yield on the note at time of purchase. The appropriate calculator steps are:

    PV = –10,440; FV = 10,000; PMT = 600; N = 5; CPT → I/Y = 4.9842%. Next, value the note at a yield of 3.9842% with four years to maturity.

    FV = 10,000; PMT = 600; N = 4; I/Y = 3.9842; CPT → PV = $10,731.99.

    Finally, calculate the holding period return. The formula is:

    $$R_t = \frac{P_t - P_{t-1} + D_t}{P_{t-1}}$$

    $$R_t = \frac{\$10,731.99 - \$10,440 + \$600}{\$10,440} = 8.5\%$$

    (Study Session 2, LOS 6.c and Study Session 16, LOS 56.c, 57.b)

21. **C** $\dfrac{195}{160} - 1 = 0.21875,$ or 21.88%

A longer approach is to calculate the holding period return for each stock for the year, then weight the returns using beginning values.

Stock A $= \dfrac{20 - 10}{10} = 100\%$

Stock B $= \dfrac{60 + 1 - 50}{50} = 22\%$

Stock C $= \dfrac{110 + 4 - 100}{100} = 14\%$

$\left(\dfrac{10}{160}\right)(100\%) + \left(\dfrac{50}{160}\right)(22\%) + \left(\dfrac{100}{160}\right)(14\%) = 0.06250 + 0.06875 + 0.08750 = 0.21875,$ or 21.88%

(Study Session 2, LOS 7.e)

22. **C** From least to most information, the ordering of measurements scales is nominal, ordinal, interval, and ratio. (Study Session 2, LOS 7.a)

23. **B** $G = [(1.10)(0.85)(1.00)(1.05)]^{0.25} - 1$

$G = (0.98175)^{0.25} - 1 = 0.9954 - 1 = -0.00459 \approx -0.5\%$

Note: Taking a number to the 0.25 power is the same as taking the fourth root of the number. (Study Session 2, LOS 7.e)

24. **B** The mean absolute deviation is the mean of the absolute values of the differences between each number and the mean. Because the mean is (45 + 20 + 30 + 25) / 4 = 30, the mean absolute deviation is $\dfrac{10 + 5 + 0 + 15}{4} = 7.5$. (Study Session 2, LOS 7.g)

25. **A** As long as the investor earns at least a 5% return over the next year, the value of her portfolio after deducting the $100,000 down payment will not fall below $950,000. We first calculate the SFRatio for each of the two possible portfolios. We know that:

$\text{SFRatio} = \dfrac{[E(R_p) - R_L]}{\sigma_p}$

$\text{SFRatio}_1 = \dfrac{17 - 5}{15} = 0.8$

$\text{SFRatio}_2 = \dfrac{12 - 5}{10} = 0.7$

$\text{SFRatio}_3 = \dfrac{8 - 5}{6} = 0.5$

The SFR is the number of standard deviations that the minimum return is below the mean (expected) return. The optimal portfolio is the one with the greatest SFR as it has the lowest probability of a return below the minimum. Based on the SFRatio, the investor would prefer Portfolio 1. (Study Session 3, LOS 9.n)

26. **A**   Triangles are thought to be continuation patterns, suggesting that the trend will continue in the same direction it was going when the triangle pattern formed. An RSI above 70 is thought to indicate an overbought condition, which can be a warning sign that the current uptrend is not sustainable. An uptrend line should act as a support level in an uptrend when the price approaches the trendline from above. If an uptrend line acts as a resistance level, the price must have broken down through the trendline, which is a sign that the uptrend may be ending. (Study Session 3, LOS 12.c, d, e)

27. **B**   An unbiased estimator has an expected value equal to the true value of the population parameter. A consistent estimator is more accurate the greater the sample size. An efficient estimator has the sampling distribution that is less than that of any other unbiased estimator. (Study Session 3, LOS 10.g)

28. **C**   According to Chebyshev's inequality, the proportion of the observations within 3 standard deviations of the mean is at least $1 - (1 / 3^2) = 0.89$ or 89%. This holds for any distribution, regardless of the shape. (Study Session 2, LOS 7.h)

29. **C**   Using the addition rule for probabilities, P(analyst or positive) = P(analyst) + P(positive) – P(analyst and positive). P(A or positive) = 130 / 200 + 110 / 200 – (70 / 200) = 0.65 + 0.55 – 0.35 = 0.85. Alternatively, CEOs that predict positive impact = 40, analysts = 130, Prob (CEO positive or analyst) = (40 + 130) / 200 = 85%. (Study Session 2, LOS 8.f)

30. **B**   There are many reasons that a statistically significant result may not be economically significant (meaningful). Besides transactions costs, we must consider the risk of the strategy as well. For example, although the mean abnormal return to the strategy over the 5-year sample period is greater than transactions costs, abnormal returns for various sub-periods may be highly variable. In this case the risk of the strategy return from month to month or quarter to quarter may be too great to make employing the strategy in client accounts economically attractive. (Study Session 3, LOS 11.d)

31. **B**   In simple random sampling, each item in the population has an equal chance of being selected. The analyst's method meets this criterion. (Study Session 3, LOS 10.c)

32. **A**   Nonparametric tests can be used in a variety of instances where the assumptions required for parametric tests cannot be sustained. A runs test can be used to test for the randomness of a sample. Both of the other tests are parametric because they test the value of a parameter of the underlying distribution. (Study Session 3, LOS 11.j)

33. **A**   The TRT/PSG cross rate is 5.5 × 8.0 = 44 TRT/PSG. Because the answer choices are quoted as PSG/TRT, we need to invert this result: 1 / 44 = 0.0227 PSG/TRT. (Study Session 6, LOS 21.d)

34. **A**   Because aggregate income is the same as aggregate output, measuring GDP by summing incomes or expenditures should produce the same value, except for a statistical discrepancy that results from using different data sources. The sum-of-value-added method of calculating GDP records the sum of the increases in value of goods and services at each stage of their production and distribution. The resulting total for GDP is the same as that reached by the value-of-final-output method because the sum of value added to a good at all stages of processing is equal to its selling price. Both methods calculate GDP based on expenditures. (Study Session 5, LOS 17.a, b)

35. **C**   The J-curve effect refers to a plot of the trade deficit over time when the domestic currency depreciates (the foreign currency appreciates). The trade deficit gets worse initially but then improves over time, either because export and import demand are more elastic in the long run or because existing contracts for future delivery are fixed in foreign currency terms in the short run. (Study Session 6, LOS 21.i)

36. **A**   Promoting economic growth and reducing world poverty are among the primary goals of the World Bank. The IMF primarily promotes the growth of international trade, supports exchange rate stability, and provides a forum for cooperation on monetary problems internationally. The WTO has a primary focus on reaching trade agreements and settling trade disputes. (Study Session 6, LOS 20.i)

37. **A**   The quantity theory of money hypothesizes that a change in the money supply, at full employment, will cause a proportional change in the price level because velocity and real output will be unaffected. According to the equation of exchange, MV = PY, output of goods and services produced, Y, at full employment cannot change, so the price level, P, must increase. (Study Session 5, LOS 19.c)

38. **C**   In a conventional fixed peg arrangement, a country pegs its currency within a margin of ±1% versus another currency or a basket that includes the currencies of its major trading or financial partners. Market-determined exchange rates are a characteristic of an independently floating exchange rate regime. (Study Session 6, LOS 21.h)

39. **A**   Quantity supplied is zero at P = 17, and quantity supplied at P = 25 is 80. The area of the producer surplus triangle is 1/2 × (25 − 17) × 80 = 320. (Study Session 4, LOS 13.i)

40. **C**   Like all price searchers, monopolists will expand output until marginal revenue equals marginal cost. Monopolists do not charge the highest possible price which would be the price resulting in only one sale. A monopolist seeks to maximize profit, not price. (Study Session 4, LOS 16.d)

41. **B**   Regardless of whether a tax is imposed on suppliers or consumers, the relative burden of the tax to each depends on the relative elasticities of supply and demand. Since demand is relatively less elastic than supply, the burden of the tax will be greater on consumers than on producers. These burdens are equivalent to decreases in producer and consumer surpluses. Total consumer and producer surpluses will be reduced by the amount of the resulting deadweight loss in addition to the total amount of tax collected. (Study Session 4, LOS 13.j, k)

42. **A**   Inflation that is unexpected, or higher than expected, shifts wealth from lenders to borrowers. Unexpected deflation has the opposite effect. Because interest rates include a premium for expected inflation, an inflation rate that matches expectations does not shift wealth from lenders to borrowers. (Study Session 5, LOS 19.g)

43. **B**   The supply curve for a firm under perfect competition is its marginal cost curve above average variable cost. As long as price exceeds AVC, the firm will produce up to the quantity where MC = Price, which is also MR in this case. (Study Session 4, LOS 16.c)

44. **A**   Long-run aggregate supply is related to the level of technology and the available quantities of labor and capital. If the prices of productive inputs increase, short-run aggregate supply decreases (the SRAS curve shifts to the left), but long-run aggregate supply (potential real GDP) is unaffected. (Study Session 5, LOS 17.h, l)

45. **C**   The matching principle holds that expenses should be accounted for in the same performance measurement period as the revenue they generate. (Study Session 8, LOS 25.d)

46. **B**   The description of the percentage-of-completion method is accurate. The completed contract method under U.S. GAAP recognizes revenue only when the entire project is complete. The installment method recognizes profit in proportion to cash collected. (Study Session 8, LOS 25.b)

47. **A**   This is the correct treatment of this change. The company must disclose the nature of the error and its effect on net income and restate any prior period results that are presented in the current financial statements. The other choices are incorrect. (Study Session 8, LOS 25.e)

48. **C**   Firms that give employee stock options as part of compensation often buy back stock to offset the dilution from option exercise. Since the cost to the firm of option exercise is more properly a part of compensation expense, the analyst should reclassify the financing cash flow to repurchase shares as operating cash flow. Neither financing payables nor securitizing receivables results in financing outflows. (Study Session 10, LOS 34.a)

49. **A**

Net income	+100
Adjustment for noncash and nonoperating items:	
Depreciation	+25
Deferred taxes (increase)	+17
Profit from sale of equipment	−5
Adjustment for working capital items:	
Accounts receivable (decrease)	+30
Inventory (increase)	−17
Accounts payable (increase)	+10
Wages payable (decrease)	−5
Cash flow from operations	+$155

Dividends paid are CFF, not CFO. (Study Session 8, LOS 27.f)

50. **C**   Interest income is considered an operating cash flow under U.S. GAAP. (Study Session 8, LOS 27.a)

51. **C**   Dilution occurs since the exercise price for the warrants ($45) is less than the average market price for the shares ($50). The incremental number of shares outstanding is found from:

$$\left(\frac{\text{market price} - \text{exercise price}}{\text{market price}}\right) \times \# \text{warrants} = \left(\frac{50 - 45}{50}\right) \times 120,000 = 12,000$$

Number of shares to use in diluted EPS calculation = 500,000 + 12,000 = 512,000. (Study Session 8, LOS 25.g, h)

52. **A**   As an example, start with CA = 2, CL = 1, and Inv = 1.2. We begin with a current ratio of 2 and a quick ratio of 0.8. If the firm increases short-term bank debt (a current liability) by 1 to buy inventory (a current asset) of 1, both the numerator and denominator increase by 1, resulting in $\frac{3}{2} = 1.5$ (new current ratio) and $\frac{3 - 2.2}{2} = 0.4$ (new quick ratio). (Study Session 8, LOS 28.b)

53. **A** With an operating lease, the entire lease payment is recorded as rent expense and classified as an operating cash outflow. A finance lease results in a lower current ratio than an operating lease because the current portion of the principal repayment component will be added to current liabilities. The lessor does not recognize any profit at the inception of a direct financing lease. (Study Session 9, LOS 32.h)

54. **B** U.S. GAAP requires R&D costs to be expensed. IFRS requires research costs to be expensed, but development costs are capitalized. (Study Session 9, LOS 30.a, b)

55. **C** LIFO will result in lower net income than FIFO in the current period, during a period of rising prices. The other choices will tend to increase current period earnings. (Study Session 9, LOS 29.c, 30.a, c)

56. **B** Securities that can be converted to common stock are said to be dilutive to earnings if conversion would result in lower earnings per share. A simple capital structure has only common stock or only common stock and nonconvertible stock. It contains no securities that could ever become or create common stock, even antidilutive ones. Whether warrants are antidilutive depends on the average stock price over the reporting period, not the value at the reporting date. (Study Session 8, LOS 25.h)

57. **A** Since this company has a simple capital structure, basic and diluted EPS are equal. The numerator equals net income − preferred dividends = 210,000 − (11,000 shares × 0.10 dividend × 100 par) = 210,000 − 110,000 = 100,000. The weighted average shares outstanding = 22,500 − (5,000 shares repurchased × 0.50 midyear) = 22,500 − 2,500 = 20,000. Then, $\text{basic EPS} = \text{diluted EPS} = \dfrac{100,000}{20,000} = \$5$ per share.

    (Study Session 8, LOS 25.g)

58. **B** FIFO companies have higher net income, lower COGS, higher inventory, and higher taxes. (Study Session 9, LOS 29.e)

59. **A** Under IFRS, inventory values are revalued upward only to the extent they were previously written down. In this case, that is from €25,000 back up to the original value of €28,000. The increase is reported as gain for the period and will increase COGS of units sold during the current period. (Study Session 9, LOS 29.f)

60. **B** Remeasurements (actuarial gains and losses, difference between actual return and expected return on plan assets) are recognized as other comprehensive income under IFRS and are not amortized. (Study Session 9, LOS 32.k)

61. **A** These relationships are reversed in the later years of the asset's life if the firm's capital expenditures decline. (Study Session 9, LOS 30.c)

62. **C** Deferred tax liability refers to balance sheet amounts that are created when tax expense is greater than taxes payable. (Study Session 9, LOS 31.a)

63. **B**   EBT / EBIT is the interest burden, the second component in the extended DuPont equation. It shows that more leverage does not always lead to higher ROE. As leverage rises, so does the interest burden. The positive effects of leverage can be offset by the higher interest payments that accompany higher levels of debt. Net income / EBT is called the tax burden and is equal to (1 – tax rate). The higher the tax rate, the lower the ROE level. EBIT / revenue is called the EBIT margin or operating margin. (Study Session 8, LOS 28.d)

64. **C**   Issuing debt results in a cash inflow from financing. Payment of debt at maturity has no effect on cash flow from operations but decreases cash flow from financing by the face value of the debt. (Study Session 9 LOS 32.a, b)

65. **A**   The liability method (SFAS 109 of U.S. GAAP) takes a balance sheet approach and adjusts deferred tax assets and liabilities to future tax rates. An increase in the tax rate increases the value of both deferred tax assets and deferred tax liabilities. (Study Session 9, LOS 31.e)

66. **B**   When a question does not specify which accounting standards apply, candidates are instructed to assume International Financial Reporting Standards (IFRS). According to IFRS, property held for the purpose of earning rental income is classified as investment property. However, when a property is transferred from owner-occupied to investment property, a firm using the fair value model must treat any increase in the property's value as a revaluation. That is, the firm may only recognize a gain on the income statement to the extent that it reverses a previously recognized loss. (Study Session 9, LOS 30.k)

67. **C**   Under U.S. GAAP, an asset is considered impaired when its book value is greater than the sum of the estimated undiscounted future cash flows from its use and disposal. (Study Session 9, LOS 30.h)

68. **B**   The four general categories are: (1) scale and diversification, (2) operational efficiency, (3) margin stability, and (4) leverage. Larger companies and those with more different product lines and greater geographic diversification are better credit risks. High operating efficiency is indicative of a better credit risk. Stable profit margins indicate a higher probability of repayment and thus, a better credit risk. Firms with greater earnings in relation to their debt level are better credit risks. While the availability of collateral certainly reduces lender risk, it is not one of the general categories used by credit rating agencies to determine *capacity* to repay. Specifically, they would consider (1) several specific accounting ratios and (2) business characteristics. The availability of collateral falls into neither category. (Study Session 10, LOS 35.c)

69. **B**   The cost of preferred stock is calculated as the preferred dividend divided by the market price, not the par value. (Study Session 11, LOS 37.g)

70. **A**   We know that at a 14% discount rate, the NPV of Project X is zero and the NPV of Project Y is greater than zero. There is no well-defined relationship between the required rate of return and ordinary payback. If Project Y is smaller in size, its NPV may be smaller than that of Project X. (Study Session 11, LOS 36.d, e)

71. **A**   Financing costs should not be included in incremental cash flows. They are reflected in the weighted average cost of capital (WACC). New business at other branches is a positive externality and the $150,000 to sell the property is an opportunity cost. (Study Session 11, LOS 36.b)

72. **C** To use the pure-play method, an asset beta is calculated by removing the effects of leverage (delevering) from the comparable company's equity beta, then a project beta is estimated by adjusting the asset beta (relevering) based on the capital structure of the company that is evaluating the project. (Study Session 11, LOS 37.i)

73. **B** An increase in days of receivables outstanding, other things equal, will lengthen both the operating and cash conversion cycles, indicating poorer working capital management. An increase in days of payables outstanding, other things equal, would decrease the cash conversion cycle. A decrease in cash and marketable securities could simply indicate better management of cash (e.g., buying back its common stock or investing excess cash in profitable business opportunities or securities). (Study Session 11, LOS 40.c)

74. **C** The marginal (or weighted average) cost of capital is the appropriate discount rate for projects that have the same level of risk as the firm's existing projects. For a project with a higher degree of risk, cash flows should be discounted at a rate higher than the firm's WACC. Since this project's IRR is equal to the company's WACC, its NPV must be zero if the cash flows are discounted at the WACC. If the cash flows are discounted at a rate higher than the WACC to account for the project's higher risk, the NPV must be negative. Therefore, the project would reduce the value of the company, so management should reject it. Choice B is incorrect because a company considers its capital raising and budgeting decisions independently. Each investment decision must be made assuming a WACC which includes each of the different sources of capital and is based on the long-run target weights. (Study Session 11, LOS 36.d, 37.a, e)

75. **A** There are benefits to both an annually elected board and a board with staggered multiple-year terms so neither can be considered a "requirement." An annually elected board provides flexibility to nominate new board members in response to changes in the marketplace. Staggered boards may provide better continuity of board expertise and leadership but are more difficult to replace. (Study Session 11, LOS 41.b)

76. **B** Capital component breakpoint = $\dfrac{\text{value at which component's cost of capital changes}}{\text{component's weight in WACC}}$

   Debt breakpoint = $\dfrac{\$200,000}{0.40}$ = \$500,000

   (Study Session 11, LOS 37.k)

77. **C** An increase in debt will increase interest expense, which will decrease net income but not operating income, which is calculated before subtracting interest expense. For a profitable firm, the decrease in net income will be offset by the decrease in equity from the repurchase of common stock, so that ROE increases. The effect of the increase in financial leverage will, however, increase the variability of ROE for a given change in operating earnings. (Study Session 11, LOS 38.c)

78. **A** Stock splits and reverse stock splits do not affect a firm's future cash flows unless dividend yields are increased as a result. These transactions change the number of shares outstanding but they do not raise capital for the firm. (Study Session 11, LOS 39.a, 40.d)

79. **A** E(R) = 7% + 0.9(11% − 7%) = 10.6%. Because the expected return of 10% is less than the required return of 10.6%, the security is overvalued. (Study Session 12, LOS 44.h)

80. **A** The correlation between the two stocks is:

$$\rho_{A,B} = COV_{A,B} / (\sigma_A \times \sigma_B) = 0.001 / (0.05 \times 0.08) = 0.001 / (0.004) = 0.25$$

Note that the formula uses the standard deviations, *not the variances*, of the returns on the two securities. (Study Session 12, LOS 43.b)

81. **B** The three major steps in the portfolio management process are planning, execution, and feedback. Rebalancing the portfolio to its desired asset allocation is part of the feedback step. (Study Session 12, LOS 42.c)

82. **B** Portfolio 1 does not lie on the efficient frontier because it has a lower return than Portfolio 2 but has equal risk. Portfolio 4 does not lie on the efficient frontier because it has higher risk than Portfolio 3 but has the same return. (Study Session 12, LOS 43.g)

83. **A** Variance is a measure of total risk. (Study Session 12, LOS 44.c)

84. **C** Greenbaum's expected return for the coming year is $(62 / 54) - 1 = 14.8\%$. Its risk premium relative to the risk-free rate is $14.8\% - 8.0\% = 6.8\%$. The market risk premium is $12\% - 8\% = 4\%$. Therefore, the beta of Greenbaum must be $6.8 / 4.0 = 1.7$. (Study Session 12, LOS 44.e)

85. **A** Financial markets are said to be operationally efficient if participants can achieve their desired purposes with low transactions costs. Markets are said to be informationally efficient if prices reflect new information rapidly, and allocationally efficient if resources are allocated to their most productive uses. (Study Session 13, LOS 46.k)

86. **C** The weak form of the EMH implies that an investor cannot earn positive abnormal returns on average using technical analysis (market information), after adjusting for transaction costs and taxes. Evidence has shown that insiders can achieve positive abnormal returns on average, but this relates to the strong form of the EMH. (Study Session 13, LOS 48.e)

87. **B** REIT indexes represent a convenient way to invest in real estate. Commodity indexes are based on futures prices of commodities, and are not replicated by investing in the commodities themselves. Hedge fund indexes are biased upward because hedge funds are not required to disclose their performance to index providers and poorly performing funds are less likely to do so (self-selection bias). (Study Session 14, LOS 47.j)

88. **A** Intrinsic value is the present value of the security's future cash flows. The market value of a share is the cumulative investors' estimation of this intrinsic value, and market value is usually somewhat in line with the intrinsic value. A company's book value per share is typically not equal to its intrinsic value per share, since book value is based on the historical cost of assets. (Study Session 14, LOS 49.g)

89. **C** *Step 1*: Determine the discount rate. $7.50\% - 0.75\% = 6.75\%$.

Step 2: Value the preferred. $V_P = \dfrac{\text{dividend}}{k_p} = \dfrac{\$6.00}{0.0675} = \$88.89$.

(Study Session 14, LOS 51.d)

90. **B** Price at which a margin call will occur:

original price × [(1 − initial margin) / (1 − maintenance margin)]

= [$32.00 × (1 − 0.5)] / (1 − 0.25) = $16.00 / 0.75 = $21.33

(Study Session 13, LOS 46.f)

91. **B** ER = RFR + beta(R_M − RFR)

k = E(R) = 0.05 + 1(0.15 − 0.05) = 0.15

Retention (b) = (1 − dividend payout ratio) = 1 − 0.4 = 0.6

g = (ROE)(b) = (0.15)(0.6) = 0.09

$$\text{Value} = \frac{D_1}{k-g} = \frac{\$2.50}{0.15 - 0.09} = \$41.67$$

(Study Session 8, LOS 28.e, and Study Session 14, LOS 51.e)

92. **C** The consumer staples industry is best classified as non-cyclical and defensive. Energy and technology are best classified as cyclical industries. (Study Session 14, LOS 50.c, i)

93. **C** If markets are efficient, investors should not earn consistently superior returns from technical trading rules such as a contrary opinion strategy. A stock price will decrease on a report of an increase in earnings if that increase is less than investors expected based on all the information previously available. An analyst's recommendations could be for stocks with more than market risk, or the analyst's industry may outperform for some period of time. Both could account for outperformance even though markets are efficient. (Study Session 13, LOS 48.e)

94. **A** The security being described here is preferred stock (preference shares). In the event of liquidation of a firm, the claims of preferred equity shareholders are senior to the claims of common stockholders but subordinated to the claims of debt holders. Preferred shares typically have no voting rights. (Study Session 14, LOS 49.a)

95. **C** Equal-weighted index portfolios require rebalancing after each return period because differences in returns among securities will drive the security weightings away from equal weighting. Changes in the security prices automatically adjust the weights in price- and value-weighted index portfolios to their correct values, so funds that track price- and value-weighted indexes do not require frequent rebalancing. (Study Session 13, LOS 47.f)

96. **A** This is essentially a two-stage dividend discount model (DDM) problem. Discounting all future cash flows, we get:

$$P_0 = \frac{1.00}{(1.103)^5} + \frac{1.25}{(1.103)^6} + \frac{(1.25)^2}{(1.103)^7} + \left[\frac{(1.25)^3}{(0.103 - 0.05)(1.103)^7} \right] = \$20.647$$

Note that the constant growth formula can be applied to dividend 8 (1.25^3) because it *will* grow at a constant rate (5%) forever. (Study Session 14, LOS 51.e)

97. **C** The embedded option can be valued by analyzing the difference between the zero-volatility spread and the option-adjusted spread. (Study Session 15, LOS 52.e)

98. **B**   Inclusion of a call feature will decrease the duration of a fixed income security. The other choices increase duration. (Study Session 15, LOS 53.c)

99. **C**   At the time of purchase, the coupon rate = the market rate, so the bond traded at par. One year later, with interest rates unchanged, the bond would still trade at par, or $1,000. Thus, there would be no capital gain or loss from the sale. (Study Session 15, LOS 53.b)

100. **B**   Intangible assets that can be sold, such as trademarks, provide collateral of good quality. A credit analyst should view as low-quality collateral any assets that are likely to be written down in value if a firm encounters financial distress, such as goodwill and deferred tax assets. (Study Session 16, LOS 59.e)

101. **C**   First find the yield to maturity (YTM) of the first bond and use it in the second bond calculation. The calculator sequence to determine the YTM is: PV = –701.22; FV = 1000; PMT = 80; N = 20; CPT → I/Y = 12.00%. We discount the cash flows of the second bond at 12.00%. The calculator steps are: PV = –701.22; FV = 1,000; N = 5; I/Y = 12; CPT → PMT = $37.12. (Study Session 16, LOS 56.d)

102. **C**   Convexity adjustment to %ΔP: convexity measure × $(\Delta i)^2$ × 100 = $(60)(-0.0025)^2(100)$ = 0.0375%. (Study Session 16, LOS 58.h)

103. **C**   YTC: N = 10; PV = –895; PMT = 80 / 2 = 40; FV = 1080; CPT → I/Y = 6.035 × 2 = 12.07%. (Study Session 16, LOS 57.b)

104. **A**   During economic contractions, the probability of default increases for lower-quality issues and their yields increase. When investors anticipate an economic downturn, they tend to sell low-quality issues and buy high-quality issues, causing credit spreads to widen. (Study Session 15, LOS 55.f)

105. **C**   A sinking fund provision is an obligation, not a right, to retire portions of the bond prior to maturity. A nonrefundable bond may be redeemable or callable through means other than refunding. Serial bonds are an issue divided into segments that each have their own maturity date. (Study Session 15, LOS 52.a, d)

106. **C**   Reinvestment is crucial to bond yield, and interest rate risk is price risk. (Study Session 15, LOS 53.a)

107. **B**   Investment grade bonds are BBB– and above. This bond is rated BB, which is below BBB–. (Study Session 15, LOS 53.j)

108. **B**   10% (1 – x) = 6%, x = 40%. (Study Session 15, LOS 55.i)

109. **A**   Effective duration and effective convexity capture the effects from changes in a bond's cash flows when the yield changes. For this reason, they are the appropriate measures of interest rate sensitivity for bonds with embedded options. (Study Session 16, LOS 58.f)

110. **B**   Bonds W and Y are most likely callable, and Bonds X and Z are most likely putable. If the option-adjusted spread is less than the zero-volatility spread, the embedded option has a negative value to the bondholder (e.g., a call option), and if the option-adjusted spread is greater than the zero-volatility spread, the embedded option has a positive value to the bondholder (e.g., a put option). Zero-volatility spreads adjust for the fact that nominal spreads (between the yields to maturity of two bonds) are theoretically correct only when the spot yield curve is flat. All of these bonds' zero-volatility spreads are nearly identical to their nominal spreads to Treasuries, which suggests the spot yield curve is, in fact, approximately flat. (Study Session 16, LOS 57.f)

111. **B** Baker's net cost of the position is 60 + 4 = $64 per share. At exercise she receives $60 per share. Her net loss on the position is –4(100) = –$400. (Study Session 17, LOS 65.b)

112. **C** Candidate 1 is incorrect. In the futures markets, margin is a performance guarantee. It is money deposited by both the long and the short. There is no loan involved (as opposed to in the equity markets) and thus no interest charges. Candidate 2 is correct. (Study Session 17, LOS 62.c)

113. **C** The put holder will exercise the option at expiration whenever the stock's price is less than the exercise price. (Study Session 17, LOS 63.h)

114. **A** A futures contract must be settled by delivery, offset, or exchange for physicals; it cannot be cancelled. (Study Session 17, LOS 62.e)

115. **C** If LIBOR, at the expiration date, is below the rate specified in the FRA, the short receives a payment from the long. FRA contracts are settled in cash. Neither party will borrow from or lend to the other at expiration. (Study Session 17, LOS 61.f)

116. **A** Decreasing volatility of returns on the underlying stock will decrease option values for both puts and calls. An increase in the risk-free rate increases the values of call options on equities and decreases the values of put options on equities. (Study Session 17, LOS 63.o)

117. **A** Leveraged buyouts are the predominant activity pursued by private equity funds. Convertible arbitrage and activist shareholder strategies are more typically associated with hedge funds. (Study Session 18, LOS 66.b)

118. **C** Hedge funds do not typically trade on exchanges. (Study Session 18, LOS 66.d)

119. **A** While commodity futures retain the risk and correlation characteristics of the underlying commodities, the investor does not incur storage costs. Derivatives cannot have higher correlation with spot prices than the commodity itself, as its price is the spot price. Convenience yield is a benefit of owning the actual commodities. (Study Session 18, LOS 66.d)

120. **B** Of the three sources of return for a long commodity futures investment, only the price return can be negative for a market in backwardation. Roll yield is positive because futures prices are less than spot prices when the market is in backwardation, so the investor realizes gains when rolling the position out of expiring contracts and into new contracts. Collateral yield is the interest earned on the T-bills deposited as margin. (Study Session 18, LOS 67.b)

Exam 3
Morning Session Answer Key

To get valuable feedback on how your score compares to those of other Level I candidates, use your Username and Password to gain Online Access at schweser.com and choose the left-hand menu item "Practice Exams Vol. 1."

1. B	31. B	61. B	91. C
2. C	32. A	62. C	92. C
3. B	33. A	63. B	93. C
4. C	34. C	64. A	94. C
5. C	35. C	65. A	95. A
6. B	36. A	66. A	96. A
7. A	37. B	67. A	97. B
8. A	38. C	68. B	98. C
9. A	39. A	69. B	99. B
10. A	40. B	70. A	100. C
11. B	41. B	71. B	101. B
12. B	42. A	72. B	102. C
13. A	43. C	73. A	103. C
14. A	44. A	74. A	104. B
15. A	45. B	75. C	105. A
16. A	46. C	76. A	106. B
17. A	47. A	77. B	107. B
18. A	48. B	78. B	108. C
19. A	49. A	79. A	109. A
20. A	50. A	80. B	110. B
21. C	51. C	81. B	111. C
22. C	52. B	82. A	112. B
23. C	53. B	83. C	113. A
24. A	54. C	84. B	114. C
25. C	55. B	85. A	115. A
26. C	56. A	86. A	116. B
27. A	57. A	87. A	117. A
28. A	58. B	88. B	118. C
29. A	59. A	89. A	119. B
30. A	60. A	90. A	120. B

Exam 3
Morning Session Answers

Answers referencing the Standards of Practice address Study Session 1, LOS 1.b, c and LOS 2.a, b, c, except where noted.

1. **B** Schute has violated the Standard by not taking steps to ensure that the nonpublic information he has received as part of his investment banking work was not shared with others in the firm.

2. **C** Under Standard VII(B) Reference to CFA Institute, the CFA Designation, and the CFA Program, candidates in the CFA Program may appropriately reference their participation in the CFA Program. However, to be considered a candidate, individuals must be registered to take the next scheduled CFA examination. Therefore, Wellington, who completed Level II of the CFA examination two years ago, does not appear to be a candidate in the CFA Program. Therefore, his reference to his status as a CFA candidate in client presentation materials violates Standard VII(B). Wellington may indicate that he passed Level II of the CFA Program and the year in which he passed.

3. **B** Global Investment Performance Standards represent ethical reporting standards, but compliance with GIPS is not a requirement of CFA Institute membership or to sit for the CFA examination. (Study Session 1, LOS 3.a)

4. **C** Michaels has violated Standard IV(C) Responsibilities of Supervisors, which requires him to make reasonable efforts to detect and prevent violations of compliance procedures. Simply making employees aware of the rules is not enough. Monitoring of employee trades, duplicate confirms, establishing blackout periods, or pre-clearance of employee trades are all methods that would have revealed the problem prior to the external audit.

5. **C** Under Standard VI(B) Priority of Transactions, since the family account is a client account, it should be treated as any other client account and trades should be entered prior to trades for the employer's account. A firm may put a stock on its recommended list without making its change in recommendation public, since there is no requirement that they do.

6. **B** To comply with Standard IV(B) Additional Compensation Arrangements, Nelson must disclose outside compensation or benefits to employers. Nelson must receive written consent, which includes e-mail and any form of communication that can be documented. Note that the additional compensation is contingent on future performance and not simply a gift for past good work.

7. **A** To comply with Standard I(C) Misrepresentation, all sources used in an analyst's report should be referenced as to the source, author, and publisher—the only exception being factual information published by recognized financial and statistical reporting services.

8. **A** Because the itinerary required charter flights due to a lack of commercial transportation, River Casino can appropriately provide them. While Standard I(B) Independence and Objectivity recommends that members pay their own room costs, it is not required and it is not unusual for members to accept accommodations.

9. **A** Portfolios must be assigned to composites before the returns are known; assigning them at the end of the year is not acceptable. The composite return must be asset weighted, not a simple average (equal-weighted). Asset weighting will ensure that the performance reported will be representative of (if not exactly equal to) the performance of all the accounts assigned to a single composite over the reporting period. (Study Session 1, LOS 3.b, 4.a)

10. **A** Smart violated both Standards. Smart violated Standard III(B) Fair Dealing because she not deal fairly and objectively with all clients and prospects when disseminating investment recommendations, giving priority to some of the firm's clients by trading for her clients first before issuing the report. She also sold her own shares before issuing the report, which violated Standard VI(B) Priority of Transactions. Smart did not give clients an opportunity to react to and benefit from her recommendation before she personally benefited from her research.

11. **B** Whatever his motivation, Jacobs' attempt to manipulate the market price of Timeco shares with the intent to deceive market participants (in this case his own client) constitutes a violation of Standard II(B) Market Manipulation.

12. **B** Under Standard III(D) Performance Presentation, members and candidates must make reasonable efforts to make sure that investment performance information is fair, accurate, and complete. Rex has misled his potential clients by not disclosing that the first four years of his performance record were achieved at another firm. There is no prohibition on presenting simulated results as long as the fact that the results are simulated is disclosed.

13. **A** If Roberts suspects someone is engaging in activities that are illegal or violate the Code and Standards, Standard I(A) Knowledge of the Law requires him to dissociate from the activities if he cannot remedy the situation. In this situation, the colleague is acting within the applicable laws but is violating CFA Institute Standards of Professional Conduct. When the Code and Standards are more strict than applicable law, the Code and Standards apply. However, Roberts is not required by the Code and Standards to report violations of laws or the Code and Standards to CFA Institute or to governmental regulators, although it may be prudent or even required by law that he do so.

14. **A** Government bonds are default risk free but are subject to price risk. Thus, Blush misrepresented the expected performance of the fund and therefore violated Standard I(C) Misrepresentation.

15. **A** Standard VII(A) Conduct as Members and Candidates in the CFA Program does not prohibit members and candidates from expressing negative opinions about CFA Institute or the CFA program. Disclosing exam content and misrepresenting information on the annual PCS are violations of Standard VII(A).

16. **A** To comply with Standard III(C) Suitability, a member or candidate should establish a written investment policy statement for a client. Because Marlow depends on the portfolio for income and she has only moderate risk tolerance, risky currency derivatives are not appropriate for her account, and thus Pate has violated Standard III(C).

17. **A** Standard VI(C) Referral Fees indicates that members shall disclose to clients and prospects any consideration or benefits received for the recommendation of services. Investment managers pay a portion of their management fees earned from client assets to Rogers as compensation for his recommendation of their services. Rogers' recommendations may be predicated on the potential increase in compensation he will receive for recommending an investment manager rather than the manager's ability to provide good investment returns for the client. Therefore, in accordance with the Standard, Rogers is required to disclose the referral fee arrangement to clients and prospects before agreeing to perform any services covered by the arrangement. The disclosure must describe the nature of the consideration and the estimated dollar value of the consideration.

18. **A** Standard III(E) Preservation of Confidentiality states that candidates and members can disclose confidential client information to authorized fellow employees who are also working for the client. Acting in the client's interest requires that her investment manager be aware of her circumstances and needs.

19. **A** First we need to find the proper rate to use in the problem. The relevant interest rate must consider the effect of quarterly compounding. We can find this effective annual rate (EAR) with quarterly compounding by solving:

$$EAR = \left(1 + \frac{\text{stated rate}}{\text{comp. periods/yr.}}\right)^{\text{comp. periods/yr.}} - 1 = \left(1 + \frac{0.05}{4}\right)^4 - 1 = 5.0945\%$$

The amount needed in the account at retirement is the present value of the desired withdrawals.

This amount is determined from N = 20; I = 5.0945; PMT = –20,000; FV = 0; CPT → PV = $247,259.14. The annual contribution must grow into $247,259.14. The required payment can be found from PV = 0; N = 15; I = 5.0945; FV = 247,259.14; CPT → PMT = $11,377.30. Subtracting the $2,000 annual employer contribution gives us the client's required contribution of $9,377.30. (Study Session 2, LOS 5.f)

20. **A** Geometric mean = $[(1.10)(1.14)(1.12)(1.10)(0.90)(1.12)]^{1/6} - 1 = 0.0766$, or 7.66% (Study Session 2, LOS 7.e)

21. **C** There are 415 members of the group in favor of the continuing education requirement. 180 of these are candidates, so the probability is 180 / 415 = 43.37%. Note that this question is quite similar to those where we apply Bayes' Theorem. The priors here are the probabilities that a member of the group is a charterholder or is a candidate. Both of these are 1,000 / 2,000 = 50%. Given the information that the member of the group favors continuing education, we can update the probability that that group member is a candidate to 43.37%. (Study Session 2, LOS 8.d)

22. C   When constructing samples, researchers must be careful not to include just survivors (e.g., surviving companies, mutual funds, or investment newsletters). Since survivors tend to be those that have done well (by skill or chance), funds that have 10-year track records will exhibit performance histories with upward bias—mutual fund companies regularly discontinue funds with poor performance histories or roll their assets into better performing funds. Time period bias occurs when the period chosen is so short that it shows relationships that are unlikely to recur, or so long that it includes fundamental changes in the relationship being observed. A 10-year period typically includes a full economic cycle and is likely to be appropriate for this test. Look-ahead bias is present if the test relates a variable to data that were not available at the points in time when that variable's outcomes were observed. (Study Session 3, LOS 10.k)

23. C   A normal distribution is a *continuous* symmetric probability distribution. (Study Session 3, LOS 9.a, e, j)

24. A   A binomial random variable has an expected value or mean equal to *np*. Mean = 12(0.4) = 4.8. (Study Session 3, LOS 9.f)

25. C   The standard normal random variable, denoted *Z*, has mean equal to 0 and variance equal to 1. (Study Session 3, LOS 9.l, m)

26. C   Portfolio X: $\text{SFRatio} = \dfrac{12-5}{14} = 0.50$

Portfolio Y: $\text{SFRatio} = \dfrac{17-5}{20} = 0.60$

Portfolio Z: $\text{SFRatio} = \dfrac{22-5}{25} = 0.68$

According to the safety-first criterion, Portfolio Z, with the largest ratio (0.68), is the best alternative. (Study Session 3, LOS 9.n)

27. A   The appropriate test is an *F*-test, where the larger sample variance (Index L) is placed in the numerator. (Study Session 3, LOS 11.i)

28. A   Events J and K are dependent. By the multiplication rule, joint probability P(JK) = P(J|K) × P(K), or P(JK) = P(K|J) × P(J). Events are independent if P(J|K) = P(J) and P(K|J) = P(K). This implies that for independent events, P(JK) = P(J) × P(K). If this condition is not met, events J and K are dependent. If events J and K are mutually exclusive, their joint probability is zero. The information given is consistent with this but not sufficient to conclude that this is the case. (Study Session 2, LOS 8.g)

29. A   The 20 quarters he has used are a sample of all the possible outcomes for the quarterly returns on the index. The difference between the true population parameter (mean index return) he is trying to estimate and the sample statistic he has calculated is called the sampling error. The arithmetic mean is the appropriate estimator of the next period's return. (Study Session 2, LOS 7.m, and Study Session 3, LOS 10.b)

30. A   The significance level of a test is the probability that a true null hypothesis will be rejected by chance because the test statistic is from a sample and may take on a value that is outside the range of critical values because of sampling error. Choice B is incorrect because the probability of making a correct decision also must account for the probability of failing to reject a false null hypothesis. (Study Session 3, LOS 11.b)

31. **B**   The lognormal distribution is most appropriate for modeling asset prices because the values cannot be less than zero and are not bounded on the upside. A binomial distribution allows only two possible outcomes over a period. (Study Session 3, LOS 9.o)

32. **A**   Calculate the NPV as in any other project. Discount the cash flows back at a rate of 10%. $CF_0 = -200,000$; $CF_1 = 50,000$; $CF_2 = 60,000$; $CF_3 = 70,000$; $CF_4 = 80,000$; $CF_5 = -20,000$; $I/Y = 10$; $CPT \rightarrow NPV = -\$10,144$. (Study Session 2, LOS 6.a)

33. **A**   Increases in expected future incomes will decrease savings, which will decrease the supply of financial capital and increase the equilibrium interest rate. If the demand for financial capital rises, interest rates also rise; so both changes tend to increase the equilibrium interest rate. (Study Session 5, LOS 19.d)

34. **C** $$\text{Potential expansion multiplier} = \frac{1}{\text{required reserve ratio}} = \frac{1}{0.2} = 5$$

   (100)(5) = 500

   (Study Session 5, LOS 19.c)

35. **C**   At a minimum wage above the equilibrium wage, there will be an excess supply of workers, since firms will not employ all the workers who want to work at the minimum wage. Firms will substitute other productive inputs for labor and use more than the economically efficient amount of capital. The result is increased unemployment because even though there are workers willing to work for less than the minimum wage, firms cannot legally hire them. (Study Session 4, LOS 13.j, k)

36. **A**   The opportunity cost of one unit of leather for Ymer is 20 / 25 = 0.80 units of cheese, and the opportunity cost of one unit of cheese is 25 / 20 = 1.25 units of leather. The opportunity cost of one unit of cheese for Hokah is 30 / 35 = 0.86 units of leather, and the opportunity cost of one unit of leather is 35 / 30 = 1.167 units of cheese. Ymer has an absolute advantage in both cheese and leather, but has a comparative advantage only in leather. (Study Session 6, LOS 20.c)

37. **B**   An industry with a downward-sloping long-run industry supply curve is a decreasing-cost industry. In such an industry, input costs decrease as output quantities increase. In the short run, this causes firms to earn economic profits. In the long run, these economic profits attract new entrants to the industry, which reduces the equilibrium selling price of the industry's output. (Study Session 4, LOS 15.i)

38. **C**   Average cost pricing is meant to force a natural monopolist to reduce price to where the firm's average total cost intersects the market demand curve. This results in higher output and a lower price than would prevail for an unregulated natural monopoly. (Study Session 4, LOS 16.e)

39. **A**   We can calculate the current USD/EUR cross rate as 104.2 / 76.6 = 1.3603 USD/EUR. The original USD/EUR cross rate was 100 / 80 = 1.2500 USD/EUR. Thus, the USD has depreciated relative to the EUR. While it is correct to say that the EUR has appreciated 4.2% relative to the JPY (104.2 / 100 − 1) = 4.2%, it is not correct to say that the JPY has depreciated by the same percentage. To calculate the percentage change in the JPY relative to the EUR, we need to invert the quotes. One year ago, the quote was 0.0100 EUR/JPY and now the quote is 0.0096 EUR/JPY. (0.0096 / 0.0100 − 1) = 0.0403 or 4.0% depreciation in the JPY relative to the EUR. (Study Session 6, LOS 21.c, d)

40. **B**   Colluding restricts output and puts upward pressure on price, but cheating actually increases output and ultimately, if enough cheating occurs, puts downward pressure on the price. Colluders cheat to increase their share of the profits. (Study Session 4, LOS 16.d)

41. **B**   Decreasing costs of factors of production cause a supply curve to increase (shift to the right). An increase in wages would shift the supply curve to the left. A decrease in the price of cars is represented as movement along the supply curve to a lower quantity supplied. (Study Session 4, LOS 13.c)

42. **A**   The LM curve illustrates a positive relationship between real income and the real interest rate, holding the real money supply constant. The IS curve illustrates a negative relationship between real income and the real interest rate, holding the marginal propensity to save constant. (Study Session 5, LOS 17.f)

43. **C**   An inferior good is one that experiences a decline in demand when income rises. (Study Session 4, LOS 14.f)

44. **A**   According to the Keynesians, policymakers can use the budget to diminish aggregate demand through restrictive fiscal policy. Reducing government expenditures and/or increasing tax rates should lead to a decline in the expected size of the budget deficit or an increase in the budget surplus. (Study Session 5, LOS 19.r)

45. **B**   Firms usually support the idea of having a single set of reporting standards because having one set of standards would reduce the cost and the time spent on reporting. Disagreement among different standard-setting bodies and regulatory authorities does hamper agreement on a single set of standards, as does political pressure from business groups and others who would be affected by changes in reporting standards. (Study Session 7, LOS 24.c)

46. **C**   Foreign currency translation gains and losses are not reported on the income statement as a component of net income, but affect owners' equity because they are included as other comprehensive income. The other items are included on the income statement so they affect both net income and owners' equity. (Study Session 8, LOS 25.l)

47. **A**

Sale of common stock	45
Issuance of bonds	25
Financing cash flows	$70

(Study Session 8, LOS 27.f)

48. **B**   Since the value of newly released DVDs will typically fall most rapidly in the first year after their release, some form of accelerated depreciation is appropriate. The declining balance method is the only accelerated depreciation method among the answer choices. Straight-line depreciation is appropriate when the decrease in value is uniform over an asset's life. Units-of-production depreciation assumes that there is a given amount of service that an asset will provide. (Study Session 8, LOS 25.d)

49. **A**   When a firm has a controlling interest (>50%) in a subsidiary, but less than 100% ownership, it includes (consolidates) the assets and liabilities of that firm on its own balance sheet. Noncontrolling (or minority) interest in the equity section of the balance sheet represents the portion of the subsidiary that is not owned by the reporting firm. (Study Session 8, LOS 26.d)

50. **A** FCFF = Cash flow from operations + interest expense net of tax − net capital expenditures

FCFF = $800 + 80(1 − 0.35) − 40 + 30 = $842

Depreciation and amortization do not have to be added when calculating FCFF from CFO. They are added when calculating FCFF from net income. (Study Session 8, LOS 27.i)

51. **C** Securities held with the intent to profit over the short term are classified as trading securities, and changes in their market values are reflected in their balance sheet values and also reported on the income statement. Debt securities issued by the firm, and debt securities that the firm intends to hold until maturity, are both reported at amortized cost, not market value. Debt and equity securities that the firm does not expect to hold to maturity or to sell in the near term are marked to market on the balance sheet, but unrealized gains and losses do not affect the income statement. (Study Session 8, LOS 26.e)

52. **B** IFRS and U.S. GAAP both require discontinued operations to be reported on the income statement separately from continuing operations and net of tax. U.S. GAAP permits unusual and infrequent items to be treated as extraordinary items, but IFRS does not permit extraordinary items. Fixed assets can be revalued upward under IFRS but not under U.S. GAAP. (Study Session 8, LOS 25.e, 26.d)

53. **B** COGS FIFO = COGS LIFO − (ending LIFO reserve − beginning LIFO reserve)

COGS FIFO = 27,000 − (1,400 − 1,200) = $26,800. (Study Session 10, LOS 35.e)

54. **C** The listing of all the journal entries in order of their dates is called the general journal. The general ledger sorts the entries in the general journal by account. "Trial ledger" is not part of an accounting system. (Study Session 7, LOS 23.f)

55. **B** When the capital structure contains options or warrants, the treasury stock method uses the average price. In this situation, the warrants are antidilutive because the exercise price of the warrant ($25) is higher than the market price of the stock ($20). Thus, warrants are excluded. Otherwise, common shares would be reduced.

$$\text{original shares of common stock} = 1,000,000\left(\frac{12}{12}\right)$$

Then add the impact of the bond conversion:

(10,000)(20) × (6/12) = 100,000

Thus, the adjusted denominator for fully diluted EPS is:

1,000,000 + 100,000 = 1,100,000 (Study Session 8, LOS 25.g, h)

56. **A** During periods of rising prices, the last units purchased are more expensive than the existing units. Under LIFO, the cost of the last units purchased is assigned to cost of goods sold. This higher cost of goods sold results in lower income, as compared to the FIFO method. As the name suggests, the weighted average method is based on mathematical averages rather than timing of purchase/use. Thus, cost of goods sold using this method falls between that of LIFO and FIFO. (Study Session 9, LOS 29.e)

57. **A** If convertible bonds are dilutive, interest expense multiplied by (1 − tax rate) must be added back to the numerator to calculate diluted EPS. (Study Session 8, LOS 25.g, h)

58. **B** Net income is higher with capitalization because it does not decrease by the full amount spent, as it would with expensing. Capitalizing an expenditure changes its cash flow classification from an operating cash outflow to an investing cash outflow. As a result, CFO is higher and CFI is lower than they would be if the expenditure had been immediately expensed. Total cash flow, however, is unaffected (assuming the tax treatment of the expenditure is independent of the financial reporting treatment). Equity is higher in the period of the expenditure with capitalization. Assets are higher because they include the capitalized asset. Debt is unaffected by the decision to capitalize or expense. Thus, the debt-to-equity and debt-to-assets ratios are lower with capitalization. (Study Session 9, LOS 30.a)

59. **A** The three-part DuPont approach is as follows: net profit margin × asset turnover × leverage ratio, where the leverage ratio is assets-to-equity. (Study Session 8, LOS 28.d)

60. **A** Impairment writedowns are reported losses "above the line" and are included in income from continuing operations. (Study Session 8, LOS 25.e)

61. **B** Material changes in the firm's cost of debt capital should be included in the Management Discussion and Analysis section of the financial statements. If the firm does not use fair value reporting of debt obligations, net income and shareholders' equity are not affected by changes in the market value of the firm's debt, and disclosing its gain or loss in market value is not required. (Study Session 9, LOS 32.e)

62. **C** Deferred tax assets and liabilities are adjusted for changes in expected tax rates under the liability method. (Study Session 9, LOS 31.e)

63. **B** Whether a lease is an operating or a finance (capital) lease, both U.S. GAAP and IFRS require disclosure of the minimum lease payments for each of the next five years and the sum of minimum lease payments more than five years in the future. (Study Session 9, LOS 32.i)

64. **A** Under IFRS, past service costs (changes in defined benefit plan obligations that result from a change in the plan's terms) are reported as part of service costs, a component of net income. Under U.S. GAAP, past service costs are recognized in other comprehensive income and amortized over time to the income statement. (Study Session 9, LOS 32.k)

65. **A** Complex or unstable organizational structures and ineffective internal controls over accounting and information technology are among the risk factors related to opportunities for fraud. (Study Session 10, LOS 33.c)

66. **A** Sensitivity analysis is based on hypothetical ("what if") questions about a single variable, such as "what if sales decline by 10%?" Simulation is a technique in which probability distributions for key variables are assumed and a computer is used to generate a distribution of outcomes based on repeated random selection of values for the key variables. Scenario analysis is based on one or more specific scenarios (a specific set of outcomes for key variables), which include changes in multiple variables. (Study Session 8, LOS 28.f)

67. **A** The balance sheet reports the company's financial position at a point in time. In contrast, the income statement reports on financial performance over a period of time and the cash flow statement reports a company's cash receipts and payments over a period of time. (Study Session 7, LOS 22.b)

68. **B** Lessors that are dealers or manufacturers of the leased assets typically recognize sales revenue at the inception of a lease and thus account for their leases as sales-type capital (finance) leases. Dealers of high-value items that can be distinguished one from another, such as large earth movers, typically use specific identification to account for inventory. (Study Session 9, LOS 29.b, 32.h)

69. **B** Business risk is the combination of sales risk, which is the variability of a firm's sales, and operating risk, which is the additional variability in operating earnings (EBIT) caused by fixed operating costs. (Study Session 11, LOS 38.a)

70. **A** WACC = $(w_d)(k_d)(1 - t) + (w_{ce})(k_{ce})$

   WACC = $(0.5)(6\%)(1 - 0.33) + (0.5)(12\%) = 8.0\%$

   The increase in after-tax cash flows for each year is $3,000 \times (1 - 0.33) = \$2,010$.

   I = 8; N = 8; PMT = $2,010; CPT → PV = $11,550.74

   NPV = PV income − cost = $11,550.74 − $10,000 = $1,550.74

   (Study Session 11, LOS 36.d, 37.a)

71. **B** For a board to be independent, it should not have a majority of members who are firm executives. Board members should not be closely aligned with customers, suppliers, or pension advisors since their interests may conflict with those of shareholders. The board should meet regularly *outside* the presence of management. (Study Session 11, LOS 41.c)

72. **B** The investment opportunity schedule is a downward sloping curve of the internal rates of return (expected returns) of potential projects ranked from highest to lowest. This curve intersects the company's upward sloping marginal cost of capital curve at an amount of capital where the marginal project's IRR just equals the firm's cost of capital. The firm should accept projects with IRRs that exceed the marginal cost of capital (lie to the left of the intersection) and reject projects with IRRs less than the marginal cost of capital (lie to the right of the intersection). (Study Session 11, LOS 37.d)

73. **A** An increase in the weighted average collection period indicates that customers are taking longer to pay their outstanding accounts. This represents a drag on the company's liquidity. A vendor that changes its payment terms from "net 30" to "net 60" is allowing the company 60 days to pay instead of 30. This extension of trade credit is a source of liquidity for the company. An inventory turnover ratio that is increasing relative to the industry average is a sign of good inventory management, which can also be a source of liquidity for a company. (Study Session 11, LOS 40.a, f)

74. **A** The earnings yield on the firm's shares is $2 / $25 = 8%. Because both the firm's after-tax yield on excess cash and its after-tax cost of borrowing are less than the earnings yield, financing a share repurchase either with excess cash or with debt will increase earnings per share. (Study Session 11, LOS 39.d)

75. **C** Using the CAPM approach, the estimated cost of common equity = 3% + 0.89(12% − 3%) = 11%. Using the dividend discount model approach, the growth rate = (0.3)(0.2) = 6% and the estimated cost of common equity = $3 / $50 + 6% = 12%. To get a cost of common equity of 14%, Harlan most likely added a risk premium to Cyrene's bond yield. (Study Session 11, LOS 37.h)

76. **A** The cash conversion cycle is equal to the operating cycle minus the number of days of payables. If Quixote is extending the time it takes to pay its suppliers, its number of days of payables will increase, and its cash conversion cycle will decrease. Its operating cycle (days of inventory plus days of receivables) is unaffected by the increase in days of payables. Changes in inventory or receivables management would affect both the operating cycle and the cash conversion cycle. (Study Session 11, LOS 40.c)

77. **B** If the total undiscounted cash flows from two projects are equal, their NPV profiles intersect the vertical axis at the same value. The NPV profile will have a steeper slope for Project Smith, which has more of its cash inflows occurring later in its life, and therefore the IRR of Project Smith (its intersection with the horizontal axis) must be less than the IRR of Project Jones. The NPV for Project Jones will be greater at any rate of discount, and Project Jones will be preferred over the entire range. However, if the discount rate applied to the cash flows is greater than the IRR of Project Jones, both projects will have negative NPVs and the company should reject both of them. (Study Session 11, LOS 36.e)

78. **B** Other Board experience can be beneficial. Choice A is incorrect because this may present the board member with a conflict of interest. Choice C is incorrect because a substantial stock position in the firm aligns the board member's interests closely with those of other shareholders. (Study Session 11, LOS 41.d)

79. **A** Property and casualty insurers typically have a short-term time horizon, since claims are expected in the near term, and low risk tolerance. (Study Session 12, LOS 42.b)

80. **B** $(1+HPR)^{1/n} - 1 = (1+1.70)^{1/20} - 1 = 0.050916$ (Study Session 12, LOS 43.a)

81. **B** The investment guidelines section typically contains information about specific types of assets prohibited in the portfolio and the permissible use, if any, of leverage and derivatives. (Study Session 12, LOS 45.b)

82. **A** Of the five categories of investment constraints, the four matters listed are related to Pope's time horizon (years to retirement), liquidity needs (available cash), legal and regulatory factors (required copies of account statements to Pope's compliance officer), and unique needs and preferences (no investments in Lower Pannonia). None of these constraints address Pope's tax situation or the taxable status of the investment account. (Study Session 12, LOS 45.e)

83. **C** This statement is not correct; the standard deviation of returns for the resulting portfolio is a weighted average of the returns standard deviation of the risk-free asset (zero) and the returns standard deviation of the risky-asset portfolio. (Study Session 12, LOS 44.a)

84. **B** From the fact that $beta_i = Cov_{i,mkt} / Var_{mkt}$, we have $Cov_{i,mkt} = beta_i \times var_{mkt}$.

$Cov_{i,mkt} = 1.2 \times 0.14^2 = 0.02352$. (Study Session 12, LOS 44.e)

85. **A** This grouping is most likely the result of a cluster analysis and may have arisen by chance. The two firms clearly offer different products and services. An industrial machinery manufacturer is likely to be a cyclical firm, while a grocery retailer is likely to be a non-cyclical firm. (Study Session 14, LOS 50.b, c)

86. **A** Value-weighted indexes do not need to be adjusted for stock splits because the market capitalization of the company remains the same. (Study Session 13, LOS 47.e)

87. **A** The numerator of the formula for the P/E is the payout ratio, which is unchanged (both expected earnings and dividends increase by the same percentage). The denominator $(k - g)$ doubles from 3% to 6%, which will decrease the P/E by half. (Study Session 14, LOS 51.h)

88. **B** $k = RFR + \beta(R_M - RFR) = 0.08 + 1.2(0.13 - 0.08) = 0.08 + 0.06 = 0.14$

$$P_0 = \frac{P_1 + D_1}{1 + k} = \frac{25 + 1.10}{1.14} = \$22.89$$

(Study Session 14, LOS 51.e)

89. **A** In an equity swap, one party pays a fixed amount periodically in return for a payment that is calculated using a specific amount and the return on a stock or portfolio of stocks. (Study Session 13, LOS 46.c)

90. **A** Asset-based models are often used to value natural resources companies and companies that are being liquidated. Because Visser is unprofitable, an earnings multiplier model or a dividend discount model such as the Gordon growth model may not produce a meaningful value for the firm. (Study Session 14, LOS 51.b)

91. **C** Value @ t = 2 $= \dfrac{D_3}{k - g} = \dfrac{D_0(1 + g)^3}{k - g} = \dfrac{\$6.25(1.07)^3}{0.12 - 0.07} = \$153.13$

(Study Session 14, LOS 51.e)

92. **C** Management buyout refers to a situation where an investor group that includes the firm's key management purchases all the outstanding shares (not just a controlling interest) of a public company in order to take it private. Once this is done, the shares are no longer registered for public trading and, as a result, are no longer traded on exchanges or in other public markets. (Study Session 14, LOS 49.c)

93. **C** The maturity phase of an industry life cycle is not typically characterized by excess capacity or price competition. The conditions described may be consistent with a concentrated industry (typically characterized by low levels of price competition, since firms in the industry seek to avoid it) that is moving into the decline phase of an industry life cycle (excess capacity leads to aggressive price cutting, especially when barriers to exit are high). These conditions could also be consistent with an industry that is moving into the shakeout phase (characterized by developing excess capacity and intense price competition) following the growth phase (during which price competition is low). (Study Session 14, LOS 50.h)

94. **C** $P_2 = \dfrac{D_3}{k - g} = \dfrac{2.25(1.2)^2}{0.15 - 0.05} = 32.40$

$$P_0 = \frac{\$2.25}{1.15} + \frac{2.70}{(1.15)^2} + \frac{32.40}{(1.15)^2} = \$28.50$$

(Study Session 14, LOS 51.e)

95. **A** Restrictions on short sales remove some of the selling pressure on overvalued securities that would otherwise drive their market values down toward their intrinsic values in an efficient market. Market inefficiency caused by high transactions costs or restrictions on arbitrage trading may allow market values that are different from intrinsic values to persist both for overvalued and undervalued securities. (Study Session 13, LOS 48.b, c)

96. **A** The investor is short the stock and will experience losses if the stock price increases. A stop buy order at $44 will execute if the stock price rises to $44 or higher. A limit buy order at $44 would execute immediately because the stock price is less than $44. (Study Session 13, LOS 46.e, h)

97. **B** CMOs redistribute prepayment risk and/or the expected repayment term of the underlying MBS among the CMO tranches. If some tranches have less prepayment risk, others must have more. (Study Session 15, LOS 54.f)

98. **C** This question can be answered without calculations. Since the spot rates are less than the coupon rate, the price must be greater than par value, so C is the only possible correct choice.

This is a four-period bond with $50 cash flows each period. Divide each spot rate by two to get the semiannual rate.

PV_1: N = 1; I/Y = 3.00; FV = $50; CPT → PV = $48.54
PV_2: N = 2; I/Y = 3.25; FV = $50; CPT → PV = $46.90
PV_3: N = 3; I/Y = 3.50; FV = $50; CPT → PV = $45.10
PV_4: N = 4; I/Y = 3.75; FV = $1,050; CPT → PV = $906.23

or $\dfrac{50}{1.03} + \dfrac{50}{1.0325^2} + \dfrac{50}{1.035^3} + \dfrac{1,050}{1.0375^4} = \$1,046.77$

Sum to get $1,046.77. (Study Session 16, LOS 57.e)

99. **B** The change in price due to a change in yield is only approximate because the calculation of effective duration does not reflect all of the curvature of the price-yield curve (convexity). It is a linear approximation of a non-linear relation. (Study Session 15, LOS 53.f)

100. **C** Issuing asset-backed securities allows a corporation to dedicate the assets' cash flows to specific debt issues. This enables the issue to receive a higher credit rating than that of the corporation. (Study Session 15, LOS 54.i)

101. **B** absolute yield spread = yield on Bond A – yield on Bond B = 7.5% – 7.0% = 0.5%

$\text{yield ratio} = \dfrac{\text{Bond A yield}}{\text{Bond B yield}} = \dfrac{7.5\%}{7.0\%} = 1.071.$

(Study Session 15, LOS 55.e)

102. **C** The duration/convexity approach provides an approximation of the interest rate sensitivity of a bond/bond portfolio. This approach estimates the risk for a parallel shift in the yield curve and allows the analyst to express interest rate risk with the summary measures of duration and convexity. The full valuation approach is more precise and can be used to evaluate the risk from more complex interest rate change scenarios than a parallel shift in the yield curve. Both approaches account for the curvature of the price-yield relation. (Study Session 16, LOS 58.a)

103. **C** $\sqrt{\dfrac{(1.07)^4}{(1.05)^2}} - 1 = 0.0904$, or $\dfrac{(4 \times 7) - (2 \times 5)}{2} = 9$ as an approximation

(Study Session 16, LOS 57.g)

104. **B** EBIT / interest is a coverage ratio and debt / capital is a leverage ratio. Higher interest coverage and lower leverage are favorable for creditworthiness. Of the three companies given, Knight has the highest interest coverage and Lawrence has the lowest leverage. EBIT / revenue (operating profit margin) is a profitability ratio and revenue / assets (asset turnover) is an operating ratio. (Study Session 8, LOS 28.e, Study Session 9, LOS 32.l, and Study Session 16, LOS 59.f, g)

105. **A** When the yield curve is flat, all spot interest rates are equal, and the spot rates will equal the YTM of the bond. The static spread and the YTM spread will diverge when the yield curve gains shape (upward-sloping, humped, or downward-sloping). The option-adjusted spread is the spread *without* the option. Hence, to compare the relative valuation of these two securities, we would compare their OAS and buy the bond with the biggest OAS (Bond Q). (Study Session 16, LOS 57.f)

106. **B** A company may refund the debt as long as they do not issue cheaper debt to do so. The firm could not refund the bonds by issuing zero-coupon bonds. (Study Session 15, LOS 52.d)

107. **B** This bond has no cash flows for the first five years. It then has a $100 cash flow for years 6 through 10. Additionally, the accrued interest ($500) that wasn't paid in the first five years would have to be paid at the end, along with the principal. A financial calculator using the CF/NPV worksheet can handle this type of problem. The required inputs are $CF_0 = 0$, $CF_1 = 0$, $F_1 = 5$, $CF_2 = 100$, $F_2 = 4$, $CF_3 = 1{,}600$, $F_3 = 1$, NPV, I = 10%, CPT = 813.69. Note that CF_3 is made up of the principal ($1,000) plus the remaining $100 coupon plus the accrued interest ($500) that was not paid during the first five years of the bond's life. (Study Session 16, LOS 56.c)

108. **C** The market segmentation theory states that the shape of the yield curve is determined by the supply and demand for bonds within certain market segments. If the demand for long-term bonds exceeds supply, prices will be forced up and yields down. Hence, a large demand for long bonds could force a downward-sloping yield curve. (Study Session 15, LOS 55.c)

109. **A** Floating-rate securities are subject to interest rate risk because their coupon rates are not reset continuously. The longer the time until the security's next reset date, the greater its potential price fluctuation away from par value (to a discount or premium). Other reasons that the price can differ from par include caps and floors on the floating rate, changes in the issuer's credit risk that are not reflected in the coupon's margin over LIBOR, and changes in the market's required yield premium for the firm's level of credit risk. A decrease in the yield premium for credit risk would be likely to cause the security to trade at a premium rather than a discount. Liquidity risk is much less likely to change than default risk and market interest rates. (Study Session 15, LOS 53.e)

110. **B** PVBP represents the change in the price of the bond when its yield changes by one basis point, or 0.01%. PVBP = duration × 0.0001 × bond value. This calculation ignores convexity because for a small change in yield, the curvature of the price-yield relationship typically has no material effect on the PVBP. (Study Session 16, LOS 58.j)

111. **C** In a currency swap, the *full* notional principal is exchanged at the beginning and termination of the swap. (Study Session 17, LOS 64.b)

112. **B** Interest rate caps are designed to protect floating-rate borrowers from higher interest rates by paying the borrowers when rates reach a certain level. The combination of a long cap and a short floor is called a collar and offers downside protection at the cost of a sacrifice of upside. (Study Session 17, LOS 63.g)

113. **A** When the stock's price (S) – the strike price (X) is positive, a call option is in the money. 35 – X = 3, so X = 32. (Study Session 17, LOS 65.a)

114. **C** The word "hedge" means to reduce risk. Since the investor is short the portfolio, he will have gains as stock prices fall and will have losses as stock prices rise. Hence, hedging requires a position that provides gains as prices rise and losses as prices fall. If the investor buys calls and writes puts in the correct proportions, he will have offset the market risk of his short portfolio. (Study Session 17, LOS 65.b)

115. **A** Writer of put's maximum loss = $50 – $4 = $46 (Study Session 17, LOS 65.a)

116. **B** In the first year, the net payment for the fixed-rate payer will be (0.06 – 0.05) × $10,000,000 = $100,000. In the second year, the net payment will be zero if the interest rate is indeed 6%. (Study Session 17, LOS 64.b)

117. **A** The description relates best to the early stage wherein the capital that is supplied helps speed up product development and also helps pay for the beginning of a marketing campaign. (Study Session 18, LOS 66.d)

118. **C** Quantitative directional strategies employ technical analysis and may have net long or short exposure. A market neutral strategy maintains approximately equal values in long and short positions and is typically based on fundamental analysis. Special situations strategy is an event-driven strategy that involves investing in firms that are selling divisions or assets, distributing capital, or issuing or repurchasing securities. (Study Session 18, LOS 66.d)

119. **B** In a hedge fund's fee structure, a hard hurdle rate means that incentive fees are earned only on returns in excess of the benchmark return. A soft hurdle rate means that incentive fees are calculated on the entire return, but are only paid if the return exceeds the hurdle rate. A high water mark specifies that incentive fees are only paid on returns that increase an investor's account value above its highest previous value. (Study Session 18, LOS 66.f)

120. **B** Investing in farmland may provide income over the life of the investment from crops produced and sold. Investing in commodities typically does not provide income. Commodities and real estate investments such as farmland may both provide a hedge against inflation. Direct investments in real estate are less liquid than investments in commodities, which are typically made through highly liquid exchange-traded derivatives. (Study Session 18, LOS 66.d)

EXAM 3
AFTERNOON SESSION ANSWER KEY

To get valuable feedback on how your score compares to those of other Level I candidates, use your Username and Password to gain Online Access at schweser.com and choose the left-hand menu item "Practice Exams Vol. 1."

1. B	31. B	61. B	91. C
2. A	32. A	62. A	92. B
3. A	33. B	63. A	93. C
4. B	34. C	64. B	94. A
5. B	35. B	65. C	95. B
6. A	36. A	66. C	96. A
7. C	37. A	67. C	97. A
8. A	38. C	68. C	98. A
9. B	39. C	69. C	99. C
10. C	40. A	70. B	100. C
11. A	41. C	71. B	101. C
12. C	42. C	72. A	102. A
13. C	43. B	73. A	103. C
14. A	44. B	74. B	104. B
15. C	45. C	75. A	105. C
16. A	46. C	76. C	106. B
17. B	47. A	77. C	107. A
18. B	48. C	78. C	108. C
19. B	49. A	79. A	109. C
20. C	50. B	80. B	110. B
21. A	51. A	81. A	111. B
22. A	52. C	82. C	112. B
23. B	53. B	83. B	113. B
24. C	54. A	84. A	114. A
25. C	55. C	85. C	115. A
26. B	56. A	86. B	116. C
27. B	57. C	87. A	117. C
28. C	58. A	88. A	118. A
29. B	59. B	89. B	119. B
30. C	60. A	90. A	120. B

Exam 3
Afternoon Session Answers

Answers referencing the Standards of Practice address Study Session 1, LOS 1.b, c and LOS 2.a, b, c, except where noted.

1. **B** Members can accept or reject a disciplinary sanction proposed by the Designated Officer. If the member rejects the sanction, the matter is referred to a hearing by a panel of CFA Institute members. The other statements are accurate. (Study Session 1, LOS 1.a)

2. **A** According to Standard I(B) Independence and Objectivity, members and candidates may accept gifts from clients but must disclose them to their employers. Because Miguel did not disclose the gift to his employer, he has violated Standard I(B). In addition, Standard I(A) Knowledge of the Law states that members and candidates are not to commit any act that they know or should know violates the Code and Standards. Miguel is a CFA charterholder and should know that his actions violate Standard I(B). Thus, by violating Standard I(B), Miguel also has violated Standard I(A).

3. **A** Jones violated Standard I(C) Misrepresentation when he used the work of others without acknowledgment, which is plagiarism. It did not matter that Smith gave Jones the information verbally or that she said he was "welcome to it." Jones used another's work without crediting the source, which constitutes plagiarism. Jones also violated Standard V(A) Diligence and Reasonable Basis because he did not have a reasonable and adequate basis for his recommendation.

4. **B** Watson's excessive drinking is unfortunate but we have no evidence that it has affected his work, professional integrity, judgment, or reputation. His arrest for public intoxication occurred while he was away from work. If he commits an act involving fraud or dishonesty, he would violate the Standard on misconduct.

5. **B** GIPS require a firm to show a GIPS-compliant history for a minimum of five years, or since inception of the firm or the composite if in existence for less than five years. If Reliable has been in business for less than five years, it may still claim compliance with GIPS on a since-inception basis, provided the firm follows all other aspects of compliance. The other choices are requirements for a firm to claim compliance with GIPS. (Study Session 1, LOS 4.a)

6. **A** The recommended procedures for compliance with Standard I(B) Independence and Objectivity include the recommendation that analysts on company visits pay their own travel expenses and use commercial transportation if it is available.

7. **C** Standard VII(A) Conduct as Members and Candidates in the CFA Program and the Code of Ethics. By writing down information from the Candidate Body of Knowledge and taking it into the exam room, she compromised the integrity of the exam, whether she used the notes or not. Her actions are also in violation of the Code of Ethics by not acting "with integrity, competence, diligence, respect, and in an ethical manner."

8. **A** The requirement that members and candidates place their clients' interests before their employer's or their own is in Standard III(A) Loyalty, Prudence, and Care. The other choices are included in the CFA Institute Code of Ethics.

9. **B** Kramer violated Standard V(B) Communication with Clients and Prospective Clients. The problem is with the word "will." Kramer should have used "is estimated to be" to separate fact from opinion. Statistical estimates of future events are subject to change and should not be presented as certainties. She need not give complete details of the statistical model but should indicate its general characteristics and the important factors involved in her projections.

10. **C** Standard III(B) Fair Dealing requires that all clients be treated fairly. Members and candidates should not discriminate against any client. A family member who is a fee-paying client should not be treated differently from other clients when taking investment action. Following up changes in recommendations with phone calls to larger clients is not a violation of the Standard if the changes have been disseminated fairly.

11. **A** According to Standard II(B) Market Manipulation, members and candidates cannot attempt to distort prices or artificially inflate trading volume. Thompson's misleading internet postings violate Standard II(B) since the intent is to manipulate the price of the bond issue. In addition, Thompson did not consider the suitability of the investment for his clients when he chose to recommend Ibex based only on his client's account size rather than investment objectives and constraints. Since some of the clients to which he recommended the investment have low risk tolerances and are unlikely to find a highly risky junk bond issue suitable for their portfolio, Thompson also violated Standard III(C) Suitability.

12. **C** According to Standard VI(A) Disclosure of Conflicts, Elliott should disclose his beneficial ownership of TECH to his employer and to clients and prospects, because such ownership could interfere with his ability to make unbiased and objective recommendations. Selling his shares or declining to write the report are not required and are more extreme than simply disclosing the potential conflict.

13. **C** Mendoza has not violated the Standards of Practice or GIPS. Because the presentation was introductory and brief, Mendoza was not required to give any supporting documentation, but he made it available to clients and prospective clients upon request. His claim of GIPS compliance is in the required format. (Study Session 1, LOS 3.c)

14. **A** According to Standard II(A) Material Nonpublic Information, members and candidates who possess material nonpublic information must not act or cause others to act based on the information. A conference call with several analysts does not constitute public dissemination, and Franklin should urge Level Tech to publicly disseminate the information.

15. **C** Standard III(C) Suitability requires that members and candidates update client information (the IPS) at least annually. The IPS can be updated more frequently if there are significant changes in the investment strategy or client characteristics.

16. **A** To comply with Standard III(E) Preservation of Confidentiality, Johnson must not discuss with her charitable foundation anything regarding her client and her client's intentions. It does not matter that her client intends to give money to charities in the near future.

17. **B** Standard III(A) Loyalty, Prudence, and Care does not require the voting of all proxies. A cost-benefit analysis may support the conclusion that the voting of all proxies is not beneficial to the client in light of the time and effort required. Voting on nonroutine issues that have a material impact is required.

18. **B** According to Standard I(A) Knowledge of the Law, Gold must comply with the most strict of the laws of Country T, laws of Country U, and the CFA Standards of Practice. In this case, the most strict rules are those in the Standards of Practice. Standard VI(C) Referral Fees requires the disclosure of all referral fees and Standard II(A) Material Nonpublic Information prohibits acting or causing others to act on the basis of material non-public information.

19. **B** It's best to break this problem into parts to accommodate the change in the interest rate.

    Money in the fund at the end of ten years based on deposits made with initial interest of 5%:

    (1) The total value in the fund at the end of the fifth year is $3,152.50:
       PMT = –1,000; N = 3; I/Y = 5; CPT → FV = $3,152.50. (calculator in END mode)

    (2) The $3,152.50 is now the present value and will then grow at 4% until the end of the tenth year. We get: PV = –3,152.50; N = 5; I/Y = 4; PMT = –1,000; CPT → FV = $9,251.82

    (Study Session 2, LOS 5.e)

20. **C** With more than one compounding period per year, $FV_N = PV\left(1 + \dfrac{r_s}{m}\right)^{mn}$

    $PV = \$5,000$; $r_s = 6\%$; $m = 12$; $\dfrac{r_s}{m} = \dfrac{6\%}{12} = 0.5\%$; $n = 3$; $m \times n = 12 \times 3 = 36$.

    To compute FV_3, enter PV = –5,000; I = 0.5; PMT = 0; and N = 36 to get $5,983.40. (Study Session 2, LOS 5.d)

21. **A** A t-distribution with sufficiently high degrees of freedom is approximately normal and a normal distribution has thinner tails compared to a t-distribution. The less the degrees of freedom, the fatter the tails. (Study Session 3, LOS 10.i)

22. **A** $R_1 = -10/100 = -10\%$; $R_2 = +9/90 = +10\%$

    $\text{geometric mean} = \sqrt{(0.9)(1.1)} - 1 = -0.005 \text{ or } -0.5\%$

    An alternative way to get the geometric mean is:

    $\left(\dfrac{\text{ending value}}{\text{beginning value}}\right)^{\frac{1}{n}} - 1 = \text{geometric mean return}$

    $\sqrt{\dfrac{99}{100}} - 1 = -0.005 \text{ or } -0.5\%$

    (Study Session 2, LOS 7.e)

23. **B** $R_L = \dfrac{2.0 + 151 - 150}{150} = 0.02$

   Choose Portfolio X because it has the larger safety-first ratio, $(0.10 - 0.02)/0.14 = 0.57$.

   Note: $\text{SFRatio(B)} = \dfrac{0.12 - 0.02}{0.20} = 0.50$

   (Study Session 3, LOS 9.n)

24. **C** To find the money-weighted rate of return, equate the present value of inflows to the present value of outflows and find the discount rate that makes them equal.

t = 0:	Buy 500 shares @ $22	=	−$11,000
t = 1:	$0.42 × 500 shares	=	+$210
	Buy 500 shares @ $24.75	=	−$12,375
	Net cash flow	=	−$12,165
t = 2:	$0.42 × 1,000 shares	=	+$420
	Buy 600 shares @ $31.25	=	−$18,750
	Net cash flow	=	−$18,330
t = 3:	Sell 1,000 shares @ $35.50	=	+$35,500
	Sell 600 shares @ $36.00	=	+$21,600
	Net cash flow	=	+$57,000

   Find the IRR with CFs as follows:
   $CF_0 = -11,000$; $CF_1 = -12,165$; $CF_2 = -18,330$; $CF_3 = 57,100$.
   The final result is IRR = 18.49%. (Study Session 2, LOS 6.d)

25. **C** The up-move factor equals one plus the percentage increase when the variable goes up, and the down-move factor is equal to one divided by the up-move factor. (Study Session 3, LOS 9.g)

26. **B** No calculations are really necessary here since the MMY involves no compounding and a 360-day year, the BEY requires compounding the quarterly HPR to a semiannual rate and doubling that rate, and the EAY requires compounding for the entire year based on a 365-day year. A numerical example of these calculations based on a 90-day holding period yield of 1.3% is: the money market yield is $1.3\% \times 360 / 90 = 5.20\%$, the bond equivalent yield is $2 \times [1.013^{182.5/90} - 1] = 0.0531 = 5.31\%$, which is two times the effective semiannual rate of return, and the effective annual yield is $1.013^{365/90} - 1 = 0.0538 = 5.38\%$. Calculating the semiannual effective yield using 180 days instead of 182.5 does not change the order. (Study Session 2, LOS 6.e)

27. **B** P(good economy and bear market) = 0.60 × 0.20 = 0.12. The other statements are true. The P(normal market) = (0.60 × 0.30) + (0.40 × 0.30) = 0.30. Given that the economy is poor, the probability of a normal or bull market = 0.30 + 0.20 = 0.50. (Study Session 2, LOS 8.f)

28. **C** Expected value = (0.4)(10%) + (0.4)(12.5%) + (0.2)(30%) = 15%

   Variance = $(0.4)(10 - 15)^2 + (0.4)(12.5 - 15)^2 + (0.2)(30 - 15)^2 = 57.5$

   Standard deviation = $\sqrt{57.5} = 7.58\%$

   (Study Session 2, LOS 8.m)

29. **B**   We can view this problem as the number of ways to choose three analysts from five analysts when the order they are chosen matters. The formula for the number of permutations is:

$$\frac{n!}{(n-r)!} = \frac{5!}{2!} = 5 \times 4 \times 3 = 60$$

On the TI financial calculator: 5 2nd nPr 3 = 60.

(Study Session 2, LOS 8.o)

30. **C**   Choice A is downgrade risk; choice B is default risk. (Study Session 3, LOS 9.n, and Study Session 16, LOS 59.a)

31. **B**   Rejecting the null hypothesis when it is true is a Type I error. The probability of a Type I error is the significance level of the test and one minus the significance level is the confidence level. The power of a test is one minus the probability of a Type II error, which cannot be calculated from the information given. (Study Session 3, LOS 11.b)

32. **A**   Type I error is rejecting the null hypothesis when it is true. The power of a test is the probability of rejecting the null hypothesis when it is false. $H_A: X \neq 0$ indicates a two-tailed test, while $H_A: X < 0$ or $H_A: X > 0$ indicates a one-tailed test. (Study Session 3, LOS 11.a, c)

33. **B**   Real business cycle theory, which derives from applying utility theory and budget constraints to macroeconomic models, is associated with the New Classical school. (Study Session 5, LOS 18.c)

34. **C**   If the quantity supplied at a given price is greater than the quantity demanded, then that price is greater than the equilibrium price. A price ceiling on electricity set above the equilibrium price will have no effect because the quantity supplied equals the quantity demanded at a price less than this legal maximum. A minimum wage causes a loss of efficiency (quantity of labor supplied is greater than the quantity demanded) when it is set above the equilibrium wage for unskilled workers. Increased search time is an example of an inefficiency that results from a rent ceiling below the equilibrium rent level. (Study Session 4, LOS 13.j, k)

35. **B**   Arbitrage-free forward rate = 1.3382 USD/EUR × (1.025 / 1.035) = 1.3253 USD/EUR. (Study Session 6, LOS 21.g)

36. **A**   The demand curve (price as a function of Q_D) is found by inverting the demand function:

P_{gas} = 20 + 2/15 P_{bus} − 1/15Q_D

The slope of this function (for any positive value of P_{bus}) is −1/15, or −0.0667. (Study Session 4, LOS 13.f)

37. **A**   Demand curves are not observable so a monopolist must search for the profit maximizing price. Because demand information is not perfect, a monopolist is a price searcher. The other statements are false. Although a monopolist can earn positive economic profits in the long run, they are not guaranteed profit. If average total costs exceed price, the monopolist will lose money. A monopolist maximizes *profit* where marginal revenue equals marginal cost. (Study Session 4, LOS 16.b, d, e)

38. C   With exchange rate targeting, a central bank's ability to increase the value of the domestic currency is limited by the amount of foreign reserves the country has available to buy its own currency in the foreign exchange market. While inflation targeting and interest rate targeting have limitations (e.g., liquidity trap conditions may exist, interest rates are bounded by zero), the central bank's resources are not typically a limitation. (Study Session 5, LOS 19.k, m)

39. C   From an initial equilibrium, an increase in real money balances will leave households and businesses with more money than they wish to hold, so they will purchase interest-bearing securities, driving their prices up and yields down until a new equilibrium short-term rate is established. (Study Session 5, LOS 19.d)

40. A   An increase in expected future incomes will cause consumers to increase current expenditures (reduce current savings) in anticipation of the higher future incomes. An increase in the money supply will tend to decrease interest rates which will lead to increased consumer spending on durable goods and increased investment by businesses. Both effects increase aggregate demand. (Study Session 5, LOS 17.h)

41. C   Either higher-than-expected or lower-than-expected inflation can cause producers to misinterpret unexpected changes in the price level as signals of increases or decreases in demand, and produce more or less than the equilibrium quantity of output. (Study Session 5, LOS 19.g)

42. C   In the Heckscher-Ohlin model, the source of comparative advantage is the relative amounts of labor and capital that are available in each country. Countries with more capital available relative to labor available will have a comparative advantage in producing capital-intensive goods, while countries with more labor available relative to capital will have a comparative advantage in labor-intensive goods. (Study Session 6, LOS 20.d)

43. B   Firms' demand curves are perfectly elastic (horizontal) in a market characterized as perfect competition, so that marginal revenue is equal to price and a firm maximizes profit by producing the output quantity at which marginal cost equals price. In monopoly markets or under monopolistic competition, firm demand curves are downward sloping so that marginal revenue is less than price. (Study Session 4, LOS 16.f)

44. B   If demand is inelastic, the percentage change in quantity demanded is smaller than the percentage change in price; quantity demanded is relatively unresponsive to price changes. A price increase increases total expenditures on a good. (Study Session 4, LOS 13.l)

45. C   These are examples of items that are typically treated as extraordinary under U.S. GAAP. There is no provision for accounting for an item as extraordinary under IFRS. Accounting errors are corrected with prior-period adjustments, which are made by restating results for any prior periods that are presented in the current financial statements. Discontinued operations are not classified as unusual or infrequent items and are reported (net of taxes) after net income from continuing operations but before net income. (Study Session 8, LOS 25.e)

46. C   Borrowing funds to purchase capital equipment will result in an increase in assets (equipment) and in liabilities (debt). The accrual of the salaries that are owed, but not paid, as of month-end will increase expenses and increase liabilities (accrued salary expense). Therefore, these two transactions taken together will result in the greatest increase in liabilities. (Study Session 7, LOS 23.c)

47. **A** Cash received from issuing securities is a financing cash flow. Income taxes paid are operating cash flows under U.S. GAAP. Interest and dividends received and interest paid are considered operating cash flows under U.S. GAAP, but dividends paid are considered financing cash flows. (Study Session 8, LOS 27.a, c)

48. **C** The easiest way to calculate CFO here is total cash flow – cash flow from investing – cash flow from financing = $13,000 + 5,000 + 4,250 = $22,250. Alternatively, CFO = $50,000 – 3,250 – 17,000 – 7,000 – 500 = $22,250. (Study Session 8, LOS 27.f)

49. **A** Cash conversion cycle (CCC) = days of sales outstanding + days of inventory on hand – number of days of payables. Days of sales outstanding = 365 / receivables turnover = 365 / 11 = 33.18; 365 / 12 = 30.42. This means the CCC decreases by 2.76 days. (Study Session 8, LOS 28.b)

50. **B** Besides the annual SEC filings, an analyst should examine a company's quarterly or semiannual filings. These interim filings typically update the major financial statements and footnotes, but are not necessarily audited. Annual reports to shareholders and press releases are written by management and are often viewed as public relations or sales materials. (Study Session 7, LOS 22.e)

51. **A** Basic EPS *does not* consider potential dilution from convertible bonds.
Original shares = 2,000,000(12) = 24,000,000
+ Stock dividend = 200,000(12) = 2,400,000
+ New shares = 100,000(3) = 300,000

$$\frac{\text{sum}}{12} = \frac{26,700,000}{12} = 2,225,000$$

Alternatively, 2 million (1.1) + (¼) (100,000) = 2.225 million. (Study Session 8, LOS 25.g)

52. **C** The gain (loss) on disposal is the amount by which the selling price exceeds (is less than) book value. Book value = original price – accumulated depreciation. Thus, gain or loss = selling price – (original price – accumulated depreciation), or selling price – original cost + accumulated depreciation. (Study Session 8, LOS 25.a)

53. **B** In the absence of taxes, there is no difference in cash flow between LIFO and FIFO. In addition, using LIFO would result in lower working capital (inventory is lower). Using LIFO would result in lower net income because of a *lower* gross margin (cost of goods sold is higher). (Study Session 9, LOS 29.h)

54. **A** Screening for high dividend yield stocks will likely include a disproportionately high number of financial services firms as such firms typically have higher dividend payouts. A screen to identify firms with low P/E ratios will likely exclude growth firms from the sample as high expected earnings growth leads to high P/Es. (Study Session 10, LOS 35.d)

55. **C** Operating cash flow that is less than net income (ratio less than one) or declining over time may indicate low quality earnings from aggressive accounting or accounting irregularities. A ratio that is consistently above one, but highly variable, is not necessarily indicative of aggressive accounting. (Study Session 10, LOS 33.d)

56. A   Under IFRS, if the outcome of a long-term contract cannot be estimated reliably, the firm should expense costs when incurred, recognize revenue to the extent of the costs, and recognize profit only when the contract is complete. The firm does not need to recognize a loss when expenses are greater than cash collected, but would need to recognize a loss if it determined that a loss on the contract was likely. (Study Session 8, LOS 25.b, c)

57. C   Useful lives and salvage values of long-lived assets are management estimates that may vary among companies. Companies typically do not disclose data about estimated salvage values, except when estimates are changed. (Study Session 9, LOS 30.c)

58. A   Interest and dividends received are reported as income, regardless of the balance sheet classification of marketable securities. (Study Session 8, LOS 26.e)

59. B   Straight line depreciation is (100,000 + 10,000 + 5,000 − 25,000) / 6 = 15,000 each year. Double-declining balance depreciation in the second year is: 115,000 (2/3)(1/3) = 25,556. The difference is $10,556. Remember that salvage value is not part of the declining balance calculation. (Study Session 8, LOS 25.d, and Study Session 9, LOS 30.d)

60. A   A decrease in the accounts receivable amount on the balance sheet indicates that cash collections exceed revenues (sales). This increases operating cash flow because receivables are being collected. An increase in the accounts payable amount on the balance sheet indicates that purchases from suppliers exceed cash payments. This increases operating cash flow because the cash was not used to pay the suppliers. (Study Session 8, LOS 27.f)

61. B   The most useful estimates of inventory and cost of sales are those that best approximate current cost. Whether prices are increasing or decreasing, FIFO provides a better estimate of inventory values, and LIFO provides a better estimate of cost of sales. If prices are stable, there is no difference between LIFO and FIFO estimates of inventory or cost of sales. (Study Session 9, LOS 29.e)

62. A   Working capital equals current assets minus current liabilities and is lower under a finance lease because the current portion of the finance lease increases current liabilities. Total asset turnover is lower because total assets are higher under a finance lease. Companies with finance leases report higher debt-to-equity ratios because liabilities increase and equity is unchanged at lease inception and lower in the early years of the lease. Return on equity is lower with a finance lease because the numerator, net income, is decreased proportionally more than the denominator, equity, from the greater expense of a finance lease in its early years. Over the life of the lease, the expenses are equal. (Study Session 9, LOS 32.h, l)

63. A   Warranty expense should be recorded when the inventory item covered by the warranty is sold. A deferred tax asset is created when warranty expenses are accrued on the financial statements but are not deductible on the tax returns until the warranty claims are paid. The full amount of the obligation, $100,000, is recorded as an expense, with a deferred tax asset of $30,000. Note that a deferred tax asset results when taxable income is more than pretax income and the difference is likely to reverse (warranty will be paid) in future years. (Study Session 9, LOS 31.d)

64. **B**   Diluted EPS = [NI – preferred dividends + convertible interest (1 – t)] / [weighted average shares + convertible debt shares].

100(1,000)(6%)(1 – 0.4) = \$3,600; convertible debt shares = 50(100) = 5,000

$$\frac{\$15,000 - \$10,000 + \$3,600}{2,000 + 5,000} = \$1.23$$

(Study Session 8, LOS 25.g)

65. **C**   Noncurrent assets are those that will not be used up during the next year or during the firm's operating cycle. Firm investment is typically in assets that are longer term in nature. (Study Session 8, LOS 26.d)

66. **C**   The initial liability is the amount received from the creditor, not the par value of the bond.

N = 8; I/Y = 11/2 = 5.5; PMT = 500,000; FV = 10,000,000; CPT → PV = \$9,683,272.

The interest expense is the effective interest rate (the market rate at the time of issue) times the balance sheet liability. \$9,683,272 × 0.055 = \$532,580.

The value of the liability will change over time and is a function of the initial liability, the interest expense and the actual cash payments. In this case, it increases by the difference between the interest expense and the actual cash payment: \$532,580 – \$500,000 = \$32,580 + \$9,683,272 = \$9,715,852. *Tip:* Knowing that the liability will increase is enough to select choice C without performing this last calculation. Entering N = 7 and solving for PV also produces \$9,715,852. (Study Session 9, LOS 32.b)

67. **C**   On a horizontal common-size balance sheet, the divisor is the first-year values so they are all standardized to 1.0 by construction. Trends in the values of these items as well as the relative growth in these items are readily apparent. A vertical common-size balance sheet expresses all balance sheet accounts as a percentage of total assets and does not standardize the initial year. (Study Session 8, LOS 28.a)

68. **C**   Covenants protect bondholders from actions the firm may take that would decrease credit quality and reduce the value of the bondholders' claims to firm assets and earnings. Examples of covenants include restrictions on dividend payments and stock repurchases; mergers and acquisitions; sale, leaseback, and disposal of certain assets; issuance of new debt; and repayment patterns (e.g., sinking fund agreements and priority of claims). Repurchases of bonds in the market do not negatively affect the interests of bondholders. (Study Session 9, LOS 32.d, Study Session 15, LOS 52.d, and Study Session 16, LOS 59.e)

69. **C**   Changing the inventory accounting method has no immediate cash flow effects and therefore should not change a firm's short-term forecast (typically 4 to 6 weeks) of its net cash position. However, because the average cost inventory method will result in lower gross profit compared to FIFO, it will also result in decreased taxes. The firm's long-term forecast (typically 3 to 5 years) of its net cash position should reflect a decrease in cash outflows for taxes, and consequently greater net cash in future periods. (Study Session 9, LOS 29.e and Study Session 11, LOS 40.d)

70. **B**   It is not uncommon for individuals to be members of the boards of directors of more than one firm. This is acceptable as long as they maintain independence and act in the interests of the firms' shareholders. A strong corporate code of ethics should discourage the company from awarding consulting contracts or finder's fees to board members or relatives of board members. (Study Session 11, LOS 41.f)

71. **B**   Introducing a new product or entering a new market involves sales and expense projections that can be highly uncertain. Expanding capacity or replacing old machinery involve less uncertainty and analysis. (Study Session 11, LOS 36.a)

72. **A**   The appropriate method for estimating the cost of equity for a firm in a developing market is to add a country risk premium (CRP) to the market risk premium, so the revised CAPM equation becomes: $k_{ce} = R_F + \beta[E(R_{MKT}) - R_F + CRP]$. The CRP is the sovereign yield spread (between yields on the country's government bonds and a developed country's government bonds) adjusted for the volatility of the developing country's equity market. An alternative approach is to add the CRP (not the sovereign yield spread) to the cost of equity as calculated from the CAPM. (Study Session 11, LOS 37.j)

73. **A**   Factoring refers to the sale of receivables without recourse; that is, the risk that the firm's customers will not pay, or will not pay in a timely manner, is borne by the factor, who purchases the receivables. Thus, the amount the factor will pay per dollar of receivables is lower (higher discount or interest rate) if the credit quality of the firm's credit customers is lower. (Study Session 11, LOS 40.g)

74. **B**   The degree of financial leverage (DFL) is the percent change in earnings per share for a given percent change in operating income. The degree of operating leverage (DOL) is the percent change in operating income for a given percent change in sales. The degree of total leverage (DTL) is the percent change in earnings per share for a given percent change in sales, and is the product of DOL and DFL. Based on the information given, Smith has a higher DFL than Jones, but we cannot conclude that Smith has a higher DTL than Jones. (Study Session 11, LOS 38.b)

75. **A**   The correct treatment of flotation costs according to the CFA Curriculum is to include their cost in the initial cash outflow of the project. Since flotation costs are included in the initial outlay, they decrease the NPV by an amount that is unaffected by the discount rate, and the discount rate and cost of capital are not adjusted for flotation costs. (Study Session 11, LOS 37.l)

76. **C**   The internal rate of return is the rate of discount at which the NPV of a project is zero. On an NPV profile, this is the point where the profile intersects the horizontal axis. (Study Session 11, LOS 36.e)

77. **C**   An increase in the tax rate will reduce Thompson's after-tax cost of debt (other things equal) and therefore reduce its WACC. With a relatively lower cost of debt the firm will likely change its capital structure to include more debt and less equity (i.e., to increase its financial leverage). (Study Session 11, LOS 37.b)

78. **C**   The payment of a stock (as opposed to a cash) dividend does not affect the firm's equity or net income, but will decrease its earnings per share because it increases the number of shares outstanding. (Study Session 11, LOS 39.a)

79. **A** The market model is expressed as: $R_i = \alpha_i + \beta_i R_m + \varepsilon_i$. In this model, beta ($\beta_i$) measures the sensitivity of the rate of return on an asset (R_i) to the market rate of return (R_m). (Study Session 12, LOS 44.d)

80. **B** The correlation between the returns of the two assets is:

$$\frac{\text{Cov}_{AB}}{\sigma_A \sigma_B} = \frac{0.03735}{\sqrt{0.031} \times \sqrt{0.045}} = 1.$$

Therefore, the standard deviation of the portfolio returns is a weighted average of the standard deviations of returns for the two assets: $0.3\sqrt{0.031} + 0.7\sqrt{0.045} = 20.13\%$.

Since the correlation of returns is +1, there are no diversification benefits. (Study Session 12, LOS 43.e)

81. **A** Open-end funds redeem existing shares or issue new shares in accordance with investor demand. Closed-end fund shares are fixed in number and trade on exchanges as though they were common stock. (Study Session 12, LOS 42.d)

82. **C** Using the CAPM, the required rate of return for each stock is:

$E(R_X) = 4\% + 1.0(10\% - 4\%) = 10.0\%$.

$10.0\% - 10.0\% = 0.0\%$ properly valued.

$E(R_Y) = 4\% + 1.6(10\% - 4\%) = 13.6\%$.

$16.0\% - 13.6\% = 2.4\%$ undervalued.

$E(R_Z) = 4\% + 2.0(10\% - 4\%) = 16.0\%$.

$16.0\% - 16.0\% = 0.0\%$ properly valued.

(Study Session 12, LOS 44.h)

83. **B** According to the CAPM, rational, risk-averse investors will optimally choose to hold a portfolio along the capital market line. This can range from a 100% allocation to the risk-free asset to a leveraged position in the market portfolio constructed by borrowing at the risk-free rate to invest more than 100% of the portfolio equity value in the market portfolio. The global minimum variance portfolio lies below the CML and is not an efficient portfolio under the assumptions of the CAPM. (Study Session 12, LOS 43.g)

84. **A** Based on the CAPM, the portfolio should earn: $E(R) = 0.05 + 1.5(0.10) = 20\%$. On a risk-adjusted basis, this portfolio lies on the security market line (SML) and thus is earning a risk-adjusted rate of return equivalent to that of the market portfolio. (Study Session 12, LOS 44.g)

85. **C** $g = (1 - \text{payout})(\text{ROE}) = (1 - 0.40)(16\%) = 9.6\%$

$$k = \frac{\$1.50(1.096)}{\$40} + 0.096 = 13.7\%$$

(Study Session 8, LOS 28.e, and Study Session 14, LOS 51.e)

86. **B**   The following formula indicates the stock price that will trigger a margin call:

$$\text{long} = \frac{(\text{original price})(1 - \text{initial margin \%})}{1 - \text{maintenance margin}} = \frac{(\$50)(1 - 0.50)}{1 - 0.25} = \$33.33$$

(Study Session 13, LOS 46.f)

Professor's Note: An intuitive way to solve minimum margin problems for equity accounts is based on the fact that while the margin amount changes with stock price changes after purchase, the loan amount does not. Stock price is $50, loan is $25, when the margin is 25% the loan must be 75% (of share price). $25 / 0.75 = $33.33.

87. **A**   Operational efficiency refers to low transactions costs in a securities market. Informational efficiency means prices change rapidly to reflect new information without predictable bias and rates of return are, on average, proportional to risk. (Study Session 13, LOS 46.k)

88. **A**   Price-weighted index $= \dfrac{4 + 10}{2} = 7$. A price-weighted index is not affected by a split. The divisor is adjusted to account for the price change.

$$\text{Value-weighted index} = 100 \times \frac{\$4(50) + \$5(20)}{\$2(50) + \$10(10)} = 150$$

(Study Session 13, LOS 47.e)

89. **B**   Required return = 5% + 1.1(8%) = 13.8%

Sustainable growth = 18%(1 − 0.4) = 10.8%

$$P_0 \Big/ E_1 = \frac{0.40}{0.138 - 0.108} = 13.33.$$

(Study Session 8, LOS 28.e, and Study Session 14, LOS 51.c, h)

90. **A**   Payment of a dividend reduces shareholders' equity and thereby increases return on shareholders' equity going forward. The repurchase of common stock with the proceeds of a debt offering will increase return on shareholders' equity only if the after-tax cost of debt is less than the earnings yield on the firm's shares. Changes in the market price of a firm's shares do not affect shareholders' equity or net income. (Study Session 14, LOS 49.g, h)

91. **C**   The shakeout industry life-cycle stage is characterized by slowing (but still positive) growth, intense competition, and declining profitability, as demand begins to approach market saturation. In contrast, the decline industry stage is characterized by negative growth. The lack of brand loyalty among customers suggests the industry has not yet reached the mature stage. (Study Session 14, LOS 50.h)

92. **B** Dividend payout = 1 − earnings retention rate = 1 − 0.4 = 0.6

$R_S = R_f + \beta(R_M − R_f) = 0.06 + 1.2(0.11 − 0.06) = 0.12$

g = (retention rate)(ROE) = 0.4(0.12) = 0.048

$P/E = \dfrac{\text{dividend payout ratio}}{k − g} = \dfrac{0.6}{0.12 − 0.048} = 8.33$

Price = E(P/E) = $4(8.33) = $33.32

(Study Session 8, LOS 28.e, and Study Session 14, LOS 51.c, h)

93. **C** Both technology and housing firms tend to be quite cyclical, that is, their profits are very sensitive to changes in overall growth. The profits of telecommunications firms, on the other hand, are less economically sensitive. (Study Session 14, LOS 50.c)

94. **A** Behavioral finance studies how market anomalies can arise from psychological traits that affect investor behavior and cause investors to make systematic errors such as exiting profitable positions too soon and holding unprofitable positions too long. (Study Session 13, LOS 48.g)

95. **B** Since the index is price weighted, the value of the stocks will match the index performance. Total returns includes dividend yield, however, and since dividends are not included in the performance of the index itself, the portfolio will outperform the index by the amount of the dividend yield. (Study Session 13, LOS 47.b)

96. **A** One of the disadvantages of present value models such as the Gordon growth model is that the required rate of return on equity must be estimated. Neither an enterprise value multiplier model nor an asset valuation model requires an explicit estimate of the required rate of return. (Study Session 14, LOS 51.k)

97. **A** Only amortizing securities with a prepayment option are subject to prepayment risk. Event risk is the possibility that some event (e.g., natural disaster, change in regulations, merger, restructuring) reduces the issuer's ability to meet its debt obligations. Liquidity risk can be important even for a bond held to maturity if the portfolio manager needs to mark its holdings to market for performance reporting purposes. Low liquidity for the bond can mean the prevailing price is not an accurate measure of the bond's value. (Study Session 15, LOS 53.i, k, o)

98. **A** Default risk is the possibility that the issuer will fail to meet its obligations under the indenture, for which investors demand a premium above the return on a default-risk-free security. Bond ratings indicate default risk. Downgrade risk is the risk that a bond will be reclassified as a riskier security by a credit rating agency. Credit spread risk is the risk that the default risk premium on a bond can increase. (Study Session 15, LOS 53.j and Study Session 16, LOS 59.d)

99. **C** A callable bond is made up of a straight bond and a written call option. An increase in volatility increases the value of the call option and decreases the value of the callable bond. On the other hand, a putable bond is made up of an option-free (or straight) bond and a long put option. An increase in volatility increases the value of the put option and therefore increases the value of the putable bond. (Study Session 15, LOS 53.n)

100. **C** A medium-term note is sold on a "best efforts" basis wherein the underwriter does not guarantee a price for the bonds to the issuer but tries to get the best price possible. Price risk is completely borne by the issuing firm. (Study Session 15, LOS 54.h, i)

101. **C** Because the coupon rate on an inverse floater increases when market interest rates decrease, there is an implicit cap on the coupon rate because market interest rates cannot decline further than zero. The bondholder always receives coupon payments made by the issuer. The opposite would correspond to a negative interest rate. The coupon rate, not the principal, is adjusted inversely with market interest rates. (Study Session 15, LOS 52.b)

102. **A** Portfolio duration is an approximation of the price sensitivity of a portfolio to parallel shifts of the yield curve (yields for all maturities increase or decrease by equal amounts). Duration can be a poor approximation of interest rate risk for non-parallel shifts in the yield curve. (Study Session 15, LOS 53.g)

103. **C** "Top-heavy" refers to a capital structure that includes a high percentage of secured bank debt. A firm with a top-heavy capital structure may be limited in its access to additional bank borrowing, which increases the likelihood of default if the firm encounters financial distress. (Study Session 16, LOS 59.j)

104. **B** First calculate V– and V+, the bond's value at 7.25% and 8.75% yields to maturity. The bond values are $1,052.70 and $950.69, respectively:

N = 20; I/Y = 7.25 / 2 = 3.625; PMT = 40; FV = 1,000; CPT PV = –1052.70

N = 20; I/Y = 8.75 / 2 = 4.375; PMT = 40; FV = 1,000; CPT PV = –950.69

$$D = \frac{V_- - V_+}{2V_0(\Delta y)} = \frac{1,052.70 - 950.69}{2(1,000)(0.0075)} = 6.8.$$

(Study Session 16, LOS 56.e, 58.d)

105. **C** $$_1f_4 = \frac{(1.055)^5}{(1.04)^4} - 1 = 0.1172$$

Note: 5(5.5) – 4(4) = 11.5%. (Study Session 16, LOS 57.g)

106. **B** Had BBB and AAA yields risen from 5% and 4%, respectively, to 6% and 5%, the absolute yield spread would have remained the same, but the yield ratios would have decreased from 5/4 to 6/5, and the relative yield spread would have decreased from 0.25 to 0.20. This is the reason that relative yield spreads are considered a better indicator of yield spread changes than absolute yield spreads. In an economic expansion, relative corporate yield spreads to Treasuries are likely to decrease. (Study Session 15, LOS 55.e)

107. **A** We know that: $r_{BD} = \dfrac{D}{F}\left(\dfrac{360}{t}\right)$

D = \$1,000,000 − \$987,845 = \$12,155
F = \$1,000,000
t = 78 days

Substituting we get: $r_{BD} = \dfrac{\$12,155}{\$1,000,000}\left(\dfrac{360}{78}\right) = 0.0561$

(Study Session 2, LOS 6.e)

108. **C** If mortgage rates decrease, prepayments will accelerate. Prepayments affect the values of interest-only and principal-only strips differently. A principal-only strip will increase in price when prepayments increase because the face value of the security will be received sooner. An interest-only strip will receive a smaller amount of total payments because interest will be paid on a smaller amount of outstanding principal. Thus, the price of an interest-only strip will decrease when prepayments increase. (Study Session 15, LOS 54.e)

109. **C** If preferred stock must be redeemed on a specific date, its future cash flows are as predictable as those of an option-free bond: the (dividend) payments are known, the principal repayment date is known, and the security is not convertible or exchangeable. The principal repayment date is not known with certainty for a callable bond and the coupon payments are not known for a floating-rate security. (Study Session 16, LOS 56.b)

110. **B** A spot rate is the appropriate discount rate for a security that makes a single payment in the future. Treasury bills and Treasury strips promise a single future cash flow and their yields represent spot rates. Treasury inflation protected securities (TIPS) have coupon cash flows, so a 2-year TIPS yield is not a spot rate. (Study Session 15, LOS 54.b, c, 55.d)

111. **B** The net cost of the position is 40 − 3 = \$37. If the stock price at expiration is ≥44, the gain on the position is \$7. If the stock price were to fall to zero, the investor would lose \$37. (Study Session 17, LOS 65.b)

112. **B** The payoff diagram from owning stock and a long put on the stock is similar to that of a long call. (Study Session 17, LOS 65.b)

113. **B** The counterparties do not exchange the notional principal on an interest rate swap. (Study Session 17, LOS 64.a, b)

114. **A** According to put-call parity:

$$c_0 + \frac{X}{(1+r)^T} = p_0 + S_0$$

$$\frac{X}{(1+r)^T} = \frac{\$45}{(1.06)^{0.5}} = \$43.71$$

Rearranging the put-call parity relationship:

$$c_0 = S_0 + p_0 - \frac{X}{(1+r)^T}$$

$$= \$43 + \$4 - \$43.71 = \$3.29$$

At a price of $4, c_0 is overvalued.

$$p_0 = c_0 + \frac{X}{(1+r)^T} - S_0$$

$$= \$4 + \$43.71 - \$43 = \$4.71$$

At a price of $4, p_0 is undervalued.

$$S_0 = c_0 + \frac{X}{(1+r)^T} - p_0$$

$$= \$4 + \$43.71 - \$4 = \$43.71$$

At a price of $43, S_0 is undervalued. (Study Session 17, LOS 63.m)

115. **A** This is a 1 × 3 FRA since it expires in 30 days and is based on 60-day LIBOR which is a 3-month period from the time of contract initiation to the end of the interest rate period. To hedge the risk of an interest rate increase, the firm takes a long position in an FRA. The payoff to the long is found from multiplying the notional principal by:

$$\left[\frac{\left(LIBOR_T - \text{forward contract rate} \right) \left(\dfrac{\text{days in underlying rate}}{360} \right)}{1 + LIBOR_T \left(\dfrac{\text{days in underlying rate}}{360} \right)} \right]$$

Where $LIBOR_T$ is the underlying rate at expiration of the FRA.

We get: $\$50,000,000 \left[\dfrac{(0.050 - 0.048)\left(\dfrac{60}{360}\right)}{1 + 0.050\left(\dfrac{60}{360}\right)} \right] = \$16,529$

(Study Session 17, LOS 61.g)

116. **C** If the margin account balance falls below the maintenance margin level, the account must be brought back up to the initial margin amount. (Study Session 17, LOS 62.d)

117. **C** Because a hedge fund database only includes the more stable funds that have survived, the risk measure of hedge funds as an asset class is biased downward. (Study Session 18, LOS 66.e)

118. **A** Real estate and commodities offer potential hedges against inflation because rents, property values, and commodity prices tend to increase with inflation in the long term. (Study Session 18, LOS 66.d)

119. **B** In a secondary sale, a private equity firm sells one of its portfolio companies to a group of investors or another private equity firm. (Study Session 18, LOS 66.d)

120. **B** The notice period is the time within which a hedge fund must fulfill a request for redemption of shares. The period during which investors may not redeem shares is called a lockup period. (Study Session 18, LOS 66.d)

Notes

Notes

Notes